McCoy

McCoy

The Autobiography

A. P. MCCOY

with Steve Taylor

MICHAEL JOSEPH
an imprint of
PENGUIN BOOKS

To Billy Rock,
who treated me like a man when I was a boy and
who saw more in the boy than any other man

MICHAEL JOSEPH

Published by the Penguin Group
Penguin Books Ltd, 80 Strand, London WC2R ORL, England
Penguin Putnam Inc., 375 Hudson Street, New York, New York 10014, USA
Penguin Books Australia Ltd, 250 Camberwell Road, Camberwell, Victoria 3124, Australia
Penguin Books Canada Ltd, 10 Alcorn Avenue, Toronto, Ontario, Canada M4V 3B2
Penguin Books India (P) Ltd, 11 Community Centre,
Panchsheel Park, New Delhi – 110 017, India
Penguin Books (NZ) Ltd, Cnr Rosedale and Airborne Roads,
Albany, Auckland, New Zealand
Penguin Books (South Africa) (Pty) Ltd, 24 Sturdee Avenue,
Rosebank 2196, South Africa

Penguin Books Ltd, Registered Offices: 80 Strand, London WC2R ORL, England

www.penguin.com

First published 2002
1

Copyright © Tony McCoy, 2002

The moral right of the author has been asserted

Set in 12/14.75 pt Monotype Bembo
Typeset by Rowland Phototypesetting Ltd,
Bury St Edmunds, Suffolk
Printed in England by Clays Ltd, St Ives plc

A CIP catalogue record for this book is available from the British Library

ISBN 0–718–14535–6

Contents

Acknowledgements

Graham Cunningham, Mark Bowers, Simon Turner, Ashley Rumney, Graham Bradley, Martin Pipe, Carol Pipe, David Pipe, Jonothan Lower, John Randall, David Cleary, John Inverdale, Noel Chance, Jim Bolger, Peter Deal, David Johnson, Willie Supple, Conor O'Dwyer, Brian Clifford, Barry Fenton, Toby Balding, Dave Roberts, Gee Armytage, Billy Rock, Tom Gallagher, T. J. Comerford, Steve McManaman, Dr Michael Turner, Patrick Hibbert-Foy, Paul Barton, Marcus Buckland, Michael Caulfield, Norman Williamson and the McCoy family.

PHOTOGRAPHIC CREDITS

© Dan Abraham: 50; © Ed Byrne: 57; © Chris Cook: 18; © Empics/ Chris Turvey: 12; Getty Images: 44, 46; Getty Images/Julian Herbert: 10, 11, 29, 32, 33, 35, 45; © John Grosswick: 55; © Healy Racing Photos: 3, 4, 5, 6, 7, 8, 28; © Trevor Jones: 17, 25, 27, 31; Trevor Martin, courtesy of the Belfast Telegraph: 49; Mirrorpix.com: 37, 41, 43; Mirrorpix.com/ Edward Whitaker: 26, 30, 34, 36, 48, 56; Mirrorpix.com/Phil Smith: 13, 14, 15; News International: 40; PA Photos: 42; © Bernard Parkin: 24; © Colin Turner: 23; © Ray Wright, 16, 21, 47

Every effort has been made to trace copyright holders and we apologize in advance for any unintentional omission. We would be pleased to insert the appropriate acknowledgement in any subsequent edition.

1. Break Point

It felt like the coldest place in all Ireland as the two-year-olds pulled out of Jim Bolger's immaculate yard in Coolcullen, Co. Carlow, one thousand feet above sea level and a slicing wind for company. A welcome Christmas and New Year holiday with my parents was fading into a pleasant memory and all my thoughts centred on the new Flat season of 1993, which beckoned in three months' time. This might be my year, the one when Anthony McCoy would come from obscurity to win the Irish apprentice championship. But a colt called Kly Green was about to change my life more than any horse before or since.

Kly Green wasn't the worst of the young ones but he'd been in 'the padded cell', a name we gave to the area inside the covered ride, which was surrounded by straw bales that stopped the lunatics damaging themselves on concrete or iron. There was nothing evil about him: he was just mad fresh that January morning as we made off to the end of the all-weather gallop, bucking and diving on a hair-trigger that might go off at any second.

But it didn't worry me, 'not a bother', as my dad was fond of saying. I was eighteen and knew I was pretty good. When it came to the tricky ones it was usually the better kids, like myself and Paul Carberry, that the head lad David Downey put on to sort them out. It was a compliment of sorts: it meant it was recognized that you knew what you were doing.

Every day was a rodeo with Kly Green, buck, plunge, buck, plunge, but this particular snow-flecked morning he saw the wooden rail at the bottom of the gallop and charged it, head down. The rail won. He staggered, I came off and heard my left leg snap. The lads who were milling around a hundred yards away heard it too and I soon knew how serious it was. As I looked down at my leg it seemed as though I had two kneecaps where the splintered bones were pressing through my jodhpurs.

Seamus Heffernan was nearest to me. One look was all he needed to see I was in serious trouble and he galloped back to the yard to get help.

In a matter of seconds I felt sick and very weak, and the boys who clustered around me saw the colour drain from my face. I was in desperate pain and so cold as the ground temperature seeped in to me. Gradually I went numb as shock set in.

It wasn't long before Jim Bolger came down from the house. He was never a demonstrative man and his first observation was a laconic 'Are you sure you've broken it?'

I was roaring in agony, and he called for blankets to be brought from the tack room to insulate me from the bitter cold. We were a long way from anywhere and I must have lain out in the open for nearly an hour before the ambulance came. When the medic put the mask over my nose and mouth the gas flooded up to my brain, the pain began to subside and I slipped into semi-consciousness. It was one of the best feelings I can remember. Even now, nine years and well over a thousand winners on, I can still remember the way the pain disappeared.

Several seasons later I crushed some vertebrae when riding Merry Gale in the cross-country race for the Marlborough Cup. I took a crashing fall and the horse finished on top of me. I couldn't even get my hand to my head to take my face out of the ground so that I could breathe, but the gas came to my rescue – again, it was the best feeling in the world.

Back on that wintry morning I still had to endure a thirty-minute ride to hospital in Kilkenny. The roads in deepest Co. Carlow aren't the best and I could feel every pothole and bump until more gas returned me to a daze.

When we finally made A&E I was still cold with shock, but a young nurse brought a warm blanket, wrapped me up in it to the neck and I felt comfortable and at ease. I can't remember being taken to theatre – I was probably put out with a strong sedative. At that stage, I didn't care so long as the pain was gone.

When I came round I was in a side ward on my own with my leg encased in plaster from toe to thigh and elevated on a wire cage. Now I had time to think, and the thoughts that tumbled through my mind were not good. The little world I inhabited had begun to disintegrate: the bright future that had stretched before me that morning was now looking as bleak as the grey skies that covered Kilkenny, as I gazed through the window.

I spent a couple of days in hospital, but I doubt the surgeons would have been so keen to let me out had they known the standard of after-care to which I was returning. I shared a house not far from the yard with four other young lads, Ted Durcan and Calvin McCormack, who both went on to ride successfully in England, Declan O'Brien, and David Wachman, who now trains successfully. Well, looking back, you wouldn't have kept sheep in that house. It was the roughest of the rough but, then, we were only kids and housework was never high on the list of priorities. Instead of making the beds we should have mucked out in the morning, and we hardly ever went into the kitchen.

I was glad enough to be out of hospital and the boys kept my spirits up when they were around, but the hours on my own when they were at work were dire. It was also the first time I'd been on crutches and there is a knack to using them, which I took time to master. Moving about was difficult.

It clearly wasn't the ideal environment for recuperation and I must have sounded low on the phone when I spoke to my parents, because it wasn't many days before my dad, Peadar, made the four-hour journey to take me back home to Moneyglass, Co. Antrim, in the North of Ireland.

My mother, Claire, realized that this would probably be the last time she would ever have me home for any length of time. I'd been at Bolger's over two years and had only been back for the odd few days. Ma made the most of it: I was bored and she supplied the food I loved – chips and anything out of the frying-pan. To me it was the food of the gods but, on reflection, not of the aspiring champion jockey. I was comfort-eating because, no matter how well I was being cared for, there was the persistent nagging at the back of my mind that I was losing ground in my chosen career. Whenever I cared to look in the mirror or fasten my Levis I became uncomfortably aware that my body was filling out. When I went into hospital I weighed around seven stone ten, but when I finally signed off and returned south to take up the reins I tipped the scales at around nine stone two.

Once back in full work the weight came down and, with sweat and self-denial, I managed to ride at eight stone six when I returned on Bubbly Prospect, who finished eighth in a Gowran Park maiden. But my metabolism had been given a kick start and nature had taken over. It probably would have been easier to keep my weight down had I been more established. As it was I barely got a ride every two weeks, so the incentive to control it wasn't there.

I had ridden my first winner on Legal Steps at Thurles on 26 March the previous year, carrying an easily attainable eight stone eleven. I had to wait until 23 October for my second, Zavaleta, and she had eight stone thirteen. The signs weren't looking good.

Half-way through the next season I knew that the Flat dream was over: the needle on the bathroom scales was stuck at eight stone ten. I went to Jim and asked if he'd take out a jumping licence for me. He's a good man, but then he had a knack of deflating you without raising his voice, and he could cut you with a withering look and a few sharp sentences: 'You want to be a jump jockey. You're some fool. I heard you crying like a baby with a broken leg and jump jockeys get that every day of the week. You're not hard enough. You're not tough enough to be a jump jockey.'

I had to prove him wrong.

2. School's Out

'Anthony! School! Will you get into the car or I'll redden your bum!' The same scene is played out in a million homes each morning and it was no different in a small bungalow in Moneyglass, Co. Antrim in the late seventies. The battle of wills between my mother and me each weekday morning at eight thirty was a pantomime without any laughs as far as I was concerned. The daily ration of lessons and discipline held no silver lining for me.

'I'm not going, I feel sick.'

'You'll be sick, all right, if I have to come and get you. Now get into the car and let's have no more of it.'

Bottom lip turned out and slouching down the hallway, I was a picture of misery as I made my way to the Volkswagen Beetle parked out on the road. My two older sisters, Anne-Marie and Roisin, took the bus for the mile and a half journey to Toome Primary. I did the same for the first two weeks of the summer term of 1979 but the novelty soon wore off. After that I made sure to miss it, which meant Ma had to take me in the car. However, I still wouldn't give in gracefully to the education system. After a lot of huffing and puffing I'd throw myself on to the back seat, but when we arrived outside the school I'd push out my arms and legs, wedging myself into the back and, no matter what Ma did, I could not be winkled out. She couldn't get a good hit at me either, so it was a swift about-turn back home and my dad would be called in. He's more reserved than Ma and a good bit stronger, too, so he managed to prise me out of the car and carried me bellowing up to the school entrance. It was there that, aged five, I sank my teeth into him and even this most placid of men fast began to lose his temper.

But I still had one card to play in the unequal struggle of Anthony Peter McCoy against the world. You needed school books to do school work and when they got me to my desk my satchel was missing. *I* didn't know where it had gone – someone with a greater need than mine must have stolen it.

The headmaster, Brian Barry, knew Ma and Dad quite well and phoned to say that my satchel had gone and I was saying nothing. Unfortunately, they had apparently limitless supplies of those damn school books, although it wasn't until two weeks later that my satchel was discovered half submerged in a ditch at the bottom of our garden. I had hurled it as far as I could in a final gesture of defiance before leaving for the day's incarceration.

In varying degrees it was going to be the same for the next ten years with flare-ups followed by an uneasy truce. There were times when the headmaster had to come to the bungalow and physically push me to school. When I got there I spent as much time standing alone and staring into a corner as I did learning at the desk. Although no one, least of all me or my long-suffering mother, realized it at the time, I was already showing the single-mindedness that would sustain me in the character-breaking world of racing. Not that there was any early indication that I would take that route, on family pedigree at least.

My dad, Peadar, came from Moneyglass and my mum, Claire, was born a few miles away in Randalstown. They were married in 1968. Dad, a carpenter with plenty of experience in the building industry, built the bungalow in his spare time before my eldest sister Anne-Marie was born in 1971. It was barely five hundred yards from his family home, the Home House. Roisin arrived a year later, with me joining them on 4 May 1974 and Jane two years after that. My brother Colm was born in 1979 with the last – and possibly the cleverest – Kelly, coming in 1984.

The growing family put a strain on the three-bedroom bungalow and when my dad's sister, Bernie, was left the Home House on the death of my grandparents it made sense for us to swap. The Home House was ideal and also had a shop attached, which served as a general store and post office to the small country community when they didn't want to make the journey to either Toomebridge or Randalstown. Anyway, we had enough relations around to keep the place in profit and, with my mum working behind the counter, there was always a trade in gossip and information. She will never use two words when twenty-two can be found.

But good as the Home House was it lacked something that the bungalow had. Stables. Although my dad and his family had no connection with horses or racing he had a strong pull towards them, like many Irishmen. Unlike the majority he did something about it and put up three stables shortly after the bungalow was complete. It wasn't long before he had a mare called Fire Forest, who was related to the 1962 Grand National winner, Kilmore.

He got her from a wealthy man he was working for in Ballymena. She'd failed to get in foal for three seasons and, after a good bit of haggling, Dad bought her with a colt foal inside for £300. That mare and her son were going to have a significant influence on my life because someone else had been keen to buy her. That man was Billy Rock, who trained some eight miles from our home at Cullybackey.

Dad and Billy formed a friendship that endures to this day and the colt, soon to be gelded, was named Apache Pass and managed a couple of point-to-point wins. Many years later it was Billy Rock and his stable of misfits who took me on the fast track to the racecourse.

Unknown to me I had a brief flirtation with horses when, aged two, I waddled out of the back door to the paddock and Ma found me crawling around the legs of Fire Forest, who was thankfully one of the quiet ones. A few years later I was pictured on the back of her daughter, Misclaire, who went on to breed Thumbs Up, winner of the 1994 County Hurdle at the Cheltenham Festival. However, at the time that looked like the only connection the McCoys were going to have with the home of steeplechasing. I had no interest in racing or horses. For me it was either football or snooker. With snooker I had the Belfast boy Alex Higgins firmly in my sights. When it came to soccer it was Arsenal and nothing else – I don't know why, perhaps it was the strong Irish element they had at that time, with the likes of Liam Brady, Frank Stapleton

and David O'Leary, but a more probable reason is that Pat Jennings
was in goal.

He was my local hero, born in Newry and one of the best keepers
the world has seen. When I found out he was opening a sports shop
in Magherafelt, Co. Derry, I wouldn't let up on Ma until she agreed
to take me. It cost her a football, too, which the great man signed
after I'd queued for half an hour. I treasured it until I went into
racing full-time. I've met Pat several times since when we've
attended sports functions and he's a very good man indeed. I always
remembered how he behaved towards the youngsters that day and
had time for all of them. No matter what the circumstances, I
always try to do the same: by sparing a few seconds of your time
you can make someone's day.

That trip outside Antrim was a rare treat, and visits to Belfast
were rarer still. The troubles that have put Northern Ireland on the
front pages of the world's newspapers for all the wrong reasons had
been raging way before I was born and I grew up with them. Like
all of those my age and older I never knew anything else. Although
the country area I came from was largely Nationalist I hardly ever
encountered sectarianism while I was growing up.

When the troubles reached our area we watched with detached
interest. I heard the bomb go off that ripped through the police
station at Toomebridge. It was early evening in winter and I was at
my uncle Brendan's farm, not far from our home and somewhere
I often went to make a nuisance of myself. I heard a *whump* and ran
to the top of the hill that overlooks the town, which was plunged
into darkness as the power supply went down. All I could see was
blackness and a faint glow topped with a pall of smoke that rose
from the smashed building.

It was the only topic of conversation over dinner. Later in the
evening Uncle Brendan asked Dad if he would go down to the
town and secure the doors and windows of the chemist's, which
had been blown in; it was in danger of being robbed as there were
drugs on the premises. There was no way I was going to miss out,
aged seven, on my first experience of the troubles and I pleaded
with Dad to take me with him. We had to wait until midnight,

which made it even better, and my mind was doing overtime as we negotiated each checkpoint.

The nervous soldiers with camouflage paint on their faces and automatic rifles across their chests waved us down and asked our business before letting us through. That it was a Nationalist area didn't mean we would be any safer. There was a barracks in Toomebridge and for that reason alone the town was at risk. Shortly after the first bomb the security forces found an arms cache not far from the back of our house and the whole area was cordoned off. The police helicopters carried on sweeping the ground with lights throughout the night. It was like being in the middle of a film and I'd have given anything to be out there.

When the barracks eventually took a hit I was at secondary school, and the only thought I had as we were held at the roadblocks was, Good, a few less hours of work. You can't help being selfish as a kid.

I was gradually getting used to the education system and wasn't doing too badly at school, although Ma let me stay up late to watch the scary movies on TV while my more sensible older sisters went to bed. This meant I was never the best at rising in the morning unless it was important, a trait that is with me to this day. Both Anne-Marie and Roisin did well at Toome Primary and went on to grammar school, but I hardly completed a full week, coming up with a range of diseases and infections that would have baffled medical science. There was no reason for my lack of application except that, apart from sport, metalwork and woodwork, school bored the life out of me. When I was there, I wanted to be somewhere else.

Although Dad had mares and foals around the place I was still showing no interest in them. In fact, it was my sisters who showed me the way. Like most girls of a certain age, they decided they wanted to take up riding. My dad was keen to encourage them and took them to Miss Kyle's riding school, not far from Billy Rock's stables. I was about nine, still into football and snooker, but I tagged along on a Saturday morning for something to do before *Grandstand* started in the afternoon. I wouldn't have considered watching the racing: all I wanted to see was the football scores and then the teleprinter for the Arsenal result.

At Miss Kyle's the horses knew a lot more than the riders. After a couple of visits I was put on an old pony and had a hack round on a lunging rein. Miss Kyle said to Dad that I showed signs of natural ability – I suppose she said that about everyone – but there was nothing in it for me.

However, something was fermenting in the back of my mind. Not long after I'd turned nine I asked Dad if I could have a pony. I'm sure he was pleased that I was showing an interest at last but it is to his credit that he never pushed me towards riding, just let me come to it in my own time. He was also too clever to be sucked into buying a pony on a whim – I might have been going through a phase. He knew a fellow, Pat Liddy, who had a little white pony his son used to ride and we ended up borrowing it. The more I got to handle the pony the keener I became, so Dad took the plunge and bought me one of my own.

When professional horsemen look back over their formative years they often recall fond memories of the first pony that put them right and sent them down the road to fortune and fame. Not me. The first pony Dad bought for me came straight out of a field and was the ride from hell. She was a dark chestnut with thoroughbred looks – and an absolute cow.

At five stone wet through I was hardly a match for her, on or off the ground, and Dad had to pin her against the wall to get a bridle on. He is an incredibly patient man and as he struggled with her he looked over and said, 'Don't worry, she'll be better when we get some work into her and get her back down.' No chance. The fitter she became, the stronger she was, and her temperament got even worse. It was time to call in the professionals.

Dad was friends with Billy Rock and there was a lad in his yard who had ridden in point-to-points. He came down to put some manners on the mare. We took her to a large country estate not far from home where the roads are private and no traffic intrudes. The lad was legged up but no sooner were his feet in the irons than she was off, charging through trees and doing her best to get rid of him.

She was uncontrollable, but I persevered. I used to dread getting on her because I knew that nine times out of ten I would be heading for a fall. I never did get the better of her, but on reflection I owe that madam more than I thought at the time: nothing was ever going to be so hard again. Still, she had to go. We got as far as naming her Seven Up, as that was the average number of times I had to remount in one session.

Dad was so concerned that he contacted a local dealer, John McKeever, and said, 'We want to be rid of this pony, John. It's been spoiled when it was young, but on no account let it go to anyone with children – it's dangerous.'

McKeever had a pony to exchange. 'It's broken and ready for riding but I know nothing more about it. I'll swap it with you.'

So I was the owner of a bonny mare I named Chippy. I still had my share of falls because Chippy was quick, but she showed me that there was plenty of excitement to be had from riding. We did the round of local gymkhanas and I soon had a good collection of rosettes on my bedroom wall. But I was becoming impatient with the endless waiting in collecting rings before I went out to jump. Kids are always restless and already my eye was fixed on bigger things.

Dad had known Billy Rock since before I was born and spent his Saturday mornings at the yard watching horses school and making himself useful. I'd see Billy regularly at the pony races and gymkhana held at the back of Randalstown on Wednesday evenings in the summer. The lasting friendship of my dad and Billy gives the lie to the often misguided opinion about religious intolerance in Ulster. My family is Catholic, Billy Rock and his wife Yvonne are Protestant, like many of my dad's friends on the point-to-point circuit. But their warm relationship has stood the test of time. Ma has a well-tuned sense of humour and, during the July season of apprentice-boy parades, would greet Billy with a gleeful 'Should you not be out marching today instead of training horses?'

Not missing a beat he'd come back, 'Wasn't it you I saw on the news last night throwing stones at the soldiers?'

Ma had also been known to put sprigs of shamrock all over the cab of his horsebox on St Patrick's Day. The *craic* was always good.

Billy Rock changed my life for ever when one day he asked me the question I'd been secretly waiting to hear for weeks: 'How are you getting on with those ponies, Anthony? Would you like to sit on one of these?'

The mixed bag of chasers, hurdlers and pointers towered over me. I couldn't wait. The only problem was that I was hardly over five stone. There was no way I'd be able to hold one side of any of these brutes. Then along came Wood Louse. A rotten name for a gentleman of a racehorse.

He'd started life at the top end of Flat racing as the property of Sheikh Mohammed and was trained in England by Ian Balding. Wood Louse was transferred to John Oxx at the Curragh but a leg injury finished him on the Flat and Billy had bought him cheap at the sales. In truth, Wood Louse was a Christian, quiet as a lamb – if a bomb had gone off beside him he wouldn't have budged. But I thought he was a champion as I trotted away on him.

From that day on, my days with Chippy were numbered. It became a regular thing every Saturday morning to go the eight miles with Dad to Billy's yard. I couldn't be roused to get out of bed at eight fifteen during the week to catch the bus to St Olcan's High School, Randalstown, but I needed no prodding at seven fifteen on Saturday for my tuition at Mr Rock's. The trouble was, I liked it too much and reckoned school was intruding on my real business.

I'd never been great at homework and used the bus ride in to crib off the brighter lads. One was Kevin Docherty, a really nice fellow who was tragically hit by a car and killed in 1995. I'm sure the teachers must have known about the cheating because his and my spelling and maths mistakes were the same, but they never said anything. They were pleased enough to keep the peace.

The first couple of years went relatively smoothly but I was at the yard every day of the holidays. Gradually, I became part of

Billy's team and he did nothing to discourage me. If he was short-staffed he'd say, 'Anthony, I've got three runners to go to Fairyhouse, do you fancy going with them?' School never won. Wednesdays were often race days at Naas or Fairyhouse, so instead of the school run I'd be heading across Belfast in the box going south, sitting alongside the old driver Davey Logan. There was nothing he liked more than a drink and when we got near home he'd park the box, take me into the pub and buy me dinner.

When the attendance officer phoned to see where I was Ma would say I'd got all kinds of things. I don't think she knew you could only get measles, mumps and chicken-pox once. Often her patience ran thin and she'd refuse to drive me to Billy's. I would stand defiant on the doorstep, all five and a half stone of me, demanding, 'Right, get me the *Yellow Pages* and I'll get myself a cab!' By the time I was fourteen I didn't see how I could fit school into my schedule. Ma was furious: 'That Billy Rock is ruining you.'

Billy was certainly letting me see another side of life and, like many youngsters who are let loose in an environment they feel comfortable in, I learned fast. Billy can be argumentative and is probably best described as 'his own man', but he treated me like a son.

To supplement his training operation, Billy had a thriving business artificially inseminating cows, which meant he was away after first lot in the morning. He knew right enough that if he told me to do something I'd make sure it was done, no matter if there were five to ride out then muck out. The problem was that he gave me the instructions for the older lads in the yard and I had to be diplomatic when I passed on the boss's wishes.

He rewarded me well, too, and at the age of fourteen I was being given a hundred pounds a week, which was good money. I'd come home on Saturday night and sit counting the ten tenners. With an air of heavy sarcasm Ma would say, 'Do you think you're working in a bank? The way you're counting those notes, you'll wear the print off them.' I'd keep the smile on my face and add them to my growing bankroll.

I had to break into it sooner than I would have liked. After I decided to buck the system I had to arrange transport from Moneyglass to Cullybackey and invested a week's wages in a bike – but not just any bike: it was a hand-built Holdsworth racing cycle, whose owner had gone to England to work on the buses. It proved a reliable steed and built up my fitness level as I rode the eight miles each way. There were plenty of hills and different routes and I'd set myself imaginary targets, riding finishes against the best jockeys around – I never got beat.

I still had to make the odd guest appearance at St Olcan's and soon news of my riding aspirations leaked out. When the older lads saw me in the corridor they'd shout, 'Nice to see you turning in today, Lester.' They thought it was funny.

Around this time one of the teachers asked me what I thought I would do when I officially left school and I fired straight back, 'Be a jockey.'

'Ah, just like your father.'

'I said jockey, not joiner.' And felt like screaming, 'Pay attention!' But I didn't.

Eventually I'd had enough. When pressure from the attendance officer became too strong I'd be there under protest, but my mind would drift off to what I could be doing at Billy's.

One day after school I announced to Ma that I wasn't going back. 'I've finished.'

'You can't.'

'It's done.'

Ma, as always, was trying to do the right thing but Dad understood. I'm like him in many ways and we've got the same outlook. Once I'd made my thoughts clear he was with me: 'Not a bother.'

Billy was right behind me, too, and was a fine ally if the attendance officer came snooping. One morning we were working on his small round gallop when I saw a van parked by the hedge at the bottom of the field. 'Billy, I think that's the school officer looking for me.'

I disappeared into the distance and Billy dashed off to confront the enemy. The man was sitting in his van and Billy grabbed him by the lapels through the window. 'What are you doing sneaking round here? This is private property.'

'I've come to check the overhead power supply, there's been a power cut.' Then, to underline his credentials: 'I work for the electricity board.'

Billy knew he'd picked the wrong opponent. 'Well, that's OK then,' he said by way of an apology and went off to find me, leaving the electricity man staring nervously after him.

Finding me, though, wasn't the easiest task. Whenever I thought the attendance officer was around I'd hide for a couple of hours behind hedges until I thought it was safe to come out. No point in taking risks.

Although my school work was suffering I was graduating nicely at Billy's university, which had been rehoused: he'd had a new yard purpose-built near the old one, with thirty-two boxes, a horse-walker and swimming pool. I was riding in all the work and schooling over hurdles and fences. However, when Billy took horses away to work at racecourses I didn't always go because you had to be over sixteen to work on premises licensed by the Turf Club. Because of this I became a myth.

Billy often took a box of six to work at the Curragh in the south. At this time his jumpers were ridden by the emerging young star Conor O'Dwyer, and Anthony Powell. The horses were all sizes and temperaments, which meant that the boys would be run away with one week or run off the gallop the next. Conor, who is as good a rider as you'll see and went on to win the 1996 Cheltenham Gold Cup on Imperial Call, came back to Billy one day shaking his head. 'Jesus, Billy, I couldn't hold this thing.'

Billy looked up at him quizzically. 'Och! Wee Anthony can hold him all right.'

Then, after a wooden-mouthed point-to-pointer had bolted with him, he'd trotted back to the trainer. 'Billy, I couldn't steer one side of this thing.'

Billy would stroke his chin thoughtfully. 'Wee Anthony can steer it all right.'

When the horses were schooling and they ran out or jibbed,

'Wee Anthony' never appeared to have any problems with them. Not surprisingly, the boys thought Billy was having them on. They'd never seen Wee Anthony and they were convinced he was someone Billy had made up to annoy them, that there was no such person.

Then I got my first lead up when my old friend Wood Louse won at Downpatrick. As Conor was legged up, Billy said casually, 'By the way, Conor, this is Wee Anthony McCoy.' Conor didn't say much and clearly wasn't convinced that I was the figment of Billy's imagination. The partnership won and I was the proudest young man on the track as I led them back to the unsaddling enclosure. As for Conor, he looked at me sceptically – but he's still got the photo of me leading him up and if you go to his house for dinner it won't be long before he tells the story of 'Wee Anthony'.

As far as Billy was concerned, rules were there to be broken and when it came to riding work and schooling at our local tracks I was there from the age of fourteen. Even then I liked to look the part and I'd ride with my toe in the iron, American-style, and watch my reflection in any windows we passed. One day we were working four horses at Dundalk, Conor, Anthony Powell, Tom Taaffe and me. Billy was watching with a couple of other trainers and asked them to pick out the amateur. When he told me they hadn't picked me I felt ten feet tall.

However, I was still tiny, despite getting into the poor eating habits – KitKat and crisps – that have stayed with me to this day, and my outlook stretched no further than my second home at Cullybackey. But Billy Rock had indestructible faith in me. One night he called me to one side when he got back to the yard. 'Anthony, you're very light and there's no point in me keeping you here for the rest of your life. There's a good chance you could make it as a Flat jockey, but not with me.'

I was happy in my little world but had to listen to Billy, who set about planning my next move. There was talk of me going for a two-week trial with John Oxx at the Curragh, but Billy decided against that. 'You'll be off gallivanting round the streets of Dublin, drinking and not riding horses the way you should. I've seen it happen to too many young men who had a future. I think Jim Bolger's is the place for you. I'll give him a call and you can go down for two weeks and see how you get on.'

Billy is a terrific salesman but he certainly oversold me to J. S. Bolger of Co. Carlow. With a conviction that would have done an evangelist proud he proclaimed, 'I've got a fellow here that's going to be a champion jockey and I want you to have him.'

Jim Bolger, maker of champions both human and equine, received this information at his laconic best: 'That's a powerful big statement, Billy. He can come for three weeks and we'll see.'

Dad and I made the long journey to Wexford in the family Toyota Camry and I was placed in digs at Mrs Delaney's with twelve others. It wasn't a holiday camp, and for the first three days I was terribly homesick but I knew there were only three weeks to do. By the time I was due to come home I knew exactly what I was going to do when I officially finished school.

In the meantime, I had found a way to get Mum off the hook when the attendance officer came calling. She was a well-meaning young lady who battered Ma with some hard facts. 'Mrs McCoy, do you know that Anthony is due to sit his GCSEs and if he doesn't go back to school you can be fined up to five hundred pounds a week?'

This news forced me to attend a meeting with the St Oclan's principal, P. J. O'Grady, a good man, who told me with a straight face, 'I think you had better sit your exams, Anthony. If Lester Piggott had passed his maths he wouldn't be in prison now for getting his sums wrong on his tax return.'

I left his office with the best of intentions but never returned until 1997, when the hatchet was well and truly buried and I was asked to present the end-of-term prizes. My own scholastic achievements were delicately brushed over.

Now I'd gone completely AWOL and Ma gave an Oscar-winning performance when the attendance lady called: 'Sure, he's run away from home and gone to Co. Carlow. I never hear from him now. I don't know what he's doing.'

It was a great get-out because I was under another government down there and had taken the same route as countless rebels. It didn't put Mum in a good light but she could live with that. As far as my dad, Billy Rock and I were concerned, it wasn't a bother.

But, in the fullness of time, I realized I wasn't quite so clever as I thought and had underestimated Mr O'Grady. He was no one's fool and had a good idea of what was going on. He called Billy Rock. 'Mr Rock, I realize that Anthony McCoy is not going to be an academic. I'd like you to tell me how you think his life will pan out.'

Billy told him what he thought was the gospel truth. 'Mr O'Grady, if he avoids injury and bad luck I think he is going to be a very successful jockey.'

'Thank you, Mr Rock.'

From that day on a blind eye was turned on the school attendance register. Mr O'Grady would have been under some pressure, but I'd like to think I've justified his faith in me.

3. From Rock to a Hard Place

From the moment I arrived back from my summer trial with Jim Bolger I couldn't wait to get back to Co. Carlow: I had seen another, more focused approach to racing and I knew I had to become part of it if I was going to succeed. I'd created a favourable enough impression for Mr Bolger to call Billy Rock, but if Billy had been expecting a show of enthusiasm from my soon-to-be boss he was mistaken. The no-nonsense Jim Bolger told him that there was no chance I'd make it on the Flat. 'Billy, he looks all right but it's impossible to tell what he'll do.'

Billy Rock would not be thwarted: 'I'm telling you, he's something special.'

'Well, I'm telling you that he'll be too big to stay on the Flat.'

Billy kept this career-shattering observation from me, but it made him sit back. 'What do you mean? He's barely six stone.'

'Don't worry about that. I met his mother and father when he came here in the summer, and it's a genetic certainty that, unless there's a physical defect, a boy will always grow taller than his mother. If this boy grows taller than his, he's going to be too big for the Flat. Forget all this talk about the size of hands and feet, this is a certainty.'

Shortly before my sixteenth birthday I was on my way to join Jim Bolger. I'd be lying if I said I wasn't worried: it's a massive step to leave home for the first time, and although I was joining a yard that had a reputation for turning out top-class apprentices, I knew it would be tough.

Ma kept asking me if I was sure I wanted to go, and 90 per cent of me was on green. It was the other ten on red that was the problem. Billy Rock provided a safety-net.

'Jim Bolger will be a hard taskmaster but he's straight. Give it a go and if you don't like it you can come back to me and I'll pay you two hundred a week and teach you to bull the cows.'

I'd got some insurance. Like anyone who takes it out, I hoped I wouldn't have to draw on it. I knew to expect no favours but I was also aware that in Jim Bolger I had a man who would be tough but fair, who had a good reputation for making young jockeys and giving them a firm footing for the future.

In many ways Jim is like Martin Pipe: both are self-made within racing and both pursue their careers with a fierce single-mindedness. Unlike Martin, whose riding career produced just one point-to-point winner, Jim had three successes from twelve rides, all trained by himself. It would have been four if he had been able to ride his good mare Pigeon's Nest at Galway. However, he was called away to inspect a filly who was running for him at Goodwood and had suffered a knock while travelling. The amateur Peter Scudamore deputized at Galway but didn't hang around for the celebrations as he'd claimed the wrong allowance – seven pounds instead of five due to a difference in the English and Irish system of claiming. He didn't do too badly when he turned professional, and one day I'd fill his boots in more ways than one.

Jim spent his early working life in accountancy in the motor trade. He took out his first licence to train in July 1976 and it wasn't long before he made it to the top. In doing so he built up his magnificent base at Coolcullen, sending out quality horses to win some of the best races in Europe.

As far as I was concerned, though, it was the way he nurtured human talent that drew me. Each period in racing produces trainers who are great tutors of jockeys. In England during the last thirty years Frenchie Nicholson and Reg Hollinshead have stood out. Champions like Pat Eddery and Kevin Darley have come through those particular schools with many others. In Ireland, Liam Browne and Jim Bolger had no peers in the same period. Liam produced Mark Dwyer, Pat Gilson, Stephen Craine and Mick Kinane. The Bolger boys included three champion Flat apprentices, Kevin Manning, twice, Willie Supple and Seamus Heffernan. The excellent Ted Durcan would come a little later.

A month before my sixteenth birthday it was arranged for me to make the journey south, this time for keeps. Dad drove me to Punchestown for the opening day of the Festival, where the Bolger-trained and Charlie Swan-ridden Vestris Abu won the BMW Champion Novices' Hurdle. It seemed like a good omen, and although the lads didn't pay much attention to me as I was brought back to Coolcullen in the horsebox, I knew I was on a winning team.

On the whole I got on well with most of the lads – at under six stone I wasn't much of a physical threat – which was a good thing as I had to get from Mrs Delaney's to the yard every day, some of the older ones had cars and it wasn't a trip you wanted to walk. I struck up a friendship with Conor Everard that endures to this day and was priceless to me at the time.

Conor was one of the senior apprentices, about four years older than me, a lifetime at that age. Most of the lads found him quite difficult to get along with – he wasn't that big but he had a desperate bad temper. If someone gave him gyp he wouldn't think twice about getting stuck into them. But I got on well with him from the start. He never refused me a lift and if he thought someone was taking a liberty with me he'd take them into the feed room and give them a belting. His big problem was getting out of bed. Each morning was the same. If you wanted cereal and toast before you got to the yard you had to get up early and Conor was worse than me at getting up – and that's saying something. Needless to say, I ate most of my breakfast on the frantic car ride to the yard.

Conor won the 1996 Heinz 57 Phoenix Stakes on the 20–1 chance Mantovani, which Jim owned and trained. It wasn't enough to keep him in racing and he's out of it now.

There were extremely strict non-negotiable ground rules at Coolcullen: no smoking, no drinking and do not miss Mass, particularly during Lent. For every one of the forty days we were escorted to the church a mile from the yard. It certainly did us no harm. Jim put you on the odds early: 'The policy here is no smoke or drink. We have no problems with any fellow that wants to smoke or drink. He just has to make the decision and decide what he wants to do. Does he want to smoke and drink or work here?' If Jim caught the odour of either on a man's breath he was given notice. Fortunately it was never going to be a concern for me: I've never had the slightest desire to smoke. The idea of it makes me feel sick.

I'm certainly not against drink, though. Indeed, all my family have a glass of something occasionally and nearly all my friends drink to various degrees but it was never for me. However, it is a misconception that I have never touched alcohol and I tried it earlier than most. I can remember sitting with my dad at the age of six and having a sip of his 'hot one', a mixture of whiskey, hot water and sugar, and I didn't mind it at all. There was never any danger of me becoming the youngest alcoholic in Co. Antrim, though, and that brief brush with the drink wasn't repeated.

As I got older I didn't like the smell of the raw spirit, and when I felt brave enough to dip my tongue into something I shouldn't I didn't like the taste. In fact, it made me feel a bit sick. Over the years when I've been with the boys on a night out someone has tried to put a large vodka in my Diet Coke but I only have to get my nose into the glass to know it's been got at. As for anything stronger, the only thing that has been up my nose is a Vicks Sinex when a cold hits me.

But I wouldn't be the first jump jockey to abstain from drink. Three previous champions, Tommy Stack, Jonjo O'Neill and John Francome, showed little or no interest in it when they were riding. Jim would have approved.

I have no way of knowing what it's like to be in an army camp but I'd be surprised if it were much different from the yard at Coolcullen. Every lad was in jodhpurs and polished boots, every horse had its own bridle, rug, pad and girth. Each lad had the same colour skull cap. Immaculate.

Once the horses were tacked up for first lot and circling in the yard, the head lad Dave Downey would phone the boss from the tack room. 'We're waiting on you.'

About twenty-five to thirty horses would be walking around the yard and the lads would be talking freely until they heard the metallic clang of the catch on the gate at the bottom of the yard, which signalled the arrival of the boss. Then there was absolute silence. As soon as he was out of the yard, either to walk to the gallops or go in his car, there would be plenty of chat again. But when we met him on the gallops and we were circling around him, there was no speaking until you were spoken to when the work instructions were given. I don't think it's exaggerating to say that if we were not exactly frightened of him, we were certainly in awe of him. Everything had to be right, and because of his reputation for making young jockeys we wanted to please him.

It was drilled into us that every horse had to be ridden properly. Jim was a big fan of the American style and it is possible, with his application, that he might have made it as a professional rider. He would have been a terrible hard man to out-think in a race. He took time to make sure that you rode with just your toe in the iron and not the whole foot. There were persistent put-downs: 'Look at the state of you, tidy yourself up. Who's ever going to give you a ride looking like you do? Sit up straight and at least try to look like a jockey.'

I became obsessed with how I looked and never missed an opportunity to glance at my reflection in a window or the side of a car to check my appearance. After I'd been there a while I often rode out seven lots in a morning, another horse tacked up for me each time I returned. The yard routine wasn't like it is in England where lunch runs from around twelve thirty to four o'clock. Our break was from one to two fifteen and before you left the yard it had to be pristine. The walking surfaces were mainly woodchip for the safety of the horses and there couldn't be a straw left on it. Us apprentices would spend the rest of the afternoon in the yard, going round all the boxes removing the droppings. If Jim wasn't racing and was home he'd come round the yard in the afternoon to check. You minded what you were doing, all right.

Through his business dealings outside of racing Jim knew that delegation was the secret of success. He had a top-class head man in Dave Downey, and when the strain got too much for him and he stepped down, another in the same mould took over, Pat O'Donovan. The stable also had a useful amateur rider and an assistant trainer who would do quite well when he took up training. He wasn't imposing, with his quiet demeanour and wire-rimmed spectacles – which were less in evidence than they are today – but there was always something about Aidan O'Brien.

Still only in his early thirties, Aidan O'Brien has established himself at the pinnacle of world Flat racing, matching the achievements of his illustrious but non-related namesake Vincent at Ballydoyle. Like him, he made his first mark with jumpers and saddled his first Cheltenham Festival winner with Urubande in the 1996 Sun Alliance Novices' Hurdle. His handling of the triple Champion Hurdler Istabraq has been a textbook lesson in how to peak a horse continually each season for the race that matters. But it is on the Flat that Aidan has set a wonderful standard of excellence. The list of his Group race successes grows impressively each year, and in 2001 he was following the Irish greats Vincent O'Brien and Paddy Prendergast when he topped the trainers' prize-money championship in England. That magical season could hardly have been bettered by the Derby–Oaks double of Galileo and Imagine. Then came the Breeders' Cup at Belmont Park on 27 October. The previous year Aidan had seen the 'Iron Horse' Giants Causeway beaten in controversial circumstances when Mick Kinane, in a rare lapse, lost hold of the reins in the final hundred yards. This time they returned in style with the unbeaten two-year-old Johannesburg, who beat the best young horses America had in the Breeders' Cup Juvenile.

When Ballingarry won the Criterium de Saint Cloud on 13 November he became Aidan's twenty-third Grade One winner of the season, which beat the North American best of Bob Baffert by one. In achieving this, Aidan had won no fewer than nine of the ten European Group One races open to colts.

Like the rest of Ireland, I felt extremely proud as I watched him, on television, receiving his trophy after Johannesburg's success. I savoured the moment, then slipped into a steaming hot bath to sweat off three pounds for the Sunday action at Aintree – but that's another story.

Back in 1990 Aidan wore his spectacles as little as possible, I suspect so that Jim's confidence in his riding wouldn't be undermined. It wasn't. He rode his first winner as an amateur on the Bolger-trained Galacto Boy at Punchestown in January 1989 and went on to become champion amateur rider in 1993–4. I think Aidan will admit that he learned a lot at Coolcullen and Jim held him in high regard. If there was a horse with a problem he'd often say, 'Give it to Aidan.'

With most of us, Jim was usually Boss, but Aidan always called him 'sir' or even 'Mr Bolger'. I know that, until quite recently, he still referred to Jim as 'Mr Bolger' as a mark of respect. But that's the kind of unassuming man he is. He was there for my first two and a half years until he broke his shoulder and joined his wife Anne-Marie, who was training.

After I'd been in the yard five weeks I turned sixteen and was due to sign on for my apprenticeship. The Irish indentures last three years – which is different from the English ones: they run from year to year and are more flexible. Before an Irish apprentice signed he was interviewed by stewards of the Irish Turf Club in the presence of his parents and the trainer or his representative. This would happen before a race meeting and my chosen place of inquisition was a night meeting at Dundalk. My parents travelled down from the north and I went to Dundalk in the horsebox with our travelling head lad, Tom Gallagher.

I sat in the front of the lorry and didn't say much. My mind was going flat out with a mix of excitement and apprehension. However, I was with a good man. Tom's son, Dean, had graduated through the ranks at Bolger's and was doing well in England so Tom knew what I was going through. After he left Bolger's, Tom joined another pillar of Irish racing and is now head lad to Dermot Weld.

I presented myself before the stewards, who tried unsuccessfully to put me at my ease. They wanted to make sure I realized what I was signing up to. 'Mr McCoy, you realize that in signing these indentures you will be under the guidance of Mr Bolger for three years and will be bound by the Rules of the Irish Turf Club?'

'Yes, sir.'

I went through the remainder of the interview with the minimum of comment. When they asked if I had any questions I said, 'No, sir,' and the interview was terminated.

Ma said little but thought a lot. When we came out she couldn't hold her concern. She looked at me long and hard, then said, 'Are you sure this is what you want to do? You'll be tied up for three years and that's a long time.'

Although I felt apprehensive I put on the bold front: 'Look, Ma, there's no point in me going back to school. They've probably forgotten what I look like and, in any case, I'm never going to be a brain surgeon – I haven't got the brains. If I don't make a go of this I don't know what I'm going to do.'

I wasn't the only one signing on that month. Paul Carberry also joined the team. With him around I was going to have a lead horse of the worst kind: Paul came with a thorough racing pedigree. His father, Tommy, was a legend in and out of the saddle, winning the Cheltenham Gold Cup three times and the Grand National. Great things were predicted for Paul and eventually he fulfilled them, although the saying 'You can't breed tame ones from wild ones' applies to Paul. He is four months older than me and arrived a month or so later, intent on taking on life with his foot nowhere near the brake. Calvin McCormack, who rides in the north of England now, came at the same time.

It was a difficult job trying to control all us apprentices but with Carberry it was impossible. He was certainly no stylist then. In fact, he was a desperate rider but he learned quick, and he hadn't a taste for the drink – yet. As I've said, Jim had warned us off: 'If I catch any of you drinking I'll have my foot on your throat.' I still think, however, that because of Paul's pedigree there was just a little more give. He certainly got going quicker than me, although as time wore on I got the impression that Jim didn't like him that much.

Paul had already achieved more than the new intake of apprentices, having ridden in the Foxhunters' at Liverpool, but Jim had a fine way with words, and he said, of Tommy sending Paul to Coolcullen, 'Your daddy definitely doesn't like you.'

Paul Carberry is the classic case of natural ability and class coming through to the top. When he rode his first winner he had his whole foot in the iron and looked bigger on the horse than he does now, and he's grown to five foot nine. Today there isn't a more talented rider around.

I kept my head down, waiting to get the nod that I was ready for my first ride, and it came one morning in the tack room.

The tack room of any yard is the equivalent of the boot room in a soccer club. It's where everyone congregates between lots or after work to dwell on matters equine and human, what's worked well and is worth a punt, who's misbehaved and is going to get a shunt out of the door. Tack rooms come in all sizes, but the mixture of saddle soap, hoof oil and liniment is an evocative scent that once inhaled is never forgotten. No matter how successful a man becomes in racing he only needs to step into a tack room to bring himself down to earth.

Like everything else at Coolcullen the tack room was a model of its kind. Each lad had his own locker in which he kept his grooming kit, waterproofs and any personal items. Around the walls were pictures of past winners, but the most daunting and motivating sight for us youngsters were the photographs of the lads who had made it to the winner's enclosure. The champion apprentices Kevin Manning and Willie Supple were up there, cool young professionals along with Dean Gallagher and Gerry Supple, who had ridden Flat winners before moving on to jumping. I just wanted my picture to be up there too.

Jim gave me the news I'd been waiting for after first lot one morning. 'I've a ride for you on Saturday at Phoenix Park. Nordic Touch in the six-furlong handicap.'

He didn't say much else but he didn't need to. All I could reply was 'Thanks very much,' but inside I was churning with excitement. No matter what any jockey tells you, there's no feeling like getting that first ride. After that it's the first winner, the first fifty and so on, like the hamster in his wheel. At that stage, I couldn't have imagined how fast my own wheel was going to spin.

It had taken me five months to get to the first serious milestone in my career and I didn't spare the phone, calling Ma and Dad and the staunchest of my supporters, Billy Rock, who was surprised it had taken Jim so long to give me a chance. There was no way he and Dad were going to miss the Olympic Extended Handicap, which rounded off the Phoenix Park programme for 1 September 1990.

Nordic Touch had six stone eleven to carry as I had a ten-pound weight allowance, being a first-time-out apprentice, but although I was only around six stone four I wanted to ride on a seven-pound saddle. I started as I was forced to go on and watched what I ate on the days running up to the race.

There wasn't the slightest danger that I'd get delusions of grandeur. In fact, I had something of a double shift. As my race was the last on the card, I had to lead up one of the stable's other runners early in the day so I travelled in the horsebox. I got changed into the white- and purple-striped colours of Jim's wife, Jackie, leaving myself plenty of time to have my photo taken with Dad – if nothing else happened after this, there'd still be one memory.

Jim was typically thorough and walked the track with me, explaining what he expected me to do. I'm sure he knew that the six furlongs would be gone in an instant and that I wouldn't be able to tell him anything, but he wanted us all to start thinking like professionals from day one of our careers.

Willie Supple was the senior apprentice on the team and Jim told him to look after me in the weighing room. Willie was a grumpy little shit – and I think he was only happy being miserable and making everyone around him the same – but he looked after me all right, with a few grunts here and there for guidance. It was just his way. We've remained really good friends as the years have gone on and how well Willie has done is a reflection on the Bolger school: he's now second retained jockey to Hamdan Al Maktoum. Now he's based in England I see more of him, even though he's on the Flat. If he's riding local to Newbury and needs a bed for the night he usually calls in.

Jim made it his business to lead us inexperienced apprentices out of the parade ring, which meant the last person we saw on foot before the start was him. Jim always reckoned that the first ride was like letting a bird fly from the nest and it was right that he should be doing the pushing. He ran alongside for fifty yards just to make sure everything was all right.

Willie wasn't riding in the race, so Jim told Christy Roche to look after me. Christy was our stable jockey and there hasn't been a more wily customer to put his leg over a horse. Christy must have forgotten more than many jockeys ever learn, and if he'd been on a horse with a big chance that day I dare say he wouldn't have paid quite so much attention to me as he did.

As it was he was on Roesboro, relatively unfancied, but he was drawn in stall one, not far from me in five. I was in early enough and he kept calling across to me, 'Anthony, you all right? Don't worry, just relax.'

Some chance! Lining up against me that day were some of the biggest names in Flat racing, like Mick Kinane and John Reid. I sat in stall five shitting myself.

I'd been told to track Christy but I don't remember anything of the one minute 11.6 seconds it took for the race to be run, except that I was soon up with the pace and flapped around to finish sixth to Johnny Murtagh on Town Ablaze, beaten by about five lengths. When I got back to unsaddle Jim gave me a bollocking, just to let me know he'd been watching me. At the end of it he peered down at me with a look that said, 'Are you ever going to learn something?' Then, before I went back to weigh in, with the wind shot from my sails, he said to me, 'Did you enjoy yourself?'

There were times in our relationship when I thought he was looking right through me and out the back, but Jim had a kind side – it was just that he made sure he kept it well covered when we were kids.

It was a surprise to many people that Nordic Touch started 4–1 favourite, backed in from 7–1, but it wasn't stable money and Jim had a shrewd idea where the inspiration came from. 'Billy Rock was down there spoofing to everyone about A. P. McCoy. That's why the horse was favourite.' For what it's worth, Nordic Touch never won a race.

I had to wait until 23 October for my next ride, Nordic Wind in the Sea Charger Nursery Handicap for two-year-olds at the Curragh. The pressure was on because Paul Carberry had already ridden his first winner on Petronelli at Leopardstown in early August. Jim had two in the race, Nordic Wind and the much better fancied Heavy Beat, ridden by Willie Supple and the 2–1 favourite. My ten-pound allowance took the weight down to seven stone seven, and I made the most of a light weight and was soon up with the pace over seven furlongs. Willie drove Heavy Beat ahead with just under two furlongs remaining. I did everything in my limited repertoire to force Nordic Wind to close the gap, but although we took second close home we were still a length behind where it mattered.

I was gutted, no other word for it. As we pulled up I called him every name I could lay my tongue to, 'greedy bastard' being one of the more restrained. Willie just smiled. He's got the picture to this day and takes great pleasure in showing it to visitors and asking if they can name the rider finishing second.

That was me finished with race riding that season. During the whole of the 1991 season, from 4 May to 22 October I had just seventeen rides, finishing second twice. Carberry didn't do much better and I think it was Jim's way of keeping us firm-footed.

I also learned a valuable lesson that honesty is not necessarily the best policy when it comes to riding winners. Towards the end of September Jim had Heavy Beat entered for the final of the Derrinstown Apprentice Series at the Curragh on 28 September. There was another good lad in the yard, Mick Martin, whom Jim thought a lot of, and he asked us if either of us could do the weight of six stone thirteen. I said that I would do seven stone two but Mick said he'd manage seven stone. Fair enough, he could get closer to the right weight than me so he got the ride. The horse duly won but with Mick putting up five pounds overweight at seven stone four - two pounds higher than I would have done, and it wasn't as though any overweight would have mattered: Heavy Beat went well clear inside the final furlong and won by six lengths.

I was pig sick that I'd told the truth and missed riding my first winner. Ever since, I've been paranoid about putting up overweight. As for Mick, he was a nice lad who came to England but never cracked it. He returned to Ireland and, after having a few rides over jumps, he drifted out of the game.

Then came 26 March 1992 and the Silvermines Three-Year-Old Maiden. Once again, Jim had two in the race. Christy Roche was on the more fancied Northmaid and I was on the 20–1 shot Legal Steps. Jim didn't go racing that day but had a word with me before I left. He told me that he considered we had a chance. As it turned out it was one of the easiest Flat winners I'd ever ride. I was beginning to feel more at ease in a race and although this one was over a mile and a half I was never far off the pace and took Legal Steps ahead inside the final quarter-mile. We never saw another horse and strolled home by eight lengths, with me trying to look as elegant as possible. No matter what a jockey achieves, he never betters the feeling of that first win. You've justified yourself and those who had faith in you. The race was worth £2,243 and I felt like a millionaire.

Although Christy was on the wrong one and well beaten, he was generous in his praise. For a seventeen-year-old rookie, getting a pat on the back from one of the top men was as good as it could get. None of my family was able to make the journey, but they'd watched the race in the local betting shop, Toal's in Toomebridge, and were still bubbling when I called them later. It was left to Jim to bring me rapidly down to earth: 'Did you have to win so far?' he inquired.

When I got back to the yard there was no time for celebration. I'd made up my mind that strong drink wasn't for me so I watched television and dreamed of the big-time. However, any thoughts I had of being a shooting star were soon checked and I managed twenty-two rides for no more wins before the season ended.

Although the season had finished, the hard work was just beginning, with the yearlings coming in from stud and needing to be broken – but it was my leg that shattered when Kly Green got rid of me that icy January morning.

4. Cuckoo Back in the Nest

I was in the depths of depression. Just as my career had taken off it had been cut down, and I faced six months on the sidelines when I'd hoped to be making headlines. The leg break was a bad one but in Jim Bolger I had the right kind of boss. If you served him well, then only the best would do for you.

He realized that living with four other lads in a house that resembled a pig-sty was not the best place to recuperate so I returned home to Moneyglass with his blessing. Dad said that he would make arrangements for me to attend the Royal Hospital in Belfast for my rehabilitation but Jim would have none of it. 'You'll bring him down to Mr Kenny at Navan. He's the best there is and I'm paying. You'll bring him down whenever he wants to see him.' That was virtually every fortnight and the journey took up to two hours each way. Sometimes Dad would drive and on other occasions it was my sister Anne-Marie. She and I have always been close and it's just as well that she has a forgiving nature.

When I was no more than thirteen we were having an argument at home and I fled upstairs with one of Dad's shotgun cleaning rods in my hand. As she came after me howling abuse I launched the rod at her like a spear. It caught her in the mouth and broke several teeth. I was ashamed then and not proud of it now. Fortunately, today you'd never know.

As I was always good at sleeping, I'd doze through most of the journey to hospital, and when I returned home I was like a cuckoo, causing increasing resentment as I took up the space of three, sprawling on the sofa. And all the time my weight was rising with my height.

By March I was relatively mobile and settled down in front of the television to watch the Cheltenham Festival. It was the last race of the three days that held the attention of the McCoys. To all intents and purposes, a member of the family was performing at the greatest jumping show on earth: Thumbs Up was in the County Handicap Hurdle. The race wasn't televised, so we went down to Toal's and swelled with pride as the horse we had seen mature from a foal came with a smooth challenge at the final flight to beat High Baron by six lengths. Just to make it an all-Ulster victory my idol of the time, Richard Dunwoody, was on board. The last line on that race in the 1992–3 form books records 'bred by Peadar McCoy'. Indeed, that was the first time our name was associated with the home of jump racing, and it would be another three years before I made my first trip to the winners' enclosure there.

It was a good time to see my sisters and brother Colm growing up. Colm was doing well as an amateur boxer and won the junior all-Ireland championship at thirty-nine kilos. It was the natural sport for him as he was, and is, a fiery devil who hits first and asks questions later. Unluckily, the kind of coaching he needed to take him further was too far away and he drifted out of boxing. Like my sister Kelly, he is very sports-minded and plays hurling to a high standard. He was still too young to have any social life with me outside the house but in recent years we have formed a close bond. When I go home for a break he leads me round the local pubs, then takes the greatest pleasure in beating me on the pool table.

By the time I had the all-clear from Mr Kenny to return to work my siblings were ready to see the cuckoo fly the nest for the last time. When I returned to Coolcullen I began to slice off the excess weight with a stringent bout of self-denial. I managed to rid myself of nineteen pounds and was able to ride at seven stone twelve, but I knew I could only hold back nature for a limited time. Once again Jim Bolger was proved right: I'd be too big to become a Flat jockey.

I was lucky at this time that I had plenty of distractions from eating, supplied by Paul Carberry and the rest of the lads. There was lunacy and wildness in all of us, but Carberry had more. The summer nights were still light and when Carberry, Calvin McCormack and I came back from evening stables we discovered a pony in a field not far outside the village. It was wild and Carberry came up with the bright idea of seeing who could stay on it longest without a saddle or bridle. It took us an hour to catch it, then a few seconds later it buried whoever was on it before it disappeared into the distance, farting and kicking its legs out like pistons. We laughed our bollocks off.

We knew that if we three had trouble staying on then the other lads in the yard were 100–1, so we began to get them down to the field after work and took bets on how long they'd last. Well, there's always one bright spark in the bunch and one lad must have seen plenty of rodeos in films. He thought he'd tie some cord round the pony's neck to hold on to when we let him go, but the rope almost severed his index finger as the pony turned itself inside out getting him off.

We were always out looking for mischief so one day we ventured further afield on our bikes and found three Clydesdale–hunter crosses. They were slow enough but we couldn't catch them and hold on to them, so the next time we arrived with three bridles borrowed from the yard – if Jim had caught us God knows what the punishment would have been. There were hedges and ditches and we needed bridles to jump them, but we didn't bother with saddles, helmets or whips.

On another excursion we discovered a field of unbroken ponies. We got on three and the others began to run wild around us. The noise alerted the farmer who owned them. He came roaring after us in his four-wheel-drive. We thought we were Jesse James and his gang and made a getaway on the ponies, jumping in and out of fields over fences and wire. Unfortunately, Carberry had seen one too many cowboy films and thought a big stone wall with a strand of wire above it was a possibility. The pony was a better judge and stopped dead. Carberry sailed over on his own and ended up tangled in barbed wire, like Steve McQueen in *The Great Escape*. Carberry made more noise.

Being kids we thought it was funny, but we didn't fancy explaining the joke to the farmer so we hid in a ditch until he tired of looking for us. It was hard stopping Carberry moaning. Somehow he managed to cycle home but it wasn't until we went inside and turned on the light that we saw how bad he was. He was so white he was nearly blue. 'Just put me to bed and don't tell anyone I'm dying.'

After he'd been lying down for about an hour he got up, went to the toilet and came back really worried: 'I'm pissing blood!'

Jesus, we had to tell someone so we chose the landlady, Mrs Murphy, who wasn't best pleased at nearly eleven o'clock at night. She called a doctor who gave Carberry some pills and told him to rest, so he called in sick the next day but was back the following morning. It's as well Carberry was durable and just as well that Jim never found out. If he had I've no doubt that our careers would have stalled for a bit.

Nearly all the friendships I made at that time still hold firm to this day and one of the strongest is with TJ Comerford – he was always TJ, nothing else. He and I often hit the local Kilkenny disco, the imaginatively named Itchycoo. It ended at two a.m. but unless we got lucky, which wasn't often, we'd leave half an hour early to be sure of a spot in Supermacs, the burger bar nearby. TJ came over to England and rode for a time up north for Mary Reveley, but he went back to Ireland and is now one of the cogs in Aidan O'Brien's machine, travelling the horses world-wide.

Jim was a great tutor of men but he also had an incredible eye for a horse. He saw things that others would miss and it was this gift that enabled him to train some of the best horses in Ireland during the eighties and nineties. One of the best was St Jovite. Aidan rode him most of his work, and although the horse was never spectacular Jim never lost faith in him. He never overrated his horses either, as he proved when sending Jet Ski Lady over to win the 1991 Oaks at Epsom.

The next year it was St Jovite's turn to contest the Derby. Although he had developed into a useful two-year-old, winning the Group Three Anglesey Stakes at the Curragh and rounding off with a close fourth in the Grand Criterium at Longchamp, St Jovite didn't sparkle in the early work of his three-year-old career and finished a disappointing fourth when odds-on for the Gladness Stakes. This was where Jim Bolger came into his own. He worked

him with the slowest horses in the yard so that the horse knew
what it was like to quicken to win a gallop. In the Epsom Derby
he ran with great credit to finish two lengths second to Dr Devious,
but Jim was adamant that there was better to come and he was
right.

In the Irish Derby at the Curragh, three weeks later, he beat
the same horse by twelve lengths and won the most important
middle-distance weight-for-age race in Britain, the King George
VI and Queen Elizabeth Diamond Stakes at Ascot, by six lengths.
He was the first top-class horse I'd been connected with, albeit
loosely, but pride spreads like scent through a yard when you get a
champion, Flat or jumping. It's like following a football team,
identifying with them in victory or defeat.

I was ready to ride again in early August 1993, but even then I
knew my time on the Flat was over. It is impossible to cheat nature
and five of my first six rides on returning were in maiden races
where the weight was nine stone, which with my eight-pound
apprentice allowance meant my mounts would carry eight stone
six. My bodyweight had to be around eight stone three, which was
becoming harder and harder to achieve even though I boiled myself
in the sauna at Carlow.

I was coming towards the end of my three-year apprenticeship
and I made up my mind to leave Jim. Carberry had left six months
earlier to concentrate on jumping and I knew it was time for me
to go. However, you can't keep such things quiet in a yard and I'm
sure Jim got to know of my plan. He decided to hook me once
more and put me on his useful two-year-old Zavaleta in the
Autumn Nursery at the Curragh on 23 October.

The comeback win on Zavaleta was easy on all counts. The
weight was eight stone thirteen and I was able to ease the filly
considerably after taking the lead one and a half furlongs out to win
by two lengths. Despite this brief flirtation with success I knew I
was only staving off the inevitable. There was no future for me on
the Flat, and I went to tell Jim I was quitting.

Jim can be persuasive, though, and I was in awe of him. 'You're
some fool. There'll be plenty of opportunities for you here on good

horses.' He reasoned that if I kept my weight in check there would be rides for me in maiden races and on horses that were high in the handicap when my eight-pound allowance would come in handy. By the time the conversation was over I was hooked again and signed on. But this time it was only for another year on the understanding that I would take out a jumping licence.

It was five months before I was given my first ride over hurdles aboard a good old stable servant, Riszard. He had won Britain's longest Flat race, the Queen Alexandra Stakes at Royal Ascot, under Christy Roche in 1993, and was now a five-year-old.

It was not a dream début. The race was over two and a half miles at Leopardstown, which would hardly have got him warm over hurdles, but we began to make progress after the fifth and were bearing down on the leaders two out. Then Fate stuck out a hand. We were travelling well enough but Anabatic fell directly in front of us and we were brought down. I felt frustrated and miserable as I trudged back to the weighing room – where I didn't get an easy ride from Jim.

'You're some greenhorn. You should have known that horse was ready to fall.' Part of his frustration was due to my stupidity. 'And once you've fallen, you get straight up and stand there like a tree. You could have got flattened again!'

It was a day to remember for more than one reason. Twenty minutes earlier we had crowded round the changing-room television and watched The Fellow beat Jodami to win the Cheltenham Gold Cup before we dashed out to the paddock. If I had looked up towards the winning post as I got to my feet that day I would have seen Imperial Call galloping to victory. Two years later he, too, would win the Cheltenham Gold Cup under Conor O'Dwyer. Me? I'd have to wait a year longer, and at that moment such glory seemed a lifetime away.

I got round on my next three rides over hurdles and was back on Riszard when he made his next appearance in the Thomastown Maiden Hurdle at Gowran Park on 20 April. Because of the balls-up at Leopardstown I was feeling plenty of pressure and Jim was in no mood to ease it when he told me I'd kept the ride. 'I'm letting you ride that horse tomorrow. You know that Charlie Swan is wanting to ride it, and there's a few others have been on the phone for it as well.'

I didn't need this. Charlie Swan was the main man among Irish jump jockeys and I didn't want his long shadow cast over me.

But Jim hadn't finished sharpening me up. He brought in the owner, one of the biggest around at the time in both Flat and jumping, Henryk de Kwiatowski. 'I've told Henryk that I think you're capable of riding this horse and winning on it.'

Henryk de Kwiatowski was such a big player that I doubt he even knew Riszard was running, but nearly all my waking moments were spent going over that two-and-a-half-mile hurdle.

In the event there were only two worries. The first came when we made a mistake four out. The second came at the last flight when I could hardly believe we were so far in front and allowed Riszard to fiddle his way over rather than make his mind up and go for a big leap. The subsequent fumble never looked like stopping us and we came home by a distance, justifying 6–4 favouritism.

Jim still used me on the stable heavyweights on the Flat and I rode two winners on Gallardini within four days in May. I also returned home to ride my first winner in Northern Ireland when Huncheon Chance won a hurdle at Down Royal. This was also my first winner from an outside yard – not that I was any stranger to the trainer, Ian Ferguson.

Ian is one of the biggest point-to-point trainers in Northern Ireland and I'd seen plenty of him during my formative years with Billy Rock. It was great to come back and ride a winner at Down Royal, where I'd ridden gallops as a kid with Billy. It meant that Ma and Dad didn't have too far to travel either.

Ian switched Huncheon Chance back to the Flat and we won an apprentice race at Sligo in June and again at Bellewstown on 7 July. That was my last Flat win. The scales were now winning every round, and I had made up my mind to move to England. The way I looked at it, Charlie Swan had the best rides tied up in Ireland, and I'd seen how successful Adrian Maguire had become since he'd been in England. I'd seen him first when he used to arrive at Coolcullen to call on my immediate boss, Sabrina, who eventually became his wife. I'd bellowed him home in the 1992 Cheltenham Gold Cup on Cool Ground, and his rise to the top of the British-based jockeys alongside Richard Dunwoody made me aware of what could be achieved. Norman Williamson was also becoming a sought-after rider, and I set about making it known that I wanted away from Ireland.

The last hurdle winner I rode before I departed was Mollie Wootton at Kilbeggan. However, the most significant was a short head defeat on Havin' A Ball in the Harp Lager Handicap Hurdle at the Galway Festival. Although once I began earning my living as a jockey I was not one for having heroes I had a strong admiration for Richard Dunwoody. I didn't want to copy him – I was working things out for myself – but I did want to beat him, and from two flights out I felt I just had the edge over his mount, Ballyhire Lad. We were still locked together up the run-in but Woody had his horse's head down where it mattered on the line and we were beaten by a short head. I came back to the weighing room pig sick and began to change for my next ride. Unknown to me, Conor O'Dwyer was deep in conversation with one of the legends of the weighing room, Graham Bradley. Brad is a rarity in an English jockey in that he was sought after by Irish trainers and was in action during most of the big meetings. 'Who's the kid who just got beaten by Woody?' he asked Conor.

'Young lad called McCoy. He's with Jim Bolger but looks like coming to England.'

'Well, he can ride a bit,' said Brad, and made his way over to me. He could see how depressed I was, and put his hand on my shoulder. 'Don't worry, son, you'll get the better of him before long.'

It gave me a lift that someone of his standing had bothered to say something encouraging to me. It was the beginning of a friendship I value.

Other friends had been looking out for English opportunities on my behalf: the brilliant racing photographer Pat Healy and his friend Norman Williamson set about getting me a job as conditional jockey to Kim Bailey in Lambourn. Also, a friend who trains in the north, Paddy Graffin, was on good terms with Richard Dunwoody, who said he'd try to fix me up with a job at Martin Pipe's.

All this talk was bound to find its way back to Jim and he told me in no uncertain terms that he thought I was running before I could crawl, let alone walk. 'You should spend another year here.'

I told him I thought that Charlie Swan and Conor O'Dwyer had the game tied up.

Jim was at his most silver-tongued and explained that with another year I would be a stronger and better rider. I felt it would be time wasted. Then came the emotional blackmail harking back to Riszard: 'I put my licence on the line for you and this is how you repay me!' It was an exaggeration but, looking back, it probably showed how keen Jim was to keep me. He finished off with a verbal left and right: 'I spend four years teaching you to ride, then you go off and let someone else take the benefit!'

He had a sound point, but I only had thoughts for myself. In the years since, I have come to respect Jim Bolger even more than I did then: he is a man whose opinion I value and he is still convinced that I made the move a year early. On reflection he says: 'I wanted to be sure that the leg was strong. The move was twelve months premature. As it was, things worked out but a bad fall could just as easily have finished things. It was just like going jumping with a three-year-old. There are certain types you can rush and get away with and others you can't. The fact that A. P. McCoy got away with it does not make the decision right.'

Another who heard of my intentions was the former jockey-turned-bloodstock-agent Eddie Harty, who had won the 1969 Grand National on Highland Wedding, trained by Toby Balding.

The first job offer to go to the wall was Kim Bailey's. Norman Williamson had thought the deal was virtually done but then told me Finbarr Leahy had been taken on.

Des Scahill, the leading race-caller – whose opinion I often seek – is big friends with Jimmy FitzGerald, who trains at Malton in the north of England, and said he had a job for me, but I didn't fancy being based up there. The first fledgeling jump jockey that Des tried to steer towards Jimmy was Adrian Maguire and, like Adrian, I was ultimately to tread the same path to Toby Balding's yard.

But it wasn't all losers for Des: a certain Kieren Fallon lived a few doors away from him near the Curragh and was apprenticed to Kevin Prendergast. He called in to see Des one night and said he'd had enough and was going home to County Clare. 'Why not try it in England?' said Des.

'And where would I get a job?' asked a dejected Kieren.

Des phoned Jimmy. The following Monday Kieren was in Malton and two weeks later rode a winner on Evichstar. The rest is developing into a rather large chapter of racing history. Kieren's free spirit and single-mindedness have enabled him to win four jockeys' championships and to come back from a career-threatening fall at Royal Ascot in June 2000. He's won countless big races, including the Derby, the Oaks and the One and Two Thousand Guineas. On the debit side, he's lost top retainers with Henry Cecil and Sir Michael Stoute, but through it all I'm certain he has received the wisest counsel from Des.

Unknown to me, Toby Balding was showing an interest in me. Like many trainers in England he has excellent contacts in Ireland who uncover talent on four legs and two. As well as Eddie Harty, Toby also had a good man in the north, James McNicol, who knew of me through the racing grapevine. He called Toby: 'You ought to pay attention to this boy McCoy who's with Jim Bolger. I've known him all his life and he wants to go jumping in England.'

Toby had already brought Adrian Maguire to England and was interested enough in me to attend an evening meeting at Wexford on 19 July. He'd been looking at horses with Eddie and Dermot Day. I had one ride that night, finishing second on Havin' A Ball, nine days before the galling Galway near-miss. We were beaten three-quarters of a length in a mares' maiden hurdle after being upsides at the last.

I was still throwing the race around in my mind when Eddie Harty came into the changing room. 'I've got Toby Balding outside. Would you like to come out and meet him?'

I can imagine that I felt like quite a few kids would when the chief scout from a big soccer club comes up to them after a game for the local side. At that time Toby was a big player in jump racing, training a quality stable of jumpers at Fyfield, near Andover, and I was flattered he'd made contact.

I met Toby with a firm handshake and we looked each other straight in the eye. This was no time for bullshit. Toby cut an imposing figure. After the formalities were over Toby said, 'I've brought Adrian Maguire through to the top and now I'm looking for the one to follow him.' He went on to name some of the other jockeys who had begun with him, and the list was impressive.

Bob Champion, who won his battle against cancer and the 1981 Grand National on Aldaniti, was in his care for a long time. Richard Linley, who became retained rider for Sheikh Ali Abu Khamsin – one of the biggest jump owners of the seventies and eighties – was also a Balding boy. Then there was Richard Guest, who won the 1989 Champion Hurdle for Toby on Beech Road and subsequently the 2001 Grand National on Red Marauder, and plenty of others including Brian Reilly, Tony Charlton and Martin Coyle.

I was aware that, after some good seasons, the one just past had been only moderate by Toby's standards. He didn't attempt to fudge it. 'Why don't you come over for a couple of weeks and see if you like it? If you don't there's nothing lost and you can either come back here or try somewhere else. Last season wasn't the best but I've got plenty of horses for the new one. Adrian's gone to David Nicholson and, as you know, I've been known to give lads a chance.' If I had any inward misgivings Toby shot them away with his trump card: 'I've got access to Dave Roberts.'

This was like telling a footballer you were mates with Sir Alex Ferguson and he could have a place in the Manchester United first team. In jump racing, Dave Roberts is *that* influential. With the exception of Richard Dunwoody, Peter Scudamore and Tony Dobbin, he has acted as agent for most of the top jump jockeys over the last decade. It was through a Jim Bolger old boy, Dean Gallagher – whose father Tom had taken me to get my first licence at Dundalk – that Dave had got started. He was managing a few horses in training at Epsom with Geoff Lewis and was keen to get a job within racing. At that time Jason Swift, grandson of the great Australian jockey Scobie Breasley, was trying to get going as a rider on the Flat and Dave took over booking his rides. Dean was sharing lodgings with Jason and soon Dave was working with him and doing well. Before long, Richard Guest asked Dave to look after his interests and the transformation was dramatic. Guesty went from riding thirteen winners in a season to thirty-three then forty-three. When Adrian came to England and joined Toby – he had been brought over as a relatively unknown amateur by Martin Pipe to win the Fulke Walwyn Kim Muir Chase at the 1991 Cheltenham Festival – there was only one man to handle his rides.

Toby explained, 'I've got a good relationship with Dave, and I am sure he'll help you.'

Even though agents weren't so high profile then as they are now, I knew this was a big plus. Besides, there was nothing else on the table. In four years I'd ridden in 103 races, winning six on the Flat and seven over hurdles. I'd ended on the floor at the seventh when Paddy Graffin provided my first chase ride on No Sir Rom in a novice chase at Galway on 30 July. It wasn't the brightest CV in racing, so what did I have to lose?

I told Ma and Dad I'd be moving to England and honoured my obligations to ride through July. My career in Ireland ended when I weighed in after finishing second on Bellecara in a two-mile handicap hurdle at Gowan Park on Saturday 6 August. I'd been beaten a head by Brendan Sheridan on Sense Of Value, which rankled, but I had bigger things than a race on my mind.

I packed my kit with a sense of foreboding, that disappeared when Christy Roche and Willie Supple wished me luck. Then I slung my bag over my shoulder and headed for the battered old Peugeot van that had been mine for the previous two years. I put my foot down and headed for the Rosslare ferry to Fishguard. I was on my way.

5. Call Me Anthony

I made the two-hour journey to Rosslare, drove the old van into the hold and settled down for the three-hour crossing. I slept until we docked at Fishguard on the Welsh coast early on Sunday morning. I'd never been to England before. Armed with a large road atlas, I found my way across country and picked up the M4.

Toby had arranged temporary lodgings for me with a friend of his called Stafford Kent who lived nearby. Next morning I made my first appearance in the yard. It was a world away from the regimentation that marked Jim Bolger's operation. At Coolcullen I would not have dared enter the yard without wearing jodhpurs and highly polished boots. At Toby's jeans and wellies were the norm.

My boots kept their shine for the first three days, but the easy-going nature of the place suited me and I slipped into it like a comfy pair of slippers. In many ways it was reminiscent of Billy Rock's, where I'd spent the happiest, most carefree days of my life. At Coolcullen we'd never had to go on a road to get to the private gallops, but here the horses had to walk a mile or so to do their work and quite often there would be two or three abreast along the road with the lads smoking and chatting. If anyone had dared behave like that at Jim's they'd have been sacked before second lot went out.

When a lad joins a new yard it is rather like starting at a new school. I've never been outgoing, so when anyone asked my name I answered, as I always had, 'Call me Anthony.' That's what I'd been christened, it's what my family call me, and to this day Billy Rock calls me 'Wee Anthony'. Jim Bolger had always called me Anthony. I had never been addressed as Tony – until now. From day one at Fyfield I was Tony McCoy, and although Toby tried his best to stem the tide it was hopeless. He split the difference by calling me AP. It's quite easy to chart how long someone has known me from the form of greeting: Anthony pre-August 1994, Tony post-August 1994.

I hadn't been at Fyfield a week when I received a call from Paddy Graffin in Northern Ireland. 'Anthony, Richard Dunwoody has got back to me. He's arranged for you to see Martin Pipe about a job.'

I'd forgotten the kind gesture of my fellow countryman to get me on the road to being a jump jockey. Now I didn't know what to do. I couldn't ignore the offer of an interview with one of the most influential trainers jump racing has ever seen. On the other hand, I'd just started a new job with a trainer who had a reputation for getting a young jump jockey noticed.

I went down the usual escape route that jockeys use in uncomfortable situations: I put it out of my mind, hoping it would go away. There was no chance of that. Toby's secretary was Shirley Vickery who, at that time, was going out with Martin's son, David. She knew the situation and arranged for me to see Martin a week later. It was the right thing to do: it's only good manners to talk to someone when they offer you the chance of a job, but I didn't know whether to tell Toby.

Fortunately, the man was always approachable and easy to talk to. I was due to travel on the Sunday and the Friday before I told him what was happening. Toby was as sound and forthright in his advice as he has always been. 'I think you should go down and see him. You might regret it if you don't.'

The thought of an audience with the man who was turning centuries of training theories on their heads was intimidating. Martin Pipe had already won the trainers' championship in six of the previous seven seasons with many of jump racing's major races to his credit, including that year's Grand National with Miinnehoma and four of the previous five Welsh Nationals. He had trained Granville Again to win the Champion Hurdle in the season just gone. He had elevated Peter Scudamore to a position of near invincibility as champion jockey, and now Scu had retired he was doing the same for Richard Dunwoody.

Martin and his wife, Carol, made me welcome in their home. In some ways he reminded me of Jim Bolger. Like Jim, Martin would ask questions then ponder your answer, giving little away as to what he thought. It was unnerving so I wasn't completely comfortable. Anyway, I was just another raw chancer from Ireland who had ridden a few winners and thought he could make it. As we had lunch I was in awe of the man. Every ten minutes or so a little voice at the back of my mind would say, 'This man trains hundreds of winners a season. He makes champion jockeys.'

It soon became clear that Martin had done his homework on me. He knew some of the winners I'd ridden and, before lunch was over, he offered me a job as conditional jockey. This was heady stuff. Jonothan Lower and Martin Foster had been champion conditional jockeys under his guidance and if I took up the offer I would have a tremendous chance to do the same.

I pulled myself back to reality. 'Mr Balding has been very good to me, Mr Pipe. He came to Ireland to see me and arranged for me to come over. I'll talk everything over with him and get back to you.'

That didn't seem to worry Martin. 'Fine, it's up to you. Let me know.'

After first lot on Monday morning I went straight into the office to see Toby and explained how the meeting had gone. It is at times like this, when all aspects need to be considered, that Toby comes into his own.

'There's a fair chance that if you go there you will be conditional champion. He made a champion out of Jonothan Lower, but once you've lost your claim the rides might not be so plentiful. After that, the best you can hope for is to be second jockey to Dunwoody and, remember, Lower will still be around. There will also be a lot of hype with the job and I'm not sure you're ready for that at present.'

Toby's argument was subtly slanted towards keeping me at Fyfield.

'Here I will put you on whatever horses I can and, providing things work out, I've no doubt that Dave Roberts will get you plenty of rides. You can gamble on being champion conditional and then second jockey at Pipe's, or stay here and ride nearly all of mine.'

There was silence for a few seconds. Then he said, 'I think you should stay here.'

In the end I knew I wanted to stay where I was – for the time being, at least.

Now I had to tell the champion trainer that I didn't want to work for him and I didn't know where to start. I kept putting off phoning to give Martin my decision. Under normal circumstances I'm sure it would have been forgotten, but Shirley Vickery knew I hadn't called and reminded me: 'Look, you can't keep putting it off, you've got to phone him. It's bad manners that you haven't.'

I have been accused of many things but bad manners is not one of them. I dialled the phone number a hundred other young jump jockeys would have loved to be ringing to take up a job offer that I was turning down. 'Mr Pipe, I'm terribly sorry but I'm staying where I am. Mr Balding's been very good to me and I think it's only fair that I try and repay him a bit.'

I needn't have worried. If Martin Pipe was remotely concerned about the non-arrival of A. P. McCoy he covered it up uncomfortably well. 'I understand, thanks for letting me know.' His life could clearly continue without my help – for the time being, at least.

After the first two weeks I shifted digs from Stafford Kent, who lived virtually next door to Toby, and into lodgings with Trish Fox at Luggershall, a village about three miles from the yard. Trish was the mother of another claiming rider, Sean, and the ex-wife of Jimmy Fox, who had ridden good winners for Toby and been his assistant before branching out to train in his own right.

In the yard I was put under the care of one of the younger senior jockeys, Brian Clifford, known as Barney. He was a more than capable jockey, but the right breaks did not come his way and my emergence didn't do his prospects in the yard any good. The better I did, the fewer rides went Barney's way, but he never grudged me my success. He has since become a respected clerk of the course at Kempton Park.

Back in August 1994, though, he was my team leader and, of course, there was Shirley. In any large racing yard the secretary is the person to see if you want something done that doesn't involve tack or horse ailments. If there was anything I needed sorting out, a P45 or my van taxed, I went to her.

However, when it came to rides I was in the hands of Toby and Dave Roberts. I had to wait just a week before getting my first ride in England, although it came from Northern Ireland. Paddy Graffin trained for a big owner, Robert McCoubrey, who also came from Ulster. Together they had given me my only ride so far over fences on No Sir Rom at Galway five days before I left Ireland. It wasn't the ideal start and we fell at the seventh.

Robert liked to have a smack at the bookmakers and had a large string of horses, which he maintains to this day. The best of them in 1994–5 was the hurdler/chaser Strong Platinum. In England Robert had several in training with John Jenkins at Royston in Hertfordshire, and he gave me a public vote of confidence by putting me on his two runners, Arctic Life and Crews Castle, at Stratford. Toby detailed Barney to take me there. With due deference to Shakespeare, there is nothing classical about Stratford racecourse. However, as far as I was concerned it was the most important place in Britain that bright August afternoon.

The first thing a new jump jockey needs when he begins his career is a valet. I'd had one in Ireland and needed a new one. A valet is much more than a butler-cum-dresser: he is often counsellor, confidant and comforter throughout the day and can be counted on never to break a confidence.

Barney wasted no time in getting me sorted out with two of the best in the business, John and Tom Buckingham. John was the better known: he had won on the 100–1 shot Foinavon in the 1967 Grand National, then switched to valeting on his retirement. Several other riders have taken the same path, including Allen Webb and, quite recently, Chris Maude. Chris bought John and Tom's business in 2001 and continued to mix riding with valeting; John assisted him when required. Sadly, in 1999 Tom was diagnosed with cancer and died two years later.

From that first day John and Tom looked after me like older brothers, although our relationship did not get off to the best start. I'd only brought a thin pair of Flat boots with me – I'd left the jumping ones in Ireland and hadn't managed to buy a new pair. No sooner had we been introduced than I was asking to borrow some kit.

John, who had done most of his riding in the sixties around the Midlands, has a quick sense of humour and it surfaced as he handed me a well-used pair of boots. 'Here, try these. Even if they fit you you'll never fill them like the person who owned them before.'

They fitted well enough but I didn't ask John whose they were – I wouldn't give him the satisfaction of letting him know I was intrigued or the chance of a quick payoff line. Later in the afternoon I spoke to one of the other valets. 'So, whose boots are these he's given me?'

He gave me a knowing smile. 'Peter Scudamore's.'

Scu, who with Martin Pipe had shredded previous records in jump racing and had retired the previous year with eight championships behind him. OK, I thought. I might not fill them yet, but I'll give it a bloody good go.

Not that the first day provided any encouragement. Arctic Life, who had finished second under Adrian Maguire on his previous start at Worcester, started 9–4 second favourite for the novice hurdle but was always trailing the 4–6 favourite Wilkins and Darren O'Sullivan, who beat us an easy ten lengths. My second outing in the yellow and purple diamond colours of Mr McCoubrey was even less inspiring: Crews Castle finished last of four in the three-mile three-furlong handicap hurdle. Filling those boots wasn't going to be easy.

John Jenkins supplied my third ride sixteen days later on Omidjoy in a selling handicap hurdle, the lowest grade in racing, at Plumpton. Although my ride was fourth on the card I arrived early and met Dave Roberts for the first time. He seldom goes racing and prefers to monitor his team on television at his Reigate base. Before the introduction of satellite TV he spent the afternoons in his local betting shop, keeping quiet about his line of business.

I spent the early part of the afternoon standing in the course betting shop, seeing the results roll in from the other meetings and watching Dave's team log up winner after winner. But this was Adrian Maguire's day at Plumpton. He won the first, then the second, which made me wince. John Jenkins and Robert McCoubrey had decided to run Crews Castle in the novice chase and, with my record of one fall from one ride in that department, they sensibly used Adrian. However, I'd be lying if I said my stomach didn't turn a little when they scored by a length and three-quarters.

By the time I'd gone to change, Adrian had ridden the first three winners and I didn't see much of him in the seller. I pushed and scrubbed on Omidjoy throughout the two and a half miles, but Adrian was away on Heretical Miss from two out and beat us by six lengths. I got changed quickly and joined Dave to watch the closed-circuit TV. Sure enough, Adrian made it five out of five on Wayward Wind in the two-mile handicap chase. I stood watching the screen, then turned to Dave. 'Jeez, I'd just love to do that.'

Dave just looked at me and smiled.

In the end Adrian failed to go through the card. In a truly sporting gesture Darren O'Sullivan offered to swap rides with him in the last race, giving him the chance to ride the 4–6 favourite Sir Norman Holt and go through the card. However, the stewards blocked the plan, and Adrian was denied every jockey's dream. Instead he had a hairy ride on Drama Critic, who was tailed off when Adrian pulled him up before the eighth. There was no mistaking the pride Dave took in Adrian's achievement that day: he had brought him through to the head of his profession after making him champion conditional jockey. As usual, Toby Balding summed it up best: 'Dave Roberts made Adrian Maguire and Adrian made Dave.'

He was right. Between them they had set about revolutionizing the way jump jockeys booked their rides. In fact, theirs was the first partnership that threatened to take rides off other jockeys.

Although this was the first time I'd met Dave he had made it his business to find out everything he could about me. After what Dave had achieved with Richard Guest and Dean Gallagher, Toby had faith in him and vice versa. Dave has contacts in Ireland and one of them had sent him a tape of me in action so he could assess what he was taking on.

Five days later Toby gave me his first public vote of confidence and put me on Southampton in the Garrick Jubilee Handicap Hurdle at Stratford, my fourth ride. It was a major frustration. I brought the horse to track the leaders at the last flight but, through a mixture of inexperience and enthusiasm, we hit it hard and lost vital ground. I managed to get us back on an even keel and set off after Suivez. We began to get closer with each stride but as we swept across the line I knew we had been beaten. And we were: Norman Williamson had kept Suivez in front by a short head.

There was no lengthy post-race interrogation from Toby. 'Bad luck. If you'd jumped the last you would probably have won. You came pretty close together at the last and on the run-in. It's worth objecting.'

As a conditional jockey I had Toby standing beside me at the inquiry, but we were on flimsy ground and the protest was thrown out. I learned from the experience, though: I saw how eloquent Norman was when giving evidence. However, he didn't get away with the lot – he got a two-day ban for excessive use of the whip.

I'd finished second on three of my four rides in England and I was getting restless. Would I never ride a winner? The answer came sooner than I expected, four days later at Exeter.

Her name was Chickabiddy, and she was trained by Gordon Edwards, who had a few horses for his family under permit near Minehead and whose main job was as a blacksmith. 'This one's got a real chance,' Dave told me.

I travelled with Toby, who had a runner at the meeting, against my better judgement. Toby timed his arrivals to the minute and if there were any hold-ups you were late. I had to have a sweat to make the correct weight the night before, rather than at the course, because I knew that with Toby there wouldn't be any spare time.

While we were travelling together he'd tell me how to ride the track and I always ride horses slightly differently for Toby than for anyone else. He usually likes his horses to be dropped in behind in a race then come through and learn something.

Gordon Edwards didn't tie me up with too many orders, just said that it would be best if I produced the mare with her challenge at the last. Looking at the form before the race I couldn't see why Dave thought she had such a good chance. She had been beaten by thirty lengths on her seasonal comeback and had only one behind her in the betting in the six-runner field.

Exeter racecourse, so high on Haldon Hill that low cloud can envelop it in the winter months, is a big galloping course where you can ride a waiting race. It is a fine chase course too, where young horses learn how to jump.

On that September afternoon I did exactly as I was told by Gordon Edwards and bided my time. Chickabiddy was travelling well as we turned out of the back straight about five furlongs from home with three hurdles remaining. When Simon McNeill sent Just Rosie to the front going to the second last I moved Chickabiddy closer and went for everything at the last. She took a narrow lead a couple of strides after then battled on gamely to win by a length. Dave Roberts had been right about her.

I was blowing a fair bit when I came back to unsaddle, and although I'd ridden winners at more significant meetings in Ireland, it struck me that this one had been really important. It was like the beginning of a new phase in my life, and from here events moved fast.

Toby provided my first chase ride in England on Barracilla at Huntingdon nine days later, and we overcame a serious mistake at the twelfth to finish about twelve lengths fifth to Real Progress. He gave me my second winner in England when Anna Valley won a two-mile five-furlong handicap hurdle at Worcester on 24 September.

Then, just five days later, I achieved something I had fantasized about for the previous two years: I rode my first winner at Cheltenham. It's strange riding there because the track is so undulating, but I knew how to handle it: Jim Bolger had taught me on some of the switchback tracks in Ireland. He'd go mad if you tried to make ground going uphill and went for me when I tried to improve my position on an incline at Clonmel. 'You're some fool. Don't you realize that it's much easier for the horse going downhill instead of up?'

'Sorry, boss.'

On the bare facts available, Wings Of Freedom did not have outstanding claims to winning the Frenchie Nicholson Conditional Jockeys Handicap Hurdle, having finished a tailed-off third under Norman Williamson on his previous start. Like my first rides in England he was trained by John Jenkins, who told me to hold the gelding up in rear, keep him interested and produce him late. Even though this was only a minor meeting held on the now defunct 'Park' course, I still felt a sense of occasion as I received my instructions in the paddock and cantered to the start. This was what it was all about.

I didn't deviate from John's instructions and came through from the rear to challenge at the last, then drove Wings Of Freedom ahead on the run-in to hold the strong challenge of Borrowed And Blue, ridden by Glenn Tormey, by a neck. I relished the moment as I returned to the unsaddling enclosure, certain that I wanted more of this – and that Ma would have gone to Toal's betting shop to watch the race. It was also a defining moment in how I would be known in public throughout my career. The reporter from the *Sporting Life* fired questions at me as I returned from the winners' enclosure. I rattled off the answers then added: 'By the way, the name's Anthony McCoy. See if you can get that right.'

When I rode my first winner on the Flat I had appeared in the *Life* as Anthony McCoy. This time the journalist compromised by starting his report, 'The Real McCoy was on show at Cheltenham yesterday, Anthony Peter . . .' However, on every subsequent occasion I have been Tony. I got used to it in the end. Norman Williamson calls me 'Champ', and sometimes I catch just a hint of a piss-take when he says it.

As for the Real McCoy joke, I wish I had a fiver for every time it has been used in text and headline – I think journalists should be fined for unoriginal thought when they use it and the same for

sub-editors when they make it a headline. I bet none of them
knows who the real McCoy was. Just for the record, he was a boxer
in the early twentieth century who was handy when he wanted to
be, but when it suited the betting he could be extremely moderate.
When he performed at his best he was the Real McCoy. I'm not
sure the comparison is a compliment!

Incidentally, that first Cheltenham win indicates just how hard
it is to make it as a jump jockey. It's only eight years ago, but of
the thirteen who set out that day only myself and three others –
Sean Curran, Tom Jenks and Rodney Farrant – are still riding.

I've never forgotten the feeling of satisfaction I had after that first
Cheltenham win. When I went into racing as a kid with Billy Rock
and later with Jim Bolger, I always assumed it would be as a Flat
jockey, but even then I knew that Cheltenham was special. The
Irish have the name drilled into them from an early age. When I
got back to Trish Fox's that night I felt I'd really achieved something
and was on my way. I wanted it to happen again.

The following month I rode seven winners but when Dave
found me a ride on a no-hoper at Bangor, Toby told me not to
bother: I'd be more use to the head lad, Clive Bailey, if I stayed in
the yard and mucked out five boxes. If I'd been hovering off the
ground with my recent success that remark had me back on earth.

In fact, I didn't need to be brought back to reality: over the years
I have never suffered from delusions of grandeur. Quite the reverse.
I wouldn't say that the initial run of success frightened me but it
made me sit back and think. I liked it, sure enough, but what if this
was the limit to it? What if I was a racing one-hit wonder? I kept
thinking, This might stop just as quick as it started.

But then I thought, You've been doing this for a long time now.
Hey, maybe it can work out.

6. Addicted

As I've already said, I can't stand the taste of drink, I think that smoking is pure insanity, and as for recreational drugs, I find it easy to enjoy myself without artificial stimulation. However, that autumn of 1994 I got addicted to riding winners. If I went to any meeting of the anonymous variety I could stand up, hand on heart, and say, 'My name is Anthony and I'm addicted to riding winners.'

It never occurred to me until I'd had a spate of seven wins. I was on a roll – what if it stopped? The fear has never left me. If I ride three winners in a day then draw a blank on the next, I get withdrawal symptoms. What's more, I'm no more confident if I ride ten straight winners because I always think the eleventh will lose. I'm a natural pessimist.

Neither Ma nor Dad is a pessimist, they're simply realists. As far as they were concerned, the never-to-be brain surgeon was starting to pay his way.

The press were picking up on me too and the first article to prompt the notion that I might win the conditional jockeys' championship had appeared in the *Sporting Life* Weekender of 24 September, which began: 'The jumping world has been buzzing this past month with speculation about the possibility of a little-known Irishman emerging as our top conditional jockey in 1994–5 . . . Introduce yourself to A. P. McCoy.'

As the season gathered pace both Philip Hide and Rodney Farrant had ridden more winners than I had, but I was starting to pick up better-quality rides. Dave Roberts was doing a great job. It was becoming normal for me to ride out two lots then jump into the wheezing Peugeot to go racing. I also paid attention to the horses Farrant and Hide were riding. I never admitted to looking at the situation of the conditional jockeys' championship, not even to Dave, but it was always in the back of my mind. When Southampton won the Warrnambool Conditional Jockeys' Handicap Hurdle at Stratford on 22 November it was my sixteenth win from ninety-four rides and there was nothing much between the contenders for the championship. At the start of the New Year, though, I was pulling away. On 29 December Green's Fair, trained by Gerald Ham, won the opening handicap hurdle at Taunton. It was my twenty-seventh victory of the season, and my riding allowance had been reduced to the minimum three pounds. The Rules of Racing stipulated that, excluding conditional or apprentice wins, a jockey could ride fifteen winners before losing his seven-pound allowance, another fifteen before dropping to five pounds, then twenty-five more before going in on level terms. In 1997 the totals were increased to thirty-five wins as a five-pound claimer and another thirty before losing the three pounds.

The allowance is a twin-edged sword: it exists to give the novice rider a chance when he takes on his more experienced rivals; it also means that plenty of a young jockey's mounts will come from the mediocre band at the bottom of the handicap on ten stone, so to claim the full allowance the rider must keep his bodyweight at nine stone five maximum.

Because of my successes in Ireland I lost my seven-pound claim with my second winner in England, Anna Valley at Worcester, and my five-pound allowance went with Eskimo Nell at Warwick on 26 November. How I had prayed for that day. I thought it would be easier to maintain my weight.

It was a fool's paradise: nature took over and soon it was just as hard to keep myself at nine stone nine to claim three pounds. The self-denial was worthwhile and by mid-January I was pulling away in the conditional championship. But I still couldn't keep the pessimist in me quiet. No matter how well things were going I kept thinking I was only one fall away from being a never-has-been.

However, if I needed to bolster my confidence I had only to look at Toby's riding arrangements: I had moved higher up the preferred list of jockeys riding for the yard. At that time Toby was still using Adrian Maguire when he was not required by his new guv'nor David Nicholson; otherwise Jamie Railton and Jimmy Frost were getting the bulk of opportunities. But I was increasing my share by the week. Toby was also putting me on the better-class horses and I lost my right to any allowance when Romany Creek won the Sherwood Rangers Yeomanry Handicap Chase at Nottingham on 28 February.

I'd ridden my first chase win on my twenty-fourth ride in England on Bonus Boy for Bob Buckler back in early October, and Romany Creek was my ninth chase winner from a total of forty-one rides over fences since the start of the season.

I didn't want to become pigeonholed as a hurdles rider, and a race from earlier that season haunted me – it still causes me to shiver with embarrassment. I was riding Tort for Paul Dalton in a three-mile handicap chase at Leicester in November and started third favourite. Having taken up the running at the fourth we came steadily clear up the home straight and had a ten-length lead with only the last fence to negotiate. Through a combination of excitement and inexperience on my part the horse stumbled on landing and I fell off. I wished I could have crawled away but there was no chance of that: I had to walk back past the grandstand. I can't remember if there was any booing but there should have been. I felt a complete fool and could only wonder what Jim Bolger would have said to me. As it was, Paul Dalton was a gentleman: he put me on the horse twice more, although we never troubled the judge.

I took part in three more races that season, but they failed to provide any success although they meant a great deal to me. On 14 March I had my first ride at the Cheltenham Festival on Supreme Master for Claire Johnsey in the Citroën Supreme Novices' Hurdle. We had won the good-class Fernbank Hurdle at Ascot in early February and, although starting 100–1 at the Festival, we made a show until dropping away from four out.

I was still only small fry in the Cheltenham lake and, with nothing offered for the second day, I went to Nottingham and rode a welcome chase winner on The Boiler White for the former amateur champion Tim Thomson Jones. However, all I could focus on was the Cheltenham Gold Cup the following day. Toby had given me two rides at the meeting, Brave Tornado in the *Daily Express* Triumph Hurdle and Beech Road in the Gold Cup.

Brave Tornado was a serious chance in the four-year-old hurdlers' championship and it was the first time I had ever got a good ride at the expense of a friend. Barney Clifford was my guide and mentor on and off the racecourse and had won on Brave Tornado when he made his début at Newbury's Hennessy meeting the previous November. When the horse ran at Exeter in January Toby wanted to cut his seven-pound penalty using my three-pound allowance and we won by two lengths. After that I rode him to win the Grade Two Finesse Hurdle at Cheltenham later that month, a race in which I couldn't use my allowance, and kept the side in the Triumph. Barney never once complained to me about it.

Brave Tornado started equal fourth favourite at 10–1 in the twenty-six-runner field, but after being badly hampered at the first in what is always a rough race, we finished seventh behind Martin Pipe's Kissair and were promoted to sixth on the disqualification of second-placed Dr Leunt.

Only Dawn Run had managed the Champion Hurdle–Gold Cup double, and although Beech Road had managed the first leg in 1989, that was before I'd even thought of joining Jim Bolger. Now his light had dimmed and his price of 100–1 reflected it. But I couldn't have cared if he'd been 1,000–1. As far as I was concerned I had arrived. I was riding in the most prestigious steeplechase in the sport. As I walked out to the paddock I understood what it must be like to take the field for the FA Cup Final.

It was a form-book finish, not a story-book one. We never had much of a sight of the leaders and were well behind from half-way, but at least I completed the course in a distant seventh to Master Oats and Norman Williamson with the previous year's winner Jodami tailed off in eighth.

The third ride with no intrinsic reward came in April. Martin Pipe had four entries for the Grand National. Richard Dunwoody would ride the 1994 winner Miinnehoma, Charlie Swan was aboard Riverside Boy, Mark Perrett had the leg up on Errant Knight, and the champion trainer chose this as his first time to employ my services and put me on Chatam. Clearly, there were no hard feelings about my refusal to join him the previous summer and I took the booking as a move in the right direction.

Unfortunately, Chatam came into the same category as Beech Road and was on the downward path after winning such good races as the Hennessy Gold Cup at Newbury in 1991. It didn't matter to me: I was pleased to be considered good enough to work for such a high-calibre outfit. Martin took plenty of time to explain what he wanted and where I should try to be in the race.

Unfortunately, it was largely a waste of time. After being hampered at the third fence we were soon behind, eventually falling at the twelfth.

Since the New Year I had begun to pull away in the conditional-title race and by the end of March I had forty-seven winners behind me with two months of the season remaining. At that stage I was well pleased with the near certainty that I would be top claiming rider, but I had a dream run through April, which put me in line for my first record. I rode eleven winners and went into May with Adrian Maguire's 1991–2 record of seventy-one winners as a long-shot target.

The season finished at Stratford on 3 June, which meant that I needed to better my previous best monthly total and get thirteen winners. I had the right man behind me in Dave Roberts, who had done it for Adrian.

Fortunately, I had moved on from the old van, which had come off worst in an argument with a Land Rover, and now had a new Volkswagen Venta. I flogged it the length and breadth of the country throughout May, from Newton Abbot in Devon to Perth in Scotland, Hereford in the west to Fakenham in the east. I was running on adrenaline and the winners kept coming. Gradually I closed on Adrian's total, and after one unsuccessful ride at Towcester on Friday 26 May I took off for Hexham in Northumberland for two rides the next day. One, Majic Rain trained by Don Eddy, won the handicap chase and put me level with Adrian's record. I didn't get back to Weyhill until late that night but caught some of the boys in our local, the Swan.

On Sunday Dave told me I'd be going on the relatively short trip to Fontwell the next day, Bank Holiday Monday, for three rides that all had good chances. Fontwell was near enough for Dave to take an afternoon away from the office. The first of the trio, Pennine Pass, did the business in the Duggie Mack Selling Handicap Chase by ten lengths. His trainer, Dai Williams, also gave me a seventy-third success when Symbol Of Success won the next on the card, but Pennine Pass goes into the book as the record-breaker.

No sooner had I got home that night than I began wondering where the next winner would come from. If you had laid out all the trainers in England before me I would not have picked Martin Pipe as the most likely man to provide it.

I was sitting in the spartan wooden changing room at Hereford for the evening meeting of 1 June, having finished a distant third on my only ride of the night, K C's Dancer in the selling chase. However, the most significant moment of the race, as far as I was concerned, came when James Pigg fell heavily at the eleventh, burying Richard Dunwoody.

It was an open secret that the dream team of Martin Pipe and Richard was no longer working, and their partnership was destined to end when the season closed at Stratford two days later. There had been plenty of talk in the jockeys' changing room as to Richard's likely successor. Now Brendan Powell raised it again. Brendan was a brilliant survivor in a hard game. He would ride anything and his tenacity had paid off with a winning ride in the 1988 Grand National on Rhyme 'N' Reason. More recently he had partnered the late Tim Forster's bold front runner Dublin Flyer to win the Tripleprint Gold Cup at Cheltenham and the John Hughes Chase at Aintree.

Brendan, like the rest of us, knew that Richard wouldn't be able to ride the Pipe-trained Crosula, who had only Henry Cone to beat in the three-and-a-quarter-mile novice hurdle. He turned to me half smiling and said, 'We'll see who's going to be Pipe's new jockey now. Whoever rides that horse in the fourth will be favourite.'

As if on cue, Chester Barnes walked into the changing room. Chester, former child prodigy of table tennis, was now synonymous with the Pipe organization. He had had a strong friendship with Martin since the late seventies and was often the stable representative when Martin was elsewhere. He was clutching the light blue and brown colours of John Bisgrove, which still carried the grass stains from James Pigg's fall. After a brief look round he handed them to me. Brendan gave me a knowing smile.

Crosula was a typical Martin Pipe horse: he had shown little form for a small yard but progressed considerably under Martin's regime. The instructions were simple: 'Jump out and make all.' It really was as simple as that, and I never saw another horse, coming home by a distance.

There was nothing in our post-race conversation that gave any hint of a long-term arrangement. In fact, apart from the Grand National, that day was the first time I can remember talking to Martin since our brief lunch date shortly after I arrived in England. Crosula was my last winner of the season, and although I did not admit it to anyone, I was still worried that I would become just another racing statistic, a claiming rider who flew through one season and was only seen again around the minor meetings, bashing the life out of himself and some moderate horses.

Fortunately for me the rules changed for the new season and summer racing was introduced: this meant that, instead of a near two-month break until 1 August, the season would kick off again on 8 June at Perth. Toby was insistent that I take a break but my fear of failure overrode his concerns. I still had it in my mind that riders could take three seasons to get back into fashion after they'd lost their claim: even though I'd continued to ride winners after losing my allowance I could imagine everything crumbling if I took my eye off the ball. I'd sampled life near the top and I didn't fancy the other option.

While the likes of Richard Dunwoody and Adrian Maguire took time off with their families for a summer holiday I decided to stay on at the factory and get in some winning insulation to give me a buffer against them when they came back. When the 1995–6 season kicked off I gave the car a rest and flew to Perth with the best possible talisman for success.

My first ride in my first season as a full jockey was for the man who had never once lost his belief in my ability: Billy Rock. He had sent three runners on the ferry to Stranraer and I would be on them at Perth. He must have thought I'd lost my touch when the first, Della Wee, bolted going to the start. That had never happened when I was a youngster with him. Unfortunately, it was as fast as she could go and we finished a well-beaten sixth. The other ride for him that day, Joey Kelly, was soon struggling and I pulled him up before three out in the handicap chase.

I did ride a winner on the opening day, Googly for John White, but the second day of the meeting provided me with one of my happiest memories. I had one ride for Billy, Tabu Lady, who started 9–4 favourite for the Aitken's Ale Novices' Hurdle, and I have never in my life wanted to ride a winner more. When I took her ahead at the second last only bad luck could rob Billy and me of a wonderful moment. I left nothing to chance, driving her out for a five-length win.

As we trotted off the track, Billy was there on the walk-up. He said hardly anything but had a big smile on his face. He makes a conscious effort to hide his feelings, and all he said was, 'It's about time you did something for me and rode me a winner.'

I knew exactly what it meant to him – and me. This man had been like a second father to me. He had guided me, treated me like a man when I was a boy, and never once lost his faith that I would be a champion. It was only my sixth ride for him, including three in Ireland, and I haven't ridden a winner before or since for a better man.

My strategy of logging up an early-season cushion soon paid dividends: by the time the season proper began in August I already had twenty-four winners in my pocket. Significantly, Martin Pipe had contributed more than anyone else, but he was casting around for the right replacement for Richard Dunwoody and plenty of other riders were given a chance. However, largely due to the shrewd assessment of Dave Roberts, I was getting all the good ones. I won four on Shikaree between 11 June and 15 July. I also won two on Crosula and people began to talk. The first time Martin broached the subject of me riding for him as stable jockey was on Sunday 11 June after I'd ridden him a double on Crosula and Shikaree at Uttoxeter. As I came back to weigh in he was walking alongside me. In the course of the conversation he said: 'What about the job?'

Even though I had ridden a growing number of winners for him it was still a surprise.

'I'm flattered that you think I'm good enough but at the moment I don't know if I am. Although I don't doubt my ability, things have moved very quickly in the last year. I've gone from hardly getting a ride to riding winners every week. I don't want to take your job as stable jockey then get the sack through inexperience if things don't go right after three months. I'd be left with nothing. I'd lose all the contacts I've made already and be back to square one. I'd feel better leaving things the way they are with me riding for you when it suits us both.'

Martin didn't force me to make a decision, just asked me to 'think about it'.

I did as I'd done over a year ago when he offered to take me on as a conditional jockey: rightly or wrongly, I put it to the back of my mind.

Eventually I discussed the situation with Toby Balding. He was emphatic: 'Wait. You've got plenty of time and he's not going to stop wanting you.'

Still I avoided telling Martin that I wouldn't be coming. And still he kept putting me on the steering jobs, although David Bridgwater was now getting a good number too.

Ironically it was Crosula, the horse which had brought us together at Hereford, who effectively drove us apart. I rode him at Worcester eleven days after Martin had put his offer to me at Uttoxeter. The horse could be moody and had an off-day. Starting 6–4 on favourite, he smashed through the first then ran out at the third, crashing through the plastic wing.

It probably wasn't the right time to talk business after that but Martin asked, 'Have you decided about the job?'

I tried to work round the issue and said, 'I would be happier riding for you whenever I can.'

Martin didn't say much – he never does – and walked off at his brisk trot. I kept riding a few for the yard, but a couple of weeks later I read that David Bridgwater had got the job. He was well qualified, having made his name riding for Nigel Twiston-Davies, whose training partner just happened to be Martin Pipe's most successful stable jockey to date, Peter Scudamore.

When I saw Bridgy riding truckloads of winners as the season progressed I'd be lying if I said it didn't play on my mind. I was also very conscious that, for the second time, I'd given the champion trainer a knock-back. It also niggled me that Bridgy was young enough to keep going for a long time. It looked like I'd blown it. On the credit side I had the twenty-four winners banked and wanted more.

Such is Martin Pipe's significance that bookmakers delayed pricing the jump jockeys' championship for 1995–6 until after he had appointed his stable jockey. Adrian Maguire had a proven track record, minimum riding weight of an easy ten stone and the backing of David Nicholson's quality yard so he headed the list at 4–5. David Bridgwater, with the Pipe team at his back, was next at 5–2. Norman Williamson, who can do ten stone without fuss and had the in-form trainer Kim Bailey behind him, was third. I was next at 7–1, which didn't look the greatest odds in the world.

It wasn't until the end of October that people I thought should have known better kept saying to me that they'd backed me for champion. But I'd made a good start, and by the end of October Adrian and Norman were out with injuries. It was true that I had consolidated my position with a total of sixty-two but the voice of Jim Bolger was always there: I could imagine him saying, 'How could you be champion jockey in your second season? You're some fool!'

I told the punters to wise up and that it wasn't on. But on the quiet I kept an eye on what horses Bridgy was riding. I didn't discuss it with Dave Roberts, my first line of contact for winners: records, championships and targets are forbidden subjects between us. When I was going for the conditional jockeys' record we never touched on it and it was the same this season. Nothing has changed since and we are still mighty superstitious.

Perhaps the most important factor as the campaign got going was that I was becoming more confident in my ability. At the start of the season I had been less than happy with my performance in chases, something I felt was highlighted when I rode Tug Of Peace for Toby at Worcester on 23 September. We had won over course and distance earlier in the month, but this time I could not get a tune out of the gelding at his fences and one mistake followed another. The miserable effort peaked at the last where we were challenging the hard-driven Mr Jamboree, ridden by Norman Williamson. Tug Of Peace made a mistake, stumbled, and I was shot out of the saddle. I've never been frightened of falling but, looking back, I was trying too hard to make sure that the horse got round. My confidence took a severe knock, even though I won the next race, a novice chase on Polden Pride. It was well into the season before I was happy with my performance over fences.

Fortunately I kept my doubts well disguised and good rides, which will always produce winners, continued to come, plenty from Paul Nicholls.

Paul hadn't amassed the fine team of horses he would have as the millennium dawned but all the signs were there. He had begun training in November 1991 and his calibre of horse was getting better each season. Paul was a trainer going places and he gave me my first taste of a top-class young jumper on the way to the top. He had no retained rider and put plenty of winners my way.

One was See More Business in a two-and-a-half-mile novice hurdle at Chepstow on 4 November. The six-year-old had been a brilliant point-to-pointer for Richard Barber and was now in joint ownership with John Keighley. Paul told me that he thought the horse might be a bit special and he was right.

We won by fifteen lengths and I returned to unsaddle full of enthusiasm. Although I'd won a couple of races on a former star, Beech Road, this horse had given me a feel of what could happen in the future, and I said, 'This is the best jumper I've ever sat on.' Normally when a jockey says that about a young horse it puts the mockers on and they're never any good. It didn't stop this one. Next time out we won a modest two-mile six-furlong novice at Wincanton before being upped in class for the Grade Two Winter Novices' Hurdle at Sandown in early December. It was another stroll by fifteen lengths. I hadn't realized quite how accurate my assessment of See More Business would be. Two years later I caused him to miss out on the Cheltenham Gold Cup in controversial and acrimonious circumstances, but it was truly justice that he fulfilled his potential when he won the Cheltenham Gold Cup of 1999.

Paul was never a good loser. To be honest, I don't think there is such a thing when you're talking about people competing at the highest level in any sport. Some trainers and jockeys just hide it better than others. Paul let you know when he was disappointed, but at that impressionable time in my career he did my confidence nothing but good. There was never a time during that period when he wanted anyone to ride a horse in front of me. You've got to remember that the rather long shadow of Richard Dunwoody was cast over all jockeys at this time by his role as ever-available freelance, so it was very flattering for me to find I was good enough for Paul Nicholls.

I clocked up the fastest ever fifty when Rolling The Bones, trained by Paul Felgate, won a novice handicap hurdle at Ludlow on 13 October. It didn't mean much as the season now began two months early, but I was glad my good run was continuing.

I had my first serious brush with the stewards quite early in the season at Taunton, and nothing that has happened at the course subsequently has made the pill any easier to swallow. The Orchard Portman Selling Handicap Hurdle turned into a fiasco once Assembly Dancer, ridden by the conditional rider Michael Clarke, had fallen at the fourth flight, which became the last on the final circuit. In June that year the Jockey Club had finally taken the lead from Ireland and allowed a fence or hurdle to be bypassed without the race being declared void if a horse or rider was lying injured. Before that the jump had to be negotiated with only some warning markers to indicate where the injured were lying. That was a desperate state of affairs, which left many a prone jockey wondering if he would get a second whack as the field came by again.

Ironically, Clarke walked away from the hurdle but there was too little time for the ground staff to remove the bollards and fluorescent chevrons as the field came into the home straight. The rules stated that you had to pass the hurdle on the left. A couple of flagmen were waving at us in front of the hurdle, but I was too busy with my head down driving Little Hooligan to catch the leader, Tony's Mist. Coupled with that, I had senior riders either side of me in Mick FitzGerald and Mark Richards so I thought I was pretty safe to go with them to the right, especially as there appeared to be more room.

When I passed the winning line a length and a half to the good I felt certain I'd ridden another winner for Gordon Edwards, who had given me my first English winner on Chickabiddy. However, one person had read the notice as you leave the weighing room, which pointed out the right course to take: Jamie Osborne. He was virtually tailed off on Safe Secret with time to assess the situation and went through the narrow gap on the left of the hurdle with three other no-hopers following him. The stewards called an inquiry but I felt sure that in the heat of battle we had done the right thing.

We hadn't.

Jamie, one of the best jockeys never to be champion, could be extremely smug if he thought he was right about anything. He was certain he was on a winner now – and he *was* right. The five who finished behind me and came the wrong side of the flight were disqualified and Osborne was given one of the most fortunate winners of his career.

It didn't get any better, either. After the guilty six were disqualified we were brought back before the stewards and told we had been banned for seven days for taking the wrong course. I was beside myself with rage and a feeling of injustice. The ban meant I had to miss meetings at Aintree, Ascot and the Hennessy at

Newbury. I feared a much wider implication and said, 'It's ridiculous. I can't believe it. I thought they would fine us – this could cost me the championship.'

I had pumped myself up to do it at the first attempt and losing seven days at this busy time of the season seemed a hammer blow. I was on sixty-seven winners and David Bridgwater was fifteen behind me. I could see him riding two winners a day while I was off to wipe out my comfort cushion. In the event I needn't have worried. I rode six winners before the ban came into force and Bridgy only managed five while I took a seven-day break.

Time has proved that the Taunton six were right. When a hurdle is dolled off up the home straight nowadays we are diverted to the right. There's no justice.

I was still looking over my shoulder at Bridgy, and at the beginning of December he had reduced my advantage to ten with Martin Pipe stoking up winners, none of which he showed the slightest interest in putting me on.

Then came a mini-breakthrough. Martin had two entries for the Knights Royal Hurdle, which finished the card at Ascot on 16 December. Bridgy was booked for Pridwell and Jonothan Lower would ride Kissair after travelling on from Uttoxeter. Midway through the afternoon a message came through to Ascot that Jonothan had travel problems and wouldn't make it for Kissair, so Martin had to do some shuffling. Bridgy decided to switch to Kissair and Martin gave me Pridwell's colours. It was a big vote of confidence: although there was little love lost between Martin and Richard Dunwoody, the reigning champion was still available to ride, as were Adrian Maguire, Carl Llewellyn and Graham Bradley, all top-quality riders with more experience than me. Martin's door was clearly still ajar.

Mysilv, trained by Charlie Egerton, ridden by Jamie Osborne and starting 1–2 favourite, set the race up for me by forcing a strong pace. I was able to cajole Pridwell, who was narrowly favoured over his stablemate in the betting, around in the rear of the eight-runner field. He had plenty left as we came through to lead at the last, outpacing Mysilv by four lengths. I'd already won the Grade

Two Kennel Gate Novice Hurdle for Paul Nicholls on Call Equiname, but it wasn't Bridgy's day: Kissair was never in the race from half-way and was tailed off when he was pulled up before two out.

At that time Bridgy and I never spoke much and had not discussed the championship. Also I hadn't let him know that I'd been offered the job before him. It would have been unfair. He had enough on his plate without mind games – and I've never played them.

The more winners I got the more I trusted my ability, but I took nothing for granted. If I was beaten when I thought I should have won, no trainer could have been harder on me than I was on myself. Physical strength plays a big part in my game and, looking back at videos of myself in my first and second seasons, it embarrasses me to see just how weak I was. True, as I began riding more and used more muscles, I got stronger and never had to resort to gym work or running – that just puts muscle on the legs, which weighs like lard and is impossible to shift. However, looking back to that first season I was concentrating more on getting the horses to arrive at the right time – that is, at the last obstacle, or half-way up the run-in. It is now obvious to me that I wasn't getting right through the horses and wringing the last ounce of effort from them. If I went for a horse too early in a race, I couldn't keep myself going to the finish, no matter what the horse had to offer.

Midway through that second season it dawned on me that Bridgy was riding a lot of winners for Martin Pipe by dominating from the start. Fair enough, I thought. The only way I was going to beat them was to do the same. And the only way to do the same was to be every bit as fit as the horses I was riding.

I began to ride everything with all the effort I could muster, even the bad ones that had no chance and were out at the back. I didn't beat them up or harm them, but I made sure they got the maximum out of the experience and I received a thorough workout at thirty miles an hour.

It worked. When the 1996 Cheltenham Festival came round, I had 120 winners on the scoreboard. Just as important, there were 530 rides behind me and thirteen more to come over the most significant three days' jump racing of the season. The previous year I had had six rides, but now I was in thirteen of the seventeen races for which I was eligible. Then Adrian Maguire had an accident.

When Smiling Chief slipped after leaping the water jump in front of the stands at Newbury, bringing down both Bells Life and Ascot Lad, Adrian broke his right collar-bone. It was only eleven days before Cheltenham. He had smashed the bone in five places, and would miss the Festival. This would have been wicked bad luck in any circumstances but even more so given that he had missed the previous year because of the death of his mother, Phyllis.

I won the first race that day at Newbury, the Ardington Novices' Hurdle, on Monicasman, trained by Alan Jarvis. Monicasman won well enough and I hardly saw any of the other seventeen runners, once we led after the first flight to win by an easy five lengths. This was clearly a horse on the upgrade and I said that I'd like to ride him in the Sun Alliance Novices' Hurdle at the Festival. When I made the verbal agreement poor old Adrian was in one piece, but after his fall an hour later the rides situation at Cheltenham took on a different aspect. Suddenly, a clutch of top mounts was available. It didn't take long for the diagnosis on Adrian's collar-bone to become public, and in such a situation there is always a feeding frenzy to get the best rides in the big races. Although it sounds unsavoury it's nothing personal.

In a matter of days David Nicholson had booked Charlie Swan for Viking Flagship in the Queen Mother Champion Chase, he then began sorting out riding arrangements for the other nineteen he would be sending. On some he gave the chance to his up-and-coming conditional jockey Richard Johnson, with other riders called in for specific horses. Despite my immaturity I was at the top of the list and he called Dave Roberts to see if I would be available for three of his best chances, Barton Bank in the Gold Cup, Zabadi in the Triumph Hurdle and Jack Tanner in the Sun Alliance Hurdle. No problem with the first two but there was now a conflict over whether to abide by my first commitment to Monicasman or jump ship to Jack Tanner.

As always in these situations – which happen regularly during the build-up to a big meeting – Dave left the final decision to me. It didn't take me five minutes to decide I would ride Jack Tanner. He had come from Ireland with a big reputation, and a price tag to go with it after winning a bumper. He was pitched into a top-class race for his début, the Coventry City Trial Novices' Hurdle at Warwick in mid-February. The race turned into a sprint and he ran a blinder to finish three lengths second to Simply Dashing, trained by Tim Easterby after the recent retirement of his father Peter and winner of his previous five races. I never had a moment's doubt that I was doing the right thing.

Dave relayed my decision to Mr Jarvis, who was less than pleased and told him exactly what he thought of him and me. I could understand that: I'd said I'd like to ride his horse and now I didn't want to. Instead I wanted to ride for David Nicholson, who had been champion trainer and had a yard full of quality horses. He was renowned for wanting the best in men and horses, and now he wanted me.

I was left in no doubt about the strength of Alan Jarvis's feelings. When you become a jockey, it is important to acquire the thickest skin possible when it comes to dealing with such incidents, and the acrimonious debates that ensue when a fancied horse is beaten for what is perceived as jockey error. It is also wise not to bear grudges: resentment does the bearer no good. However, I vowed from that day I would never ride again for Mr Jarvis or his wife, Ann, even if they were fortunate enough to train the Cheltenham Gold Cup and Champion Hurdle favourites in walkovers. They have few jumpers these days, but I'm sure the feeling is mutual. Despite their assertion that they would not be able to find a suitable replacement, they secured Jamie Osborne, one of the best riders of the nineties who had ridden five winners at the meeting in 1992. In the event it didn't matter who was on Monicasman: the gelding ran out at the first flight.

As for Jack Tanner, he ran a sound enough race. I brought him through to track the leaders at the sixth but a mistake three out knocked him out of his stride. He eventually weakened to finish twelve and a half lengths fourth to Urubande, ridden by Charlie Swan and trained by my senior workmate at Jim Bolger's, Aidan O'Brien. My remaining rides that day didn't cause much of a stir, but I felt that the final day on Thursday might belong to me.

Zabadi had looked good in winning his two previous races and, like Jack Tanner, was owned by Sir Philip and Lady Harris, then among the most significant owners in jumping. We started 10–1 third favourites, but although Zabadi held a good position from three out, his stamina ebbed on the run to the last and we weakened to finish seventh.

Barton Bank, owned by the late Jenny Mould and her husband Raymond, was not a reliable jumper and had thrown away the King George VI Chase at Kempton the previous season when he unseated Adrian Maguire at the last fence with the race won. He had not recaptured his form in the run-up to the Gold Cup, but I went out determined to get the gelding jumping to some sort of tune. Considering some of his previous efforts, it was mission accomplished: we made only one serious error when he blundered at the seventh fence, the second ditch. Unfortunately, we couldn't get anywhere near the leaders from four out and we trailed in twenty-six lengths behind Imperial Call. However, as with Urubande there was still something to take out of the race as far as I was concerned: the winner had been ridden by Conor O'Dwyer, the first man I led up on a winner at Downpatrick when I was 'Wee Anthony McCoy'. Back then I'd have given anything to know that one day I'd be sharing the same Cheltenham stage as him.

Although there had been nothing to show for ten previous rides at the meeting I went out for the eleventh feeling that I had a serious chance in the Grand Annual Chase on Kibreet. I knew Philip Hobbs had fine-tuned the gelding for this race over his favoured two miles and from a long way out I felt confident. We had won the Manicou Handicap at Ascot back in November, and although Kibreet hadn't won since, he had put up some good performances and went into the race on a fair handicap mark.

Before the race I knew that the one to beat was Easthorpe, unbeaten in his two previous races and ridden by Jason Titley. They would be forcing the pace and I planned never to be far away from them. The ground was quick and I needed a true test of stamina for Kibreet. Running fast down the hill to face the third last was the right time to go. I urged Kibreet to quicken and his response was immediate. Turning for home and facing the second last, he began to pull away and was four lengths clear at the last. There was no way I was going to mess things up and I sat down to ride as though my life depended on it. When we crossed the line, still holding that four-length margin, I was ecstatic. I'd ridden a winner at the home of jump racing and that moment justified everything that I'd put myself and those close to me through in the preceding ten years. I could imagine the shrieks of delight from my family as they watched the race in Toal's betting shop, for this was their moment too. It's all very well riding plenty of winners each week around the gaffs, but to prove you've arrived you've got to ride winners at Cheltenham.

I didn't know then that I would ride much more significant winners at the greatest jump meeting in the world. What I did know was that this was the most wonderful feeling I had experienced.

As we walked across the paddock to the unsaddling enclosure, I leaned down and shook hands with Philip Hobbs. Philip never gets excited after winning a big race and does not overreact when things go wrong, but he wore a broad grin. In the unsaddling enclosure part-owner Peter Emery was beaming. A year earlier to the day he had seen his Dr Leunt pushed out at the third last in the Triumph Hurdle and subsequently disqualified from second.

Back in the changing room the boys gave me plenty of

encouragement to push the boat out at the traditional weighing-room party, which finishes the meeting, but the last thing I needed was drink: I was high as a kite already.

There's never time to dwell on past glories in this game and my early education with Jim Bolger had taught me that the learning curve is always quite steep in front of you. The next big target was the Grand National meeting and it was going to be even better than Cheltenham. Adrian was never going to be fit enough for Aintree, and once again I was on David Nicholson's wanted list. He offered me four quality rides: Zabadi, Baron Bank, Buttercup Joe and, the best of the lot, Viking Flagship. Barton Bank made just one bad mistake in the Martell Cup Chase when he blundered four fences from home. He was legless, slowing to a virtual walk at the last, which we clambered to claim second place to Scotton Banks.

Zabadi was a different proposition away from the buffeting of the Triumph in the eleven-runner Glenlivet Hurdle, and I was able to use the waiting tactics that suited him so well. I had Our Kris, ridden by Mick FitzGerald, in my sights as we turned for home and Zabadi was full of enthusiasm. We quickened approaching the last, then sprinted clear to win by six lengths. Any race would have been good enough to get my first Aintree winner, but to do it in a Grade Two contest gave it an extra kick.

If I thought Zabadi was tricky, he was nothing compared to Top Spin, trained by John Jenkins, who was as crafty as a wagonload of monkeys and rightly a 20–1 shot for the three mile Barton & Guestier Handicap Hurdle. The last time I had ridden the seven-year-old was as a three-pound claimer at Chepstow fourteen months earlier. I dropped him out in the desperately heavy ground that day and brought him with a steady run up the home straight to lead on the run-in so he hardly knew he'd been involved in a race. That was his last win and some of the best hands in the game, including Paul Carberry, Richard Hughes, Adrian Maguire and Tony Dobbin, have tried since.

Although the ground was much better than at Chepstow I employed the same tactics and let Top Spin run his own race, producing him with a late burst on the run-in to beat Jathib, trained by David Nicholson and ridden by Richard Dunwoody, in the last few strides to win by a neck.

That win was sweet but it was nothing compared to the exhilaration I felt on Viking Flagship in the Mumm Melling Chase. Charlie Swan, who had ridden him to finish second to Klairon Davis in the Queen Mother Champion Chase at Cheltenham, was out of the game. He had picked up a six-day suspension for irresponsible riding after finishing second on Magical Lady in the Triumph Hurdle, and the final day was the Friday of Aintree. Richard Dunwoody, who had ridden Viking Flagship successfully during his time as Nicholson's stable jockey, was contracted to ride Sound Man for Edward O'Grady, so I was in.

Although Sound Man had finished a length and a quarter behind Viking Flagship at Cheltenham he was 6–4 favourite, with my horse 5–2 second best in the betting. Even allowing for Sound Man having won the Comet Chase at Ascot over two miles three furlongs on his outing before Cheltenham, it was difficult to fathom the market. Sound Man was unbeaten in four outings that season going to Cheltenham but made too many errors jumping at championship pace. There weren't any worries in that department with my horse and the extra half-mile wasn't going to be a bother as he'd won the race the previous year.

When I went to David Nicholson's stables, Jackdaws Castle, to school my three rides, I didn't do the same before Aintree as in the run-up to Cheltenham. Not that it made a blind bit of difference when it came to Viking Flagship. I'd seen him operating since I'd come to England and loved to watch him. He was everything I ever want in a chaser – game, genuine and a brilliant jumper. A jockey can't ask for more than that. He's the type of horse you'd pay to ride. Anyone would have suited Viking Flagship but I felt that he suited my forceful style just great.

I'd had a word about him with Adrian. There were no hidden quirks, and in the paddock I wasn't tied down by Mr Nicholson: 'Ride him as you find him,' which, basically translated, means, 'Do what you like and don't fall off.' The beauty of Viking Flagship was that it didn't matter when you committed him because you knew that once you did he'd just keep galloping until you reached the line.

Once again it was his near-perfect jumping that gave me this important Grade One first. Unlike Sound Man, whose jumping was flawed, Viking Flagship was magnificent and when Sound Man virtually brought himself to a standstill with a bad blunder four fences out, it was time for us to go. We were in front at the next and clear from the second last, racing home by seven lengths.

Graham Roach has owned many good horses before and since but there has never been one quite like Viking Flagship. The rotund Cornishman, whose Roach Foods lorries are a familiar sight on the motorways, was overjoyed, and both he and David Nicholson welcomed us into the winners' enclosure. Their glowing faces were possibly the result of excitement and a few confidence boosters in the owners' and trainers' bar before the event.

Buttercup Joe ran a fair fifth in the novices' hurdle, but I went to bed at the Moat House Hotel that night with the following day's Grand National in my mind.

The next day began with the ride on Kibreet in the Martell Aintree Chase, but the handicapper had nailed him with an extra eight pounds since Cheltenham and he was a comfortably beaten fourth.

Next up for me was the Grand National and I honestly thought I had an outstanding chance on Deep Bramble, trained by Paul Nicholls. The previous season he had won the Mildmay Cazalet and Agfa Diamond Chases at Sandown. He was the right type for the National, not far off Gold Cup class, and had been specially prepared for the race. His legs were not at their best, though, and he arrived at Aintree after just one previous outing when he came a distant fourth to Lo Stregone in the National Trial at Haydock in late February. Paul had done a great job on the horse, who started a well-fancied 12–1 chance, and as we began the second circuit I could understand the optimism. We were going very well with five to jump, but crossing the Melling Road after the third last I felt his stride shorten and he began to falter. We stopped in a few strides and I was off him, and it was clear that the Grand National dream was over. So, too, were Deep Bramble's racing days: he had fractured a cannon bone.

At the start of the three-day fixture I hadn't considered that I might lift the Ritz Club Trophy for leading rider at the meeting, but going into the final day both Jonothan Lower and I were on three winners apiece. It would now depend on who had ridden most placed horses. Fortunately my last ride of the meeting, Clifton Beat, owned by the entertainer Des O'Connor and trained by Philip Hobbs, bailed me out. Despite shouldering top weight he struggled on gamely to finish a length and a quarter second to Stompin and secured my first Waterford-crystal rose-bowl trophy.

I'd finished the meeting with 135 winners behind me, thirty-eight ahead of David Bridgwater. I should have known since Cheltenham that, barring injury, I would win the jump jockeys' championship. The truth was that I could not let it sink in until Dave Roberts told me there weren't enough races left for Bridgy to catch me.

When the season closed on 1 June at Stratford I had ridden 175 winners, forty-three more than Bridgy – I had ridden in 159 more races than he had. Richard Dunwoody, who had unscrewed the pressure-cooker and decided to take things easier for his own peace of mind, finished third with 101. If there was one trainer I had to thank for that first title it was Paul Nicholls, who provided a staggering forty-two winners from 146 rides, a strike rate of 29 per cent.

However, statistics can be misleading. Two names were missing from the top six: Adrian Maguire had already cracked a bone in his leg and badly torn his knee before the broken collar-bone sidelined him for the remainder of the season; and Norman Williamson's season had mirrored exactly the roller-coaster life of a jump jockey. The previous season he had won both the Champion Hurdle and the Gold Cup on Alderbrook and Master Oats. By July 1995 he had dislocated a shoulder and in October broke a leg. He regained fitness by February, only for his shoulder to dislocate again just two days after his comeback. You can understand why a jump jockey never takes anything for granted.

It wasn't until I read the papers that I realized I was the youngest champion jockey since Josh Gifford in 1962–3.

7. Connecting up to the Pipeline

Believe it or not, I didn't feel particularly tired or stressed after winning that first championship. I can understand how it must have been exhausting for jockeys twenty years earlier when they had to make their own booking arrangements, but Dave Roberts had removed that worry. All I needed to do was make sure I was mentally and physically fit, knew about the horses I was riding and the strengths and weaknesses of the opposition. Tactics make perfect! In fact, I was so immersed in the game that I decided against a holiday to celebrate my first jockeys' championship. There was no big party to mark the occasion, although I was handed plenty of bar tabs in the following couple of weeks – it seemed that my arrival in a pub in Weyhill or Lambourn was more than enough to produce an impromptu celebration. In fact, while I enjoy a night out as much as anyone, I've always been a keen television viewer.

My idea of a good night after racing was to sit through the replays of my performances that afternoon and see where I could improve. I knew it was possible that I had won my first championship from logging up that early cushion of winners. David Bridgwater would be desperate to deny me a second title, as would Adrian Maguire, while Norman Williamson would be hungrier than ever after his bleak season. I suppose this was the start of my paranoia that success could be taken away as quickly as it had come. My watchword is, take nothing for granted and keep improving your game.

It wasn't until 16 June that I received my championship trophy, another inscribed Waterford-crystal rose-bowl – I was more than happy to start a collection. The presentation took place at the Market Rasen meeting on Saturday 15 June and was made by David Hood of William Hill, who sponsored the championship that year. They had certainly caught a cold when they laid me to the shrewdies at 7–1 when the betting had opened. They didn't make the same mistake again and I was favourite to retain my title.

In the course of that second season I earned over a million pounds in prize money for the owners who employed me and my bank balance had never looked healthier. I decided it was time to step on to the property ladder, and bought my first house, a neat three-bedroom semi in a new development not far from the yard and called appropriately Weyhill Gardens.

Now I looked around for someone to share it with me. Coming from a large family, then going straight into stables, I had always been used to having people around. It's not that I mind my own company – and after a day when the results haven't gone my way, the last thing I need is someone giving me earache about it when I get home. The right lodger was virtually on my doorstep: my minder Barney Clifford.

As soon as the deeds had been signed, Barney moved in and, while I can't remember much in the way of rent changing hands, he was good to have around. Unlike me, Barney is not a teetotaller and has been known to over-indulge from time to time. The previous November he had enjoyed a relaxing Sunday, safe in the knowledge that he had no rides on Monday. Unfortunately, I was struck down with a fierce bout of food poisoning. When Barney made his way, somewhat shakily, into the yard at six forty-five on Monday he received some news from Toby Balding that would have been good under any other circumstances. 'Right, Barney. AP's sick, so you can ride Romany Creek. Off you go.'

The trouble was, it wasn't exactly round the corner: Romany Creek was entered for the novice chase at Carlisle, five hours' hard drive up north. It would have been bad enough if Barney'd been feeling great and it was summer. As it was, he was feeling rough as a bear's bum and it was 6 November. He mumbled his thanks and dragged himself off to Carlisle. He must have felt better when he got there, because he sailed round on Romany Creek, who won by three and a half lengths. He slept well that night.

Because I was busy riding I left Barney to furnish the house. I simply signed him a couple of blank cheques and told him to get on with it. However, when it came to spending a relatively large amount he called me in: a three-piece suite wasn't going to be cheap so we rolled up together at a furniture warehouse near Andover. We hadn't been in long when a salesgirl came up and asked if she could be of any assistance. 'Yes,' I replied. 'My friend and I are looking for a sofa and chairs for our house.'

She gave us a knowing look.

I twigged it in one: She thinks we're a couple of poofs. There was no way I was going to disappoint her so I bounced up and down on a big settee, patting the cushion next to me – 'Come and try this for size,' I said to Barney. It didn't take him long to catch on and the girl got redder and redder. When I saw the price of the furniture we stopped carrying on camping. I'd won the jump-jockeys' championship, not the lottery. We ended up buying two red beanbags.

For some reason that I never quite understood, Barney returned from Ireland that summer with a pair of regulation police handcuffs. One weekend when he was away I decided to have a party, which meant all the lunatics, plus Peter Henley and Barry Fenton, came round. Peter and Barry are everything an Irish jump jockey is meant to be. They work hard and put just as much into their play. At that time Barry was following me as Toby Balding's principal conditional jockey and improving all the time. He became Toby's third champion claiming rider when he tied for the title with David Walsh in 1996–7.

Peter was doing well as an amateur with Robert Alner, who trains over the border from Toby in Dorset, and it seemed natural for him to turn professional. Unfortunately, the number of his rides diminished. It didn't take him long to realize his mistake, and as the rules allowed him to recover his amateur status, he switched back and returned to Ireland, where the opportunities are better for experienced amateurs. Happily, he is now enjoying a much more rewarding time.

However, back then he and Barry were flying and were great party animals. They were like twins: if Barry said he thought it would be a good idea to climb up a drainpipe to get a better view of the area from the roof then Peter was with him.

Now, I don't know how they found Barney's handcuffs, but around one thirty a.m. they produced them, and before you could say *The Bill*, Barry had snapped one link on his wrist and the other round Peter's. There was plenty of laughter and cracks about Houdini, but after a while they decided to take them off.

'Where's the key, then?' inquired a bleary-eyed Barry.

'I haven't got a clue,' I said. 'I thought they were with the cuffs.'

There followed plenty of pushing, pulling and wrist-turning, but better and more sober men than Fenton and Henley had tried to get free of them and failed.

'Where the hell's Barney? We'd better get him back to let us out.'

'He's away until Monday morning,' I said, forcing a straight face.

This was just what the boys didn't need to hear: they were both due to work in their yards on Sunday morning, which wasn't going to be easy under the present circumstances.

Fairy liquid, soap, Vaseline – you name it, they tried it. No luck. At three a.m., sobering up rapidly, they came up with the last resort. Barry dialled 999. 'Get me the police, we're in trouble.'

The operator put him through to Weyhill police station.

'Sorry to bother you, but could you help us out of some handcuffs?'

After a busy Saturday night the duty officer couldn't see the funny side.

About half an hour later a squad car arrived with two unamused policemen. They took one look at Barry and Peter manacled on the sofa and one asked a sensible question: 'Why didn't you get someone to drive you down to the station?'

'No chance!' bellowed Barry. 'People would be thinking we were a couple of nancy-boys playing games.'

The policeman kept cool: 'Well, I'm afraid you're going to come down the station to get those things off, unless you've got any other ideas?'

Barry and Peter were bundled into the back of the police car and taken to Weyhill nick. After a short wait the duty sergeant produced the biggest pair of bolt-cutters and snipped through the steel like it was icing sugar.

The boys got a cab back and had a large vodka to steady their nerves. As for Barney, he never explained what the cuffs had been for – and if he got another set, he kept them well hidden. Episodes like that lighten the load of a working week. When you're travelling to the races every day, unable to get to sleep in the back of a car, it's always good to recall the madness of the weekend. The handcuff incident kept us laughing for a long time.

There was no doubt that I liked being champion but I knew it was going to be hard to keep ahead of the field. A few days later I was back where it had all started the previous season at Perth. Billy Rock was there for me with Tabu Lady. The year had been slightly kinder to me than it had to her and she now wore blinkers. However, she won well enough and was the first leg of a double.

I pushed the pedal to the floor in that first month and banked fourteen winners before July. I was seven ahead of David Bridg-water, who was the only jockey of those I feared to take the first month seriously. Adrian Maguire and Norman Williamson stayed away until the season proper began at the end of July. I knew they had to have their backing yards in unbeatable form if they were going to trouble me. Bridgy, however, was another matter.

I was well aware of the tremendous strength of Martin Pipe's operation and that if he chose to blanket bomb a meeting like Taunton or Newton Abbot in August, he could supply his stable jockey with three, sometimes four winners a day. That would be a strong flood to hold back. I had no doubts that he would do it, but a little voice at the back of my mind kept asking if Bridgy truly fancied the job.

By the end of August there were signs that all was not well in the partnership. Bridgy appeared less bouncy than he had been during his time with Nigel Twiston-Davies. I had the strong impression that the pressure of riding for Martin was getting to him, as it had to Richard Dunwoody. Sure enough, the split came in late September. David Bridgwater won the two-runner handicap hurdle on Shahrani at Carlisle on 21 September and that was the last winner he rode for Martin Pipe. On 29 September he quit the position Dunwoody had shed thirteen months earlier, but in the knowledge he had a job to go to.

Bridgy had decided to take the offer to ride as first jockey to the flamboyant owner Darren Mercer, who had enjoyed plenty of success with Pipe. However, their relationship had soured after the death of two of Martin's horses on the first day of the 1996 Cheltenham Festival. Draborgie was favourite for the second race on the programme, the Arkle Chase, but broke a leg after jumping the second fence and was destroyed. Things got even worse forty-five minutes later. Mack The Knife was staying on in sixth place when he broke a leg and was pulled up before the last in the Champion Hurdle, won by Collier Bay.

Incredibly, there was booing and abuse from the crowd when Martin appeared after those sad incidents, which upset him badly. The death of the two horses hung over him for a long time after and I know that he questioned whether he wanted to continue training racehorses. It was only the counsel of owners and good friends that persuaded him to go on. Not that Darren Mercer would be with him. Several weeks before Bridgy quit, Mercer had removed his team from Martin's yard and sent the leading lights, such as Banjo and Escartefigue, to David Nicholson.

As is often the case, sanitized statements were made to the press about Bridgy's resignation, and he trotted out the usual line: 'After considerable thought I have terminated my riding arrangement with Mr Martin Pipe and decided I would be happier to ride as a freelance jockey. I have very much enjoyed my time with Mr Pipe. I have learned a great deal and it was a wonderful experience. We have parted on good, amicable terms and I wish the whole stable every success in the future.'

It was certainly a partnership that had been profitable for both and, despite the loss of Draborgie and Mack The Knife, they had come away from the Cheltenham Festival with Cyborgo winning the Stayers' Hurdle and Challenger du Luc the Cathcart Chase on the final day. However, Bridgy showed his true feelings in a revealing interview in *The Times*: 'In my last six months with Mr

Pipe I could have retired, just like that – packed up at the age of twenty-five. I had got so low you wouldn't believe it. I like to think I'm a jolly kind of bloke, but I just didn't enjoy what I was doing. I asked myself what the difference was and there was only one thing – Martin Pipe. People tell me that I am crazy and that I could have been champion. Is it worth putting yourself through all that?'

Once again the newspapers speculated as to who would be the next jockey to take over the increasingly hot seat at Martin Pipe's Pond House Stables. His riding arrangements were in a more critical state than usual as he had also lost his number-two rider Jonothan Lower earlier that season when he was diagnosed with diabetes. I had to ask myself some questions. I had knocked back Martin's advances three times now. Would he ask again and risk being turned down a fourth time? Did I want him to? Not only had he fallen out with Bridgwater, his working relationship with Richard Dunwoody had broken down despite plenty of big race wins, including the 1994 Grand National on Miinnehoma. However, I also knew that whoever got the bulk of the Pipe rides could be a massive threat to me. Jamie Osborne would be a big problem and there was also the up-and-coming Richard Johnson.

There was no official approach but, looking back, I'm sure that Martin set out to bring me gradually into the fold. There was no call down to his Pond House Stables, no dropped hints from third parties to see if I would be interested. No, what Martin did was drip-feed me with the one thing I'd find irresistible – winners, and easy ones at that.

Not that I wasn't doing just grand on my own. When he cast the first winner my way, Doctor Green in the three-year-old hurdle at Exeter on 2 October, I already had forty-two winners behind me. However, Doctor Green turned out to be one of the easiest of the whole season. We made all, never saw another horse after the start and won by an unchallenged twelve lengths. It was slightly harder on my second winner for Martin that day, Nordic Valley, but it was an appropriate one. Like me he had been trained in Ireland previously by Jim Bolger.

If Martin asked Dave for me and I couldn't ride, then the horse would appear in another race where I was available – 'I'll let him know what it's like not to have to push one out from halfway. He won't be able to resist.' He was right. There was never any summit meeting to thrash out terms of employment. Martin worked on the premise that he would provide plenty of winners for me and a percentage of the million-plus won in prize money would more than cover a retainer. In return, I knew that if I was on the majority of his horses then no one else would be and, barring accidents, I would be champion jockey for as long as I stayed in one piece. But how would I handle Martin? That was the big question.

Martin Pipe is a genius trainer. Don't let anyone tell you any different. I don't know what makes him tick and I've no doubt that a psychiatrist would have a ball if he got him on a couch – although how long he could keep him there would be another matter.

Martin's background is unconventional in racing terms but he does bear comparison to Jim Bolger, who also made his way to racing from the business world. Neither came with any precon- ceived ideas about training so had a blank canvas on which to start. Martin was never destined to train: he was a prodigy with figures at school – Queen's College, Taunton. His dad, Dave, was a well-known bookmaker in the town and around the West Country horse-racing and dog tracks and, with Martin's eye for figures, that seemed to be where his future lay. Martin worked for his father in the Taunton head office and at the holiday-camp concession at Minehead, eventually taking over the credit side of the business. It was Mr Pipe's financial astuteness that set Martin on the road to revolutionizing the training of racehorses.

In 1968 Mr Pipe bought the first half of what was going to become Pond House Stables. It was then called Tuckers Farm, in deepest Somerset, which had yet to be carved open by the M5. Five years later he purchased the adjoining Pond House Farm. Neither property bore any resemblance to the magnificent estab- lishment of today. Before that, in 1971, Martin had made his most sensible move and married Carol. Since I've been with them I have seen just how important Carol is to the administration of the yard. She keeps a steady hand on the tiller and on Martin.

It is hard for me to appreciate that the no-nonsense trainer I speak to most days once had a more reckless approach to life and safety. When he was nineteen he sat on a racehorse for the first time: 'I decided I wanted to become a jockey,' he recalled, 'and a local trainer, Eric Foster, kindly consented to teach me to ride.'

Unlike me, Martin hadn't been allowed a pony when he was a boy, which proved a distinct disadvantage. 'Eric's idea of life was do or die. The first morning I turned up he put me on a racehorse called Clown at the end of his string. In those days skull caps weren't compulsory and within a couple of hundred yards of leaving the stables the string broke into a trot. Within minutes, Clown was at the gallop and I was taken over the main Taunton road, dodging the heavy traffic.' It wasn't enough to put him off, though, and he rode out most days before going to the betting office.

Martin was a bit of a boy at this time and, in his own words, 'was burning the candle at both ends'. Driving his Volkswagen Beetle back from Exeter in the early hours of one morning he fell asleep at the wheel and crashed into a concrete lamp-post. He had to be cut from the wreckage and was unconscious for three days over Easter 1965. It was a life-and-death situation and the surgeons were contemplating amputating his right foot until his dad forbade it and instead pins were put into the ankle. However, Martin is reminded of that accident every day and of another when he smashed his left thigh in a race fall. Rather than walk he spins around his yards on a BMX bike. He keeps putting off the necessary surgery, but if he was one of his horses he would have called in the vet long ago.

Martin says he had little ability as a rider, so I can appreciate the tenacity he showed to ride as an amateur. Unfortunately it was his misplaced bravery that caused him to smash his thigh.

Towards the end of 1971 Mr Pipe brought all his horses to be trained under permit at Tuckers Farm by his brother, Tony. The sole exception was Lorac. This one was trained by Tim Handel at

Hatch Beauchamp, not far away from Pond House Stables, and on 27 December 1972 Mr M. Pipe was given the mount on the 20–1 shot in the King Wenceslas Hurdle over three miles one furlong at Taunton. The official verdict was that the horse ran out at the seventh. Martin recalls it differently: 'Nigel Wakley, father of the current jump jockey Rupert, rode for Handel at the time but had been offered the ride on second favourite Drake's Gold, trained by the late John Thorne, who won the race. That's why I was given the ride. The other professional riders in the race were Bob Davies, on 11–10 favourite Baytree, Geoff Shoemark, Brian Forsey, Peter Jones, Laurence Radmore and another amateur called Charlie Micklem. I thought Lorac had an each-way chance as she had managed two seconds for Nigel, and after a slow gallop for a mile the race began to sort itself out. I was sitting behind the main bunch. I used the same tactics as when I drove my cars and rushed her up on the inside of the others as soon as I saw a gap on the rails. The pros wouldn't have too much of this from a cheeky amateur. The gap soon disappeared and Lorac and I were put through the wings. It would have been bad enough nowadays when they are made of plastic. Then they were made of whitewashed four-by-two, which is stronger than a thigh-bone. After the incident I stayed in the saddle then fell to the ground in agony. I knew I'd smashed my thigh as the pain swept over me.' Although Martin managed one winner, Weather Permitting in a point-to-point, even he knew that he was riding up a blind alley.

For as long as I have been involved in racing Martin Pipe has been at the top of his profession, but it wasn't always like that. When Martin took out a permit to train the horses owned by his father in the season 1973–4 he was what Jim Bolger would have described as a greenhorn. Apparently, during a prolonged spell of rain he didn't exercise the horses because he didn't want to get them wet. His father pointed out to him, in explicit terms, that horses raced in the rain.

It is hard for people to believe that the man who has dominated jump racing for nearly twenty years struggled to train his first winner. At the end of the following season, 1974–5, Hit Parade won the second division of the Motorway Selling Hurdle. He was ridden by Len Lungo, who was a respected jockey on the south-west circuit. Martin bounced most of his theories off Len, and they must have been good for each other. Len is now one of the best trainers in the north of England and Scotland, sending out top-class jumpers from his Dumfries base.

Martin was lucky that his father was willing to put hard cash into racing and buck the oft-quoted line that the only way to get a small fortune out of racing is to start with a big one. Not that he paid top dollar: if Mr Pipe thought something was going cheap he bought it. Over a relatively short period the best all-weather gallop in England was laid, a heated equine pool was dug and, later, one of the largest covered rides in the country was erected. Mr Pipe left no stones unturned in his quest for the best all-weather surface on which to gallop his son's horses. He inspected as many all-weather gallops as he could, including the state-of-the-art constructions at Newmarket, where the Jockey Club estate manager Robert Fellowes was frank about the problems they had overcome.

No matter how good the facilities, horses don't win if they're not fed right. Next to the trainer the headman-feeder is the most important person in the yard. It was a shrewd move Martin Pipe made when he enticed Dennis Dummet to leave Gerald Cottrell in the 1975–6 season. Dennis is still with him today, although either Martin or his son, David, feeds the horses on Sunday morning to give Dennis a lie-in and makes sure he gets a day off in the week.

The fact that Martin Pipe did not serve as an assistant to an established trainer so had no idea about training ultimately worked to his advantage, but only because of his nimble, inquiring mind and tenacity. When he is on a subject to do with horses and he feels someone has something to offer he is like a dog gnawing a bone. In the early days he was a big reader and started with an old book he bought from a second-hand shop entitled *Modern Horse Management* and written in 1890. 'I still refer to it at times,' he said, 'and another book I picked up entitled *Veterinary Notes for Horse Owners*, first published in 1952. I also read two books called *Training the Racehorse*.' These days he has a library full of veterinary books covering the most obscure parts of the anatomy of the horse in language that would make the average trainer's head spin.

He turned the training of racehorses on its head when he decided that as human athletes did not carry excess flesh neither should horses. Big, strapping horses looked wonderful, but, like weight-lifters, they wouldn't run so fast or so long as someone lean and mean. Martin doesn't like to see horses come back from a rest looking pig fat after gorging on summer grass.

He is acknowledged as having developed the method of interval training to a fine art but he still embraces traditional methods to train winners. The training performance and subsequent coup that bring the biggest smile to his face is the victory of Carrie Ann in the Makerfield Selling Handicap Hurdle at Haydock on 5 January 1980. The mare had a decent level of ability in that lowly class and Martin had left little to chance. Having taken her to gallop after racing at his nearest courses, Taunton and Exeter, he was confident he had her ready.

Not many were in the know, but Martin's great mate Chester Barnes certainly was. He and Martin had become friends the previous year and, after Rod Millman brought Carrie Ann home by two and a half lengths from Henry Hotfoot in the last race of the day, they left a dank Haydock £53,000 richer. Their friendship has endured ever since, and although Martin's son David takes on significantly more as each season progresses, Chester Barnes is never far away from the action.

The winning totals improved each year from the 1980–81 season when Martin trained his first Cheltenham Festival winner, Baron Blakeney in the Triumph Hurdle, ridden by Paul Leach. It is testimony to the loyalty Martin inspires that, after leaving the yard and training in his own right, Paul is now back as a member of the team.

Martin's performance throughout the eighties and into the nineties was nothing short of incredible. The interval training improved horses immeasurably, but he moved forward and employed any new training aid he thought would be beneficial. He even built an on-site laboratory that became the envy of many

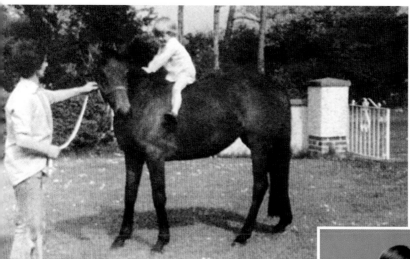

1. There's nothing like starting young. I was barely two and riding with a full length of leg when my father put me on our grand mare Misclaire.

2. An early picture of the young McCoys. From the left, Jane, myself, Roisin and Colm sitting on Anne-Marie's lap. My youngest sister, Kelly, hadn't yet joined us.

3. A very proud moment at Downpatrick, leading in my first winner, Wood Louse, ridden by Conor O'Dwyer. The lady is Yvonne Rock, wife of trainer Billy.

4. My father, Peadar, travelled from Moneyglass to see me have my first ride on Nordic Touch at Phoenix Park on 1 September 1990. If nothing happened after this there would still be one memory.

5. Explaining to the Boss, Jim Bolger, after my first ride on Nordic Touch.

6. The day I'd dreamed of. My first winner, Legal Steps, at Thurles, 26 March 1992.

7. Riszard hits the last at Gowran Park on 20 April 1994 but it's not enough to stop me having my first win over hurdles.

8. Billy Rock, who treated me like a man when I was a boy, and saw more in the boy than any other man.

9. Talking things through with Toby Balding shortly after I'd arrived in England. He always gave me sound advice.

10. First leg of the big double is landed. Make A Stand wins the 1997 Smurfit Champion Hurdle the hard way, from the front.

11. Celebrating on Mr Mulligan after winning the Tote Gold Cup.

12. One of my boyhood heroes, Richard Dunwoody, riding the brilliant but ill-fated One Man, congratulates me after the Gold Cup.

13. Winning on Petite Risk at Ludlow, 25 March 1998, and beating Peter Scudamore's record of 221 winners in a jump season.

14. (*left*) The best ride I've ever had over the Grand National fences. Cyfor Malta leads With Impunity and Ballyline at the last fence before winning the 1998 John Hughes Trophy Chase.

15. (*right*) Without doubt the best ride I've given any horse in my career – and I was banned for it! Pridwell (noseband) beats the mighty Istabraq in the 1998 Martell Aintree Hurdle.

16. (*left*) Where would I be without him? With Martin Pipe, master trainer, in the Ascot winners' enclosure. I had managed five out of six winners in a day.

17. (*right*) Sparring with Frankie Dettori. He couldn't resist a phone call after I'd missed going through the card at Ascot.

18. The most dangerous part of the race. Doing the flying dismount from Blowing Wind after winning the 1998 Vincent O'Brien County Handicap Hurdle at Cheltenham and the £50,000 bonus for owner Peter Deal.

19. Boys just wanna have fun. Ready for a game of soccer with Sean Curran, who was standing alongside me when I broke my ankle without kicking a ball.

20. Two of Arsenal's greatest fans in the weighing room. Celebrating my first championship with Willie Ryan, who won the 1997 Derby on Benny The Dip. My agent Dave Roberts and dad, Peadar, are in the background.

21. (*right*) The men who have made some impossible dreams come true: Martin Pipe and leading owner David Johnson.

22. With Brad. A friend through thick and thin.

23. With the Macca and Growler partnership, my good friends Robbie Fowler and Steve McManaman.

24. I'm in heaven, but don't tell Chanelle! With the Sisters Of Murphy's after Cyfor Malta won the 1998 Murphy's Gold Cup.

25. Going through the motions on the mechanical horse with British Racing School instructor Robert Sidebottom. I had to attend a training day at Newmarket after my suspension for whip misuse but only I could change things.

26. The race I wanted to win more than any other – and it shows. Being led into the winners' enclosure on Edredon Bleu after winning the 2000 Queen Mother Champion Chase at Cheltenham. A horse must have everything to win it.

27. A proud moment. Receiving the Champion Chase Trophy from the Queen Mother.

28. The best chaser I have ever ridden, and we will never know just how good Gloria Victis was. This wonderful shot gives you some idea of what might have been.

in racing – to the extent that whispers were heard to the effect that he was 'giving them something'. The same rumours fly around today, but I have a crude but appropriate answer to them: 'Bollocks.'

Martin soon had the capability to blood-test his horses without having to send samples away and now some leading trainers send blood to be tested by Martin's resident guru Barry Allen. Apart from the Equine Research Centre at Newmarket, there isn't a set-up like Martin's in the whole of the British Isles.

The whispering campaign against Martin came to a head when the television investigative programme, *The Cook Report*, set its sights on the then champion trainer in January 1991. They set out to attempt to prove that Martin's success, which had seen him cut the record books to pieces, had been due to illegal practices such as blood-doping. This practice had boosted the endurance of long-distance runners in the seventies and the ill-informed decided that it had been perfected by Martin and explained his horses' ability to keep galloping after others had dropped away. It was an impossibility. As Martin says: 'A horse has eighty pints of blood compared to the human's eight. How would you possibly store the amount of red cells needed to boost performance?'

The programme also tried to say that there was an abnormally high mortality rate among Martin's horses. This was totally unfounded. However, when the programme was screened on 6 May 1991 with Martin appearing to defend the accusations, it had cost him £30,000 in legal fees and preparation.

Aside from the improvement in facilities and with it the class of horse, perhaps the most significant addition to the Pond House team was a top-class jockey. Paul Leach was a solid performer and the local youngster Jonothan Lower was making his way, but Martin's link-up with Peter Scudamore was the start of something big.

Scu first took rides from the yard regularly in the 1986–7 season. He set the standard by which subsequent jockeys employed by Martin Pipe would be measured. It wasn't an easy level to reach and one that I sometimes feel I will never get to in Martin's eyes.

One reason is that Martin and Peter are more in the same age group: Martin is thirteen years older than Scu but almost thirty years older than me. Also, they were on the learning curve at the same time and moved along it together. These days, there are no better-schooled hurdlers and chasers than those trained by Martin Pipe, but it took Peter Scudamore to get it that way. Before Scu joined him, Martin had fixed ideas about schooling. He thought there was more chance of horses injuring themselves schooling than working on the all-weather track so he did much less of it than, for example, Fred Winter and David Nicholson, where Scu was regularly employed. Once Scu explained the advantages of extensive schooling Martin set about implementing changes. He extended two schooling fences to five, and now has a line of five consecutive open ditches alongside the regulation fences. Added to this he has extensive loose schooling facilities, overseen by Jonothan Lower. You can be sure that no trainer sends his jumpers to the racecourse better schooled than Martin Pipe.

Scu shared the jump jockeys' title when John Francome drew level with him in 1981–2, then stopped riding in an act of real sportsmanship after Scu was denied outright victory because of injury. However, although he won it again in 1985–6, the year before he forged serious links with Martin, it was the partnership with the trainer that made Scu virtually invincible. Perhaps the fire was burning lower in the 1992–3 season, when he was fourteen winners adrift of Richard Dunwoody and retired after Sweet Duke won a three-mile handicap hurdle at Ascot on 7 April. It would have taken a brave man to say that Scu could not have made up the difference with a back-end flourish from Martin. However, Richard was denied the satisfaction of beating Scu when he still had the sword in his hand, a frustration I can understand. Scu had made the championship his own for the previous seven years and given a new meaning to the term 'professional' jump jockey.

It was the logical move for Richard Dunwoody to take Scu's position as Martin Pipe's number-one rider and to all the world it seemed a match made in heaven. The ultimate jump trainer with the most stylish steeplechase jockey of the era. Looking back and having spoken to both parties, I can see why it didn't work. Just as Pipe and Scudamore had evolved together, when Pipe and Dunwoody joined up they were established forces in their own right with firm ideas on how things should be done. One thing I have learned since riding for Martin Pipe is that you must be a team player. Individual flair is encouraged, but everyone pulls to the same end: winners for Pond House Stables.

Martin, too, reckons he knows why it did not work: 'My relationship with Scu was great. He was more my age to start with and we'd had plenty of front running and plenty of winners from those tactics, too. Dunwoody came along and he was already more fixed in his mind. He had his own ideas and didn't like front running, he was a jockey who liked to come from behind and look good. I can remember telling him to go out and make all the running on Elite Reg in a handicap hurdle at Worcester in late May the year Scu retired. "Go as fast as you can." The horse had twelve stone two. He said it had got too much weight. I said, "So what?" Dunwoody went out in a real temper, went as fast as he could and won in a time that was below standard. He did what I told him and it worked but because it had so much weight he wanted to ride it differently.'

Richard had decided early that he didn't want to be in Martin's gang and said later: 'From the beginning my partnership with Martin was never that close; professional and businesslike but lacking any real warmth. I was not going to become part of the Pipe team as Scu had.'

The partnership, such as it was, went from bad to worse in the early months of the 1994–5 season, and in October only four of the champion jockey's fourteen winners had been supplied by the champion trainer. The most significant breach, which was only papered over subsequently, came when Martin allowed Richard to ride General Crack for Paul Nicholls in an Exeter novice hurdle on 1 November. Martin had Encore Un Peu in the race, a horse that had shown considerable promise on his previous outing under Richard at Stratford five days earlier. Encore Un Peu won by ten lengths, landing a gamble in the process. Richard thought he should have been kept more in the picture over the horse's improvement and was livid. I was only a five-pound claimer in the weighing room that afternoon so kept my head down and my mouth shut, but I remember a bad atmosphere hanging round Richard Dunwoody's corner that murky afternoon on Haldon Hill.

That day Jonothan Lower rode Encore Un Peu. He is as important today to the Nicholashayne operation as he was when riding winners for the yard, and admits that he never had as good a working relationship with Richard as he had with Peter Scudamore. 'I was there before Scu and there were only about twelve staff when I joined as a kid. You could see him and Martin growing together. The more they did, the better they got. Even though it was pissing me right off because I was missing winners I would always talk to Scu about the horses when he came down. It was different with Dunwoody. He did what he wanted to do and didn't really want to talk about it.'

Richard was all for leaving the job after the Exeter incident but wisely decided against it.

It wasn't Martin's greatest season and for the second year in succession he was beaten by Richard's former employer, David Nicholson. The patched-up partnership between him and Richard continued to the end of the season and was rewarded with the last big chase when 10–1 shot Cache Fleur won the Whitbread Gold Cup.

When I looked at the personal form book Martin Pipe did not appear the easiest trainer to get along with. There had been a breakdown in communication with two jockeys who were older than me, and I was a year younger than his son! But the winners kept coming in and, almost by stealth, I found myself becoming stable jockey to Martin Pipe.

8. The Big Double

I decided that the best way to begin my association with Martin Pipe was to make myself available whenever possible but retain the right of veto, just in case things didn't work out. I had an excellent trainer base behind me, with the likes of Paul Nicholls and Philip Hobbs and, bearing in mind the relatively rapid departures of Richard Dunwoody and David Bridgwater, I did not know how long I would last.

The 1996–7 season hadn't begun brilliantly and my total at the end of August was thirty-two. September was relatively poor with only eleven but I had a cracking October with thirty-four winners, which put me in line for the fastest hundred. Peter Scudamore had set the mark eight years earlier on 20 December and I bettered it when Class Of Ninetytwo, trained by the late Captain Tim Forster, won the Shipston Handicap Chase at Warwick on 21 November. It was the first serious record that I'd broken and I said at the time, 'I barely had a hundred rides in Ireland.' In fact it was 104, but it did give me a sense of achievement. Scu was typically gracious and said, 'It's wonderful Tony has broken the record and I've got the greatest respect for him. A few years ago you would not have mentioned him in the same breath as Richard Dunwoody but now you can. I honestly believe the standard of riding now is better than ever.'

To get that kind of accolade meant a lot to me, but my new record needed to be put into context. In fact, it would have been more accurate to call it the *earliest* hundred: when Scu completed his ton, the season had begun in August, so I'd had a two-month start. I lowered it the next season, but as the seasons click by, such milestones tend to lose their impact. A bit like an angler, I concentrate on the big ones, like Richard Dunwoody's all-time record of 1,699 career wins, and the most winners ridden in one season, which was 269 by Sir Gordon Richards in 1947.

The thread that linked Scu and me was Martin Pipe, who supplied a steady flow of winners. However, an increasing amount of the quality came from Paul Nicholls. He produced the subsequent Cheltenham Gold Cup winner See More Business to make an impressive Chase début in the Grade Two Rising Stars Novices' Chase at Chepstow on 11 November. At the same course on 7 December he sent out Belmont King to win another Grade Two race, the Rehearsal Chase. When we took the lead at the tenth fence I gave no thought to the horse we passed, and when I watched the race again later his performance was memorable for several serious mistakes. In fact, I wondered how he managed to get back to press for the lead five fences out. At that stage, Mr Mulligan looked like just another second-season novice who was going to struggle when he went in with the big boys.

I saw Belmont King in more lucrative circumstances towards the end of the season when we won the Scottish National at Ayr, but that seemed highly unlikely after I was sacked by Paul Nicholls in January.

Let's get one thing straight. A jockey's first loyalty is to himself. You are the one person you cannot deceive, and if you are not riding winners, problems set in. Your confidence goes and confidence among those who employ you ebbs away. A freelance jockey must always try to get on the horse with the best winning chance. For the season 1996–7 I was clear in my own mind that I was a freelance. I would, of course, have loyalties to honour, but in a conflict of interest Dave Roberts and I would decide on my selection of rides. This led to a major falling out with Paul and his principal owner and backer, Paul Barber.

Although Martin Pipe had provided quantity rather than quality for the first third of the season, by the time the New Year had turned he was producing some better individuals and none came with healthier credentials than Cyborgo. He'd won the Stayers' Hurdle at Cheltenham the previous March, after a long lay-off through injury, and was the kind of horse who stood out as a potential chasing star of the future. I hadn't been down to school that often at Nicholashayne, and when I went in mid-January one of the first horses Martin put me on was Cyborgo. Now, I'd ridden some good horses in my career, though never anything like a Stayers' Hurdle winner that was going novice chasing. He schooled well, and after the session Martin said, 'He's in a novice chase at Newton Abbot next week, you can ride him, if you like.'

Unfortunately it was the Bet With The Tote Novice Chase Qualifier and Paul Nicholls had entered Flaked Oats. He'd won six point-to-points and I'd ridden him to an easy win on his chasing début at Fontwell in early December. When Paul said he was going to run at Newton Abbot I said I was happy to maintain the partnership – until Cyborgo came into the equation. Both trainers wanted me and asked Dave Roberts for confirmation that they could have me. In those situations the buck stops with me. Dave said, 'You can ride Flaked Oats or Cyborgo. What do you want to do?'

There was only one answer. I wasn't retained by anyone and, good as Flaked Oats was, he didn't have the racing pedigree of Cyborgo. I screwed up my face in anticipation of the storm, took a deep breath and replied, 'I've got to ride Cyborgo. Paul and the owners aren't going to be happy, but it'll win at Newton Abbot and it's going to be a serious chance for the Sun Alliance at Cheltenham.'

Dave agreed, and I knew a row was imminent but I didn't think it was right to let Dave do my dirty work. I called Paul the day before the race and came straight to the point. 'Look, Paul, I'm going to ride Cyborgo tomorrow.'

Understandably, he was stung. 'You said you'd ride mine. We've got an agreement that you'll ride mine. You've got a gentleman's agreement with me and Paul Barber.'

'I know, and I'm sorry, but I'm going to ride Pipe's. I think it will win and it'll probably win at Cheltenham.'

'If you don't ride Flaked Oats, you won't ride any of the others tomorrow.'

'If that's how you feel, fair enough.'

Paul had another line of attack. 'What happens later on when Cyborgo is in the same race as See More Business?'

'I'll ride See More Business.'

That wasn't enough for Paul. 'I need to be able to rely on someone and so do my owners.'

Nothing I said could have repaired the damage to our relationship, which had strengthened by the week since I'd first ridden for Paul on Warfield at Sandown in the February of my first season in England two years earlier. He had been the first trainer to put me on potentially top-class horses, like See More Business, when my experience might not have warranted it. His confidence in me had persuaded others to employ me. He clearly felt I had betrayed his trust.

'You had a gentleman's agreement with us.'

'I know, but in this game things change.'

The trouble was, when Paul had been a jockey riding for David Barons he would never have considered doing what I was about to do. He rode nearly all of the horses from the yard at Kingsbridge, Devon, during the eighties, the best of them the mighty New Zealand-bred Playschool, which won the Hennessy and Welsh National of 1987. Paul wouldn't have done what I was doing even if it had meant doubling his career total of 118 winners. I was different.

Paul realized my decision was irreversible. 'If you don't ride Flaked Oats that's the end of our partnership,' he said.

'Paul, I'm going to ride Cyborgo. I think he'll win at Cheltenham.'

That was the end of the conversation and a good partnership.

On that wet and windy day at Newton Abbot Cyborgo jumped with more fluency than the usual first-time-out novice chaser and, with his proven stamina, I always had him up with the pace. We went ahead four out and he came clear from the home turn to beat Well Timed by twenty lengths. To make matters worse, Flaked Oats would have been second, albeit a well-beaten one, but fell with Philip Hide at the last. Paul took the reversal like a man, although any conversations we had that day were kept to a minimum. It would not be quite so straightforward with Paul Barber.

Paul Nicholls had made his way to the head of his profession with the backing of Paul Barber. When Jim Old decided to leave Barber's Manor Farm Stables near Shepton Mallet in Somerset in 1991 Paul Nicholls had applied to take over the operation and was given his chance. No one ever took a better one. Unfortunately for me, any slight on Paul Nicholls was keenly felt by Paul Barber, who had no involvement with Flaked Oats but clearly took what had happened personally.

Paul Barber is a farmer and a gentleman. He also makes a great success of bringing young horses through the point-to-point field ready to attain championship standard in steeplechases. There is no better example of this than See More Business, but there have been plenty of others. In Paul Barber's world a word given or a handshake is as binding as a contract made under the eye of a high court judge. The rift with Paul Nicholls healed relatively quickly and I ended the season winning the Scottish National for him on Belmont King. But it took much longer for Paul Barber to forgive and I am certain that he will never forget.

About two years later at Fontwell I took a fall at the final fence and began the walk back up the finishing hill to the weighing room. As usual, I was trying to work out why I'd ended on the floor when someone fell into stride beside me. I glanced to my right and saw Paul Barber, typically concerned about my well-being. Our pace slowed and we discussed the Flaked Oats episode for the first time since it had happened.

Hands in his pockets, looking straight at me, he said, 'I was very upset at the time by how you treated Paul. I meant it when I said you'd never ride for me again, but never is a long time and things change.'

The time was right for an apology and I said, 'I felt very badly about it and I fully understand why you were so upset. I did something that my parents brought me up not to do, broke my word. But, unfortunately, at that time I felt I had to.'

We shook hands. It was a sporting gesture that showed the calibre of the man. Paul Barber certainly didn't need me, but he had handed me a welcome olive branch. I went back to the changing room feeling good.

On reflection, the situation was magnified because Martin Pipe had been involved and it was an open secret that he wanted first call on me. Although twenty-seven of my winners that season had come from Paul Nicholls, thirty-five had been supplied by Martin. But Paul had been a supporter much longer and wanted to keep me on side.

Despite Paul Nicholls' withdrawal of support I was still on course to better two of Peter Scudamore's records, the fastest 150 and his record of 221 winners in a season, set in 1988–9. When I walked into the weighing room at Wincanton on 23 January I had 130 winners behind me. About ninety minutes later I was writhing on the ground after the first fence of the maiden chase, where Speedy Snapsgem had fallen fatally, having left me with two broken bones in my left shoulder, the clavicle and scapula.

Immediately I was on the stretcher I clamped the mask over my face to deaden the pain and went straight to Yeovil hospital to be strapped up. It was the first serious injury I'd had on the racecourse, and although I tried every gadget available to speed recovery I could not cheat nature. I knew it would be a bad mistake to come back with the bones barely knitted, as another fall would put me out of action even longer. I made sure to keep up my fitness and spent plenty of time in the Andover leisure centre on the step machines and exercise bikes. On 10 February I rode out for the first time on the quietest horse in Toby Balding's yard, Sea Freedom. I did nothing more than a hack, but it relieved the afternoon boredom.

I still put myself through the mill mentally, sitting in front of the SIS coverage and watching horses win that I would have been on. None was easy viewing, but perhaps the hardest was travelling to Newbury to see Make A Stand and Chris Maude slaughter what looked a typically tough field for the Tote Gold Trophy Handicap Hurdle sixteen days after my fall.

Make A Stand is possibly the best example of how Martin Pipe can improve a horse almost beyond the dreams of other trainers. He managed to win as a two-year-old in a handicap at Newmarket for Henry Candy in the colours of owner Robert Barnett, whose family had owned such fine horses as the Oaks winner Time Charter and Master Willie, second in the 1980 Derby and sire of Make A Stand. The colt lost his way the following season and, after one disappointing outing at Bath, was sent to Newmarket Sales where Candy bought him back for just 4,200 guineas. A syndicate, the Kingstone Warren Partners, was formed and Make A Stand won for them, easily taking an eleven-furlong claimer at Leicester in August. These are the races that Martin Pipe scans carefully for potential hurdlers, as all the runners can be claimed for an advertised price after the race. He paid £8,000 for Make A Stand and unknowingly got one of the bargains of the century.

Unknown to Martin, one of the previous syndicate owners was already on his books. It was Peter Deal. When Peter called Pond House that evening he was in typically mischievous mood and accused Martin of nicking one of his horses. Martin is a businessman and offered Peter the horse back for what he'd paid. Peter accepted half, and recalled, 'I'd had a couple of horses with Martin which were no good. To his credit, he told me early on, never kept me in the dark, which I liked. I then got on the phone to offer Martin's half to the former partners. There were no takers.'

This was particularly sad for one of them, the BBC sports presenter and racing enthusiast John Inverdale. Like the BBC footballing commentator John Motson, he loves relaxing with a day's racing, much as I like to wind down by watching football. It must have been hard for John Inverdale to see the transformation in Make A Stand. No one could have imagined just how far it would go, and it's only to be expected that John remembers the period all too well: 'Peter offered me the other half but I wasn't sure because he had a history of leg trouble. I rang Henry Candy, who I've had bits of horses with since 1989, and he said he would be surprised if Make A Stand won another race. So I rang Peter back and said I'd rather buy a leg in something else.'

Peter got back to Martin and told him he couldn't sell the other half. Martin didn't hesitate. 'I'll come in,' was his response, and he had made one of the best bloodstock investments of his life.

After winning three novice hurdles in the previous May, Make A Stand won his first handicap hurdle under Chris Maude at Stratford on 19 October with an official rating of 114. Although he missed out on his next two runs the first proved a turning point, which Peter remembers well for the way that Mark Dwyer put them on the path to glory. That was no surprise: Mark had had the same grounding as me, having served a Flat apprenticeship in Ireland before joining Jimmy FitzGerald at Malton. Mark is now a much respected figure in the bloodstock-sales world but he deserved his reputation as a great tactician and thinker when he was riding. They didn't come any shrewder.

He rode Make A Stand in a Grade Two novice hurdle at Uttoxeter over two and a half miles and he was beaten a distance by the long odds-on Jack Tanner. He was adamant when he talked to Peter after the race: 'Never, ever hold this horse up again. He's the most natural jumper, just let him go.'

Make A Stand came good in the £35,000 William Hill Handicap Hurdle at Sandown in early December, making all under Glenn Tormey off a mark of 123. After that he was virtually unstoppable. I got on him for the first time in the Grade Two Kennel Gate Novices' Hurdle, a race I'd won the previous year on Call Equiname for Paul Nicholls. In short, I had never been more impressed by a novice hurdler. He was everything you looked for, fast, fluent and game. I never saw another horse after the start and came home by an easy five lengths from Eagles Rest at 8–13 favourite. Although that was a conditional race and he was giving only seven pounds to the opposition, his official rating had now risen to 132. If he was going to win another handicap he would have to improve again. He did – and then some.

A month later, on 18 January, he started 2–1 favourite for the Lanzarote Handicap Hurdle at Kempton. Nothing got near him and we arrived at the line with an easy four lengths in hand off Gales Cavalier and Jamie Osborne. Martin Pipe knew just what he had in his hands and the Tote Gold Trophy at Newbury on 8 February was set up for Make A Stand. He had just a four-pound penalty to carry for his Kempton win, although the handicapper would have

The Big Double   103

given him seven pounds more had he been able to reassess him for that success. Having said that, it was still the hardest task Make A Stand had yet to face. It was even harder for me to watch the race.

Worth £58,000, the Tote Gold Trophy had gained notoriety in its past incarnation as the Schweppes Trophy, when it was regularly plotted up by Captain Ryan Price in the sixties. It is one of the great scalps for a jump jockey to collect outside the majors and ranks alongside the Hennessy and Whitbread Gold Cups. What's more, Newbury is one of the hardest courses for a horse to make all in a competitive race. When you turn into the home straight there are over four furlongs remaining and, believe me, you can feel vulnerable out there on your own. Not that it seemed to bother Make A Stand. Chris Maude had him well clear from the third and it was stablemate Hamilton Silk who ran through from the rear to take second at a respectable nine lengths.

Trying to salvage something from a miserable day on the sidelines, I played the race over in my mind and could hardly believe just how easily this horse had cut a competitive handicap hurdle to pieces. I also knew that he was my ride when the Cheltenham Festival came round the following month. The question now was, which race would he go for? He was qualified for both the Supreme Novices' over two miles and the Sun Alliance over two miles five furlongs. More tantalizingly still, Martin Pipe had covered every option by putting him in the Champion Hurdle.

It was no easy decision. His official mark, having been a mere 114 back in October, had now risen to 152. It still left him twenty-three pounds behind the previous year's winner Collier Bay and officially eleven pounds inferior to Large Action, who had won the 1994 Tote Gold Trophy and finished second in the Champion Hurdle to Alderbrook in 1995. On the face of it, he could win either of the novice races but Martin, who owned half of him, knew there was still more improvement. When Martin asked me my view, I said I thought he could win the two-mile novice on his head. But that was worth £45,000. The Champion was worth almost three times as much – and it wouldn't be three times as difficult to win. There was also the possibility of another big advantage: fast ground.

It would certainly be against Collier Bay, who went off second favourite.

Peter Deal had left for a holiday in Barbados immediately after the Gold Trophy and recalls, 'I got very pissed with some racing pals who were also on holiday and by the end of the session it was the Champion Hurdle. Martin needed no persuading.'

Once the decision had been taken there was another significant temptation put before owner and trainer. Martin made a call to Peter. 'We've had a big offer for the horse.'

Peter Deal was immovable: 'I don't want to know what the offer is or who made it. I don't want to sell. He owes me and you nothing whatsoever and I'm staying with him.' As he didn't want Martin to lose out on a good investment he added, 'I'll buy your half.'

Martin conceded that he had been made a fair offer.

This conversation concluded around eight o'clock and at ten thirty Peter's phone rang. It was Martin, and he never makes calls that late at night. He said, 'I'm having a sleepless night. You're absolutely right, of course we can't sell, but I had to make you aware.'

There's a saying in horse trading that the first profit is the best one. And don't forget that a hundred and one things can go wrong with any horse, let alone a jumper. But I don't think there was enough money in the Bank of England or Ireland to buy Make A Stand. It was an appropriate name for the horse and his half-owner Deal.

By the time I returned on 19 February after twenty-seven days out of action my Champion Hurdle mount was firmly established and coming down in the ante-post market. I was well pleased to be back with a win on my first ride back, which was Rare Spread for Martin in the claiming hurdle at Folkestone.

Although the Champion Hurdle arrangements had been sorted, the Cheltenham Gold Cup was going to be much less straight-forward. It had me contemplating jumping ship.

Mr Mulligan was an unlikely Cheltenham Gold Cup winner.

Norman Williamson rode him as a young horse when he was trained by Kim Bailey and had a frightening experience on him at Newbury first time out in November 1994. He remembers it well: 'I'd never seen him or schooled him before he ran in the Oxfordshire Chase and Kim told me to let him bowl along in front. I set my own pace and I was plenty busy enough trying to organize him and getting him to jump. We'd done nearly a circuit and came to the second down the back straight. He jumped it, then four strides after he turned over like someone had shot him. Once I'd checked that he was all right I went back to inspect the ground. Everyone thought he had slipped up, but there was nothing. I met Kim walking back and told him that I thought the horse had suffered a heart attack. I also said I thought he was a slow yak until Kim pointed out just how far we had been in front when we came down.

'That wasn't the end of the problems as he'd cracked his neck and had to spend nearly six months recuperating at Mary Bromiley's successful equine physiotherapy and recovery establishment at Baydon, just outside Lambourn. A couple of weeks later Kim, myself and the gelding's owner, Michael Worcester, were having breakfast and I mentioned the suspected heart attack again. Mr Worcester turned to me and said, "Funny you should say that. He did it after winning a point-to-point in Ireland and nearly fell into the crowd." He was off for ten months and went to Noel Chance, who was now training all the Worcester horses. He won his first two novice hurdles and Mark Dwyer came down to school him before he ran in his first chase at Bangor a year to the day after he fell with me.

'I was off with a broken arm, but Mark stayed with me and I drove him up to the Mandown schooling ground and said, "Listen, now, be careful. There's something wrong with him, although he's got a good engine." Mark got back into the car after he'd popped him and was of the same opinion: "He's good but he's definitely a bit wobbly."

'Richard Johnson, who was a claiming amateur then, rode him most of the time, but he didn't do much wrong for Mark and won all right at Bangor. Still, with his problems you'd never have fancied him to win a Cheltenham Gold Cup.'

After I agreed to ride him there was an uncomfortably long time when I would have endorsed Norman's opinion wholeheartedly. Mr Mulligan was very much the standard bearer for Irishman Noel Chance when he took up the position as salaried trainer to Michael Worcester at Folly House Stables, Lambourn. Noel had done his time as assistant to Neville Begg at Randwick, Sydney, and returned home to train on the Curragh with mixed success yet to no great financial gain. When Noel took charge Michael Worcester told him, 'I have a horse that will win the Cheltenham Gold Cup,' at which Noel thought but fortunately did not say, yes, you and half the other owners in Britain and Ireland.

In that summer of 1995 it didn't take Noel long to realize that Mr Mulligan was indeed something special. He was always Richard Johnson's ride and although he was beaten by Nathen Lad in the Sun Alliance Chase at Cheltenham in 1996 after a bad mistake early, he still ended the season as the best staying novice chaser. He proved that in his previous victory in the Reynoldstown Novices' Chase at Ascot, where he ran away from a quality field that included the subsequent Grand National winner Lord Gyllene. To this day, Noel reckons that was the best he ever had the horse in his life.

I'd never ridden for Noel, but I knew all about Mr Mulligan. Even though he had run sluggishly behind Belmont King in the Rehearsal Chase at Chepstow, when ridden by David Bridgwater, he was clearly a horse of some potential. When Noel asked me to ride him in the King George VI Chase at Kempton on Boxing Day I agreed on the spot.

The ride had become available because Dickie Johnson was under the wing of David Nicholson, and that meant he was required at Wetherby on what is one of the busiest days of the jumping season – weather permitting. Ironically, Kempton was the only meeting to survive severe frost, but once Michael Worcester and Noel booked a jockey they never changed. Plus, I had no obligations for the Gold Cup, so it was understood that, if things went to plan, I'd keep the ride. Noel explained the below-par effort at

Chepstow to me: 'He's a very difficult horse because you don't know if there's something wrong or whether it's just him being himself. The blacksmith was shoeing him a week after Chepstow, and when he squeezed his hoof between his knees it exploded with poison. He was the one horse in a hundred that hadn't gone lame with a stone bruise.'

The problem was that Mr Mulligan missed two weeks' work going into the King George and he was so far behind schedule that a week before he was still a doubtful runner. Michael Worcester and Noel took the gamble to run, but in Noel's words, 'We knew we were decidedly undercooked.'

Kempton on Boxing Day has a feel all of its own. People pour in, desperate to get away from a houseful of relatives, and the place is heaving. With two rides carrying eleven stone ten I'd had a full Christmas lunch blow-out at the Boot Inn, Shipton Bellinger, with a bunch of the boys, and was keen to work off the excesses of the previous day. We met in the paddock for a final round of tactics and I was adamant that there was only one way to beat the heavily backed favourite, One Man. 'The only way we can beat this grey horse is to expose his stamina.'

Noel did not want to hear this: 'Tony, this horse isn't a hundred per cent. I'll leave it to you, but whatever you do keep a bit up your sleeve or you definitely won't win.'

One Man was an exceptional horse who had won the King George the previous year, but stamina was a possible weakness. Lack of it certainly stopped him winning a Cheltenham Gold Cup. I had to go for it. If I'm realistic I don't think I'd have beaten him whatever tactics I'd used, but it was in the back of my mind that he might just empty up the home straight. The crowd launch you round the quickest three-mile chase circuit in Britain at that Christmas meeting and I took no prisoners. In front from the start, Mr Mulligan jumped from fence to fence, but when Richard Dunwoody cruised through to lead on the home turn with three fences to jump there was only one result. The best we could hope for was second. That's never been good enough for me.

Mr Mulligan, despite being short of work, had given me the lot:

there was nothing left going to the last but I decided to give him a kick as he went into that final fence and landed running. Then maybe, just maybe, we could get back if One Man weakened. Believe me, I've employed this move hundreds of times and the added momentum can bring the big pay-out. Not this time. Mr Mulligan was tired: he caught the fence and turned over, losing the consolation prize of nearly £24,000 for being second. That went to the previous season's Grand National winner Rough Quest and Mick FitzGerald.

I stayed with Mr Mulligan while he recovered his senses. By the time I had taken off my saddle and begun the walk back up the straight, Noel had come down to meet me, hands in pockets and trilby pushed back on his head. We ambled back to the weighing room, me carrying the tack. No time for excuses. 'I'm sorry, Noel, my fault entirely. But you know as well as I do how quickly the grey horse stops. If your horse was as short of work as you say, then the grey horse will never beat us again. I think we can win the Gold Cup.'

Jockeys often say the strangest things in the heat of battle and I was probably chancing my arm a bit, but I genuinely thought that it was a possibility. A tougher track and a longer trip would be tailor-made for Mr Mulligan – and just look what he'd done when nowhere near tightened up. Yes, he was more than capable of winning the Gold Cup.

'I'll ride him at Cheltenham, Noel.'

How I was going to regret those words during the course of the following two and a half months, but they were music to Noel's ears and he went straight out and backed Mr Mulligan at 20–1 for the big one. 'If he can do this in the state of fitness I have him at now, he must be a certainty.'

Now the problems started and things went from bad to worse. The Kempton fall had been so heavy that it left a massive haematoma on Mr Mulligan's hindquarter, which hardened and went right under his tail, absolutely the worst place. He'd also pulled a ligament off his spine, which was extremely painful. Mary Bromiley came in twice a day but was getting nowhere quickly. She gave Noel an ultimatum: 'I'm going to have to work on this horse five or six times a day to disperse this thing and I can't keep running down here. I've got other horses to see to as well.'

Noel knew the score: Mr Mulligan had to go into rehab at nearby Baydon. 'Right, take him, but I've got to have him back the first week in February.'

Mary sent Mr Mulligan home on 7 February. Noel didn't pull a punch with Michael Worcester: 'If we miss one day with this horse, he won't be able to run. The schedule's that tight.'

Mr Mulligan missed an intended run in the Irish Hennessy at Leopardstown and, boy, was he working bad. Noel decided to give him a racecourse gallop at Newbury after racing on 1 March, thirteen days before the Gold Cup. The omens weren't good. I didn't get near to riding a winner all day and this was the first time I'd sat on Mr Mulligan since Boxing Day.

Noel was desperate for the horse to work well and thought he'd made sure of it by selecting Sunley Secure as his galloping companion. He was only a four-year-old novice hurdler who had been well beaten on his most recent outing at Newbury back in November. There was no way this horse would be able to get Mr Mulligan out of a canter but still Noel wanted to be certain of a good public showing. As he legged me up, the last words he said to Alex McCabe, the girl on Sunley Secure, were simple and precise: 'I don't care what you do but make sure you don't finish in front of him for any reason.'

We were galloping over two miles but only doing serious work for the last ten furlongs. I was happy enough going down the back straight, but on the top bend with six furlongs to go I squeezed Mr Mulligan. Nothing happened. When we turned for home with just over half a mile to go, I was pushing for all I was worth while at the same time trying not to send out too many distress signals. They were plain enough for Noel though.

I shouted to Alex, 'Wait, wait, wait,' hoping that I could get Mr Mulligan upsides and he would take hold of his bit. Not a hope. The girl didn't twitch a muscle while I was getting a vigorous workout. As for Mr Mulligan, he virtually walked the last furlong.

This horse wasn't going to win an egg-cup, let alone a Gold Cup. I was gutted, and in those situations I'm the worst person in the world at trying to disguise my feelings. As Mr Mulligan ambled back to the Newbury paddock my jaw was in my lap.

Noel had seen the work, but my miserable face confirmed everything. I looked down at him. 'This horse cannot win a Gold Cup. Fuckin' hell, I couldn't get him out of a canter.'

This was now going to be a salvage operation. Grasping at any possible crumb of comfort, Noel said, 'Well, at least there's no reporters here.'

No such luck. No sooner had the words been spoken than a posse of Fleet Street's finest were heading for us, sensing that the best story of the day had just fallen into their laps.

Noel did a rotten impersonation of a ventriloquist and, through clenched teeth, hissed, 'What the hell are we going to say?'

Diplomacy was the only option. 'I'm not happy,' I snapped, 'but we'll say we're happy.'

'OK,' said Noel.

There was an awkward silence until the late Graham Rock of the *Observer* and the BBC led off. Eyeballing Noel, he said, 'Well, are you happy with that?'

It was then that I decided never to play poker with Noel T. Chance. Without missing a beat or losing the gaze of his inquisitor he replied, with a smile, 'Yeah, that was great. Delighted.' He warmed to his task. 'And don't forget, the horse he's worked with is a decent horse in his own right, Marching Marquis. He won a Warwick novice hurdle fifteen lengths and we're expecting a big run in the Sun Alliance Hurdle.'

But were we sick! I had the typical self-centred reaction of a jockey who wants to win big races. I was the model of misery as I trudged back to the weighing room. Although it was now forty-five minutes after the last, Carl Llewellyn was still there. I took my helmet off, threw it on the table and shouted in frustration, 'Jeez, I'm some idiot.'

At the forefront of my mind were the two horses trained by Martin Pipe, who were heading for the Gold Cup in much better form. While I had been injured, Cyborgo, who had caused my split with Paul Nicholls, had won his next two races, and had been ridden by Richard Dunwoody in both, and Challenger du Luc, a tricky individual with masses of ability, had run away with the Wessex Chase at Wincanton under Chris Maude.

I ranted at Carl, 'I could be on either Cyborgo or Challenger and I'm tied up to this yoke!'

When I got into the privacy of my car I was straight on the phone to Dave Roberts. 'Look, I don't want to be riding this horse in the Gold Cup. He's just worked like a yak and he'll win nothing. I'm going to phone Noel tonight and tell him I'm going to get off. I'll get on to Pipe's and see about their two. I reckon I can ride either if I let them know soon enough.'

Fortunately, I'd cooled down by the time I got home and decided to wait and let things quieten down, just in case something came out to explain Mr Mulligan's dismal performance. Nothing emerged, and Noel didn't want to disillusion me any further by getting me in to ride the horse work.

The next time he was due to gallop, Dickie Johnson was aboard. Noel remembers it well: 'I decided to work him on the Home Gallop, which finished going towards our yard. I said that as soon as he was heading towards home Dickie was to disappoint him and pull him in behind horses. For the last two furlongs I could see him taking hold of his bit and wanting to get back to his box and some food. As they straightened up Dickie had his hands full as the horse got into that massive stride.'

Noel didn't tell me about that. He just said the horse was going a bit better – well, he could hardly have gone backwards after Newbury – and called me in to school him over nine fences eight days after the desperate public workout. Now I was in for another surprise. Mr Mulligan was much brighter, more alert, and seemed to be enjoying what he was doing.

Four days later Timmy Murphy was riding work for Noel and the same tactics on the Home Gallop were used. Once again, Mr Mulligan worked like a decent horse. Noel gave me the good news and I decided not to make the call to Martin Pipe's office to inquire about the availability of Cyborgo or Challenger du Luc. I was going to stay with Mr Mulligan. Part of the reason was that the company who were handling my sponsorship and endorsement deals had arranged for me to carry the Guinness logo on Mr Mulligan. I hadn't given any thought to how that deal would be affected if I went for a late switch. In any case, that Cheltenham Festival would have big repercussions for me: it almost led to the break-up of my developing partnership with Martin Pipe.

The Martin Pipe Racing Club had been important to Martin ever since it began as the Pipe–Scudamore Racing Club in the 1980s. The club's black and white colours have been carried by some good horses, arguably the best of which was the prolific juvenile hurdler Hopscotch. One of the most significant dates in their calendar was lunch on the first day of the Festival at which Martin gave a talk about the day's prospects.

Although I wasn't officially his stable rider, four of my five rides on that first day were for him, including Make A Stand. Over the following two days I would be on nine more of his team, most of which had solid chances. He made it clear to me that I was expected to be alongside him and give the club members a helping hand before they sat down for lunch. 'Make sure you're there at quarter to twelve.'

The corporate circuit, for which trainers and jockeys give short talks, is partly what people pay for when they buy a day at Cheltenham or businesses arrange to entertain clients there. It would have been unthinkable twenty-five years ago but now it is normal, and well enough rewarded for most jockeys and trainers to do it if asked.

My first call that morning was to the Guinness box where I would speak to my sponsors and their guests. That was at eleven fifteen. It's probably not the ideal start to the most important race meeting of the season and I can't see many other sportsmen putting themselves through it. Imagine footballers going around the hospitality boxes before the Cup Final?! Unfortunately, I lost track of time with people anxious to quiz me about the three days ahead. By the time I looked at my watch it was ten past twelve. I knew just how Cinderella felt when the midnight chimes went.

I rushed out of the box and jog-trotted to the marquee where 150 Racing Club members had been waiting for the opinions of their trainer and his jockey. They only got one half of the double-act and I met Martin just as he was coming out of the marquee. His face was set and it was clear that he was very agitated.

I began to apologize for missing the appointment, but I was wasting my breath. Martin Pipe is not normally confrontational, but my indiscretion had tipped him over the edge. His eyes were blazing and he took me to pieces: 'If I tell you to be somewhere at quarter to twelve, you effing well be there.'

It was the first time he'd sworn at me, and although I'd had the thick end of a few bollockings in my time, it was hard to take from a man who is normally so reserved and good-natured. He then upped the tempo. 'You're riding for me, not effing Guinness!'

Having to face the crowd on his own had been bad enough, but there were many other things going on in his head at the same time. He was on the threshold of three massive days and twenty races with fancied runners in nearly all of them. There was no point in me trying to apologize any more and, despite his dodgy ankle, he was off at a brisk pace to the weighing room and left me behind. Now it was my turn for a black mood.

At the weighing room I had a word with Graham Bradley. 'You wouldn't believe it, but he's bollocked the shit out of me for not talking to his Racing Club. How big a deal can that be?'

Brad has always given me wise counsel. 'Well, it was obviously a big deal to him but it's all wound up with the pressures of this week. A winner will calm it all down, don't worry about it.'

I wouldn't let it worry me but I was mighty agitated. This was no way to go into the biggest three days' jump racing of the year.

It didn't get any better when I went out for my first ride of the 1997 Cheltenham Festival, which was Kailash for Martin in the Citroën Supreme Novices' Hurdle. Kailash was a 20–1 chance and ran accordingly. I was never able to get him into the race and we were well behind when he put the lid on things and fell at the last. This was the worst possible start to the action. Whenever I have a fall, Martin is always concerned and attentive, but this time he didn't inquire how I was when he came to get my saddle for Or Royal in the following race, the Arkle Chase for novices over two miles.

Right, two could play that game. In the paddock before mounting he barely gave me any instructions. All I did was grunt one-syllable answers: 'Sure, right.'

Or Royal was owned by David Johnson, one of the longest-serving and staunchest owners in Martin's yard. He sensed the tension. As for Or Royal, this was the big one and he would show once more why Martin Pipe is a master of his art. The horse hadn't run since 21 December at Ascot where he had hung right on the run-in and finished three lengths second to Simply Dashing. The trip of two miles three furlongs might not have suited him and I also felt that I was probably wrong to go to the front so far out at the twelfth. Martin got to work with him at home, then refitted blinkers, which the gelding had worn in his native France before David had bought him. There is never a steady pace in any race at this meeting, so I was happy to settle Or Royal in behind the leaders before surviving a mistake at the eighth. Four out, where Richard Dunwoody and the hot favourite Mulligan came down when travelling well, I was in the slipstream of Lightening Lad, ridden by Chris Maude.

Turning for home with two fences left, Jamie Osborne drove Squire Silk ahead and I swept up to challenge on Or Royal, who blundered and lost vital impetus. It was a credit to Martin and his team that the horse was in the form of his life and came back gamely at the final fence when I asked for all he had.

I still had that Ascot race in my mind and didn't want to get there too soon. Head down, but knowing where the line was, I drove Or Royal to cut down Squire Silk close to home to win by half a length. It's one thing to have a plan and another to make it work. I felt I'd done the job well. As we walked back in front of the packed stands I wondered what reception I'd get from Martin.

He met me as we turned to walk across the paddock before entering the unsaddling enclosure. He was smiling, clearly much happier. He patted my leg, looked up and said, 'Well done, a great ride.'

I was still smarting inside. Now it was my turn to let him know that he had hurt me with his outburst, no matter how justified. Without altering my expression I said, 'The next time you speak to me like that, you'll be getting someone else to ride your horses.'

Martin didn't say any more but he knew now that I'd been upset by his attitude. It was a tribute to his strength of character that the incident was never mentioned again, although, like any long relationship, we would have our moments in the future!

Communications were virtually back to normal for the Champion Hurdle, which came forty minutes after the Arkle. For once there wasn't much need to discuss tactics or worry about the opposition. There was only one way for Make A Stand to go and that was from the front. It was just a question of how long he could keep it up and if anything was good enough to get near him.

The ground had certainly come in his favour and was riding fast. I knew this would be against the previous year's winner Collier Bay, and it was a worry to his trainer, Jim Old, and Graham Bradley, who had won on him twelve months earlier.

I was staying with Brad for the three days. Travel to and from the meeting is a nightmare and he always rented a converted barn at nearby Toddington. It made sense and was a great place to wind down away from the action. We discussed the Champion Hurdle and Brad was concerned about the fast ground for Collier Bay, who had a history of joint problems. While I felt sorry for him, it was a plus point for Make A Stand. Large Action would be the big danger. He was unbeaten in three runs that season in the best company. He'd been second to Alderbrook in the 1995 Champion and was at the height of his powers. Maybe I'd set the race up for him, but there was nothing I could do about it.

In fact, Large Action was the first horse ruled out of the race. After jumping the second flight Jamie Osborne felt him falter and pulled him up lame. The following season he raced on after surgery but was a shadow of his former self.

That day Make A Stand was a tiger. By the time we'd gone past the stands and reached the third flight we were clear of a pack, including several horses that needed holding up. Collier Bay, however, wasn't one of them. He could never get competitive from half-way – Brad pulled him up when he was well behind three hurdles from home.

We were still clear and although the hold-up horses were making their move they had given me too much rope. Space Trucker, ridden by John Shortt, tried to get to us from the fourth last but they were making no progress after jumping two out as Norman Williamson came through from the rear on Theatreworld. Norman made his effort after jumping the second last but I never saw him. The only thought I had was that Make A Stand might stop as he met the hill. Normally when you jump the last hurdle five lengths clear you're entitled to feel you've got the race won, but I didn't ease up for a second and drove Make A Stand out for the line, which explains why he still had five lengths to spare over Theatreworld as he lowered the two-mile course record by 1.1 seconds.

Peter Deal and Martin were ecstatic. They'd hit the jackpot and justified turning down the big-money offer to sell the horse. It was the culmination of many years' ownership for Peter, who had owned such good young chasers as Fettimist and Fort Belvedere, and the decent staying hurdler Hebridean. Looking back, he said, 'I honestly didn't think we'd win but I felt reasonably confident we'd get placed.'

Me? It was sheer bliss. I'd won a championship race at the biggest jumping meeting in the world just under three years after riding my first ever hurdle winner at Gowran Park. I knew my ma and dad would have seen it on television and couldn't wait to speak to them. I didn't have to wait long. Ma was on the mobile, bubbling with pride and pleasure, and Dad was bouncing too.

So it was all change. The day that had started so badly was now more than on an even keel. It was hard not to feel more than a little sorry for John Inverdale. The man who had declined Peter Deal's offer of a half-share in the now Champion Hurdler had to put on the bravest of public faces. He was hosting BBC Radio Five Live's broadcast from the course that afternoon and had to interview the winning owner. In a career that has seen John interview the famous and, perhaps, the infamous, this one stands out. Not surprisingly, he remembers it all too clearly: 'I was born in Bristol and the first time I knocked off school to go to the Cheltenham Festival it was 1972, the year that Glencaraig Lady and Frank Berry just beat Royal Toss and The Dikler in the Gold Cup. After that I'd dreamed of having a runner there, let alone a winner. Rugby is my first sport, but National Hunt racing is close behind it. I think people who are involved in those sports are similar because of the ups and downs and the knocks you inevitably get. It's that line about treating triumph and disaster just the same.

'When I was introducing the programme part of me wanted the horse to win because of my friendship with Peter. But, inevitably, there's five per cent of you that thinks, Well, perhaps if it just got brought down, safely but unluckily . . . If he had been brought down at the first he had still won all those other good races, so it wouldn't have hurt quite so much. My co-presenter on the day was Charlie Brooks, who was still training at the time, and he was giving me plenty as the race approached. Then, when Make A Stand came up the hill clear, I thought, Oh, bollocks.

'I was in the action up to my ears and I had to do the interview with the winning owner, Peter. All I could do was put on a smile. It didn't get any better that night. Brooks and I ended up at Nigel Twiston-Davies's pub, the Hollow Bottom, not far from the course, and I probably had a beer or two more than I should have done. Brooks still thought it was all very funny and kept introducing me as the equine equivalent of the man who didn't sign the Beatles. I told him it was wearing a bit thin and that I was on the verge of a sense-of-humour failure. And, of course, he kept on doing it. I don't know what I'd have done if Make A Stand had come back and won it for a second year.'

That wasn't to be. Make A Stand got a knock during the Champion and I was sidelined in controversial circumstances when he ran for the final time that season at Liverpool in the Martell Hurdle over two and a half miles. Chris Maude rode him again, but the horse went out tamely before finishing third to Bimsey.

Peter Deal took the gentleman's way out when the horse failed to recover his former sparkle two seasons later. He retired him. 'Although he was athletic rather than big he would have jumped a fence, but we decided to retire him at the top.'

Make A Stand was a career landmark for me and I am delighted to say that he lives in happy retirement with Martin.

Mr Mulligan was not so lucky.

On Wednesday we came within a short head of winning the Coral Cup with Allegation, owned by the Racing Club, although the pain was eased for Martin as he had also trained the winner, Big Strand, ridden by the Australian Jamie Evans. There were no excuses for Eudipe, who was beaten fair and square by Hanakham and Richard Dunwoody in the Royal Sun Alliance Chase.

Despite the decent schooling session I'd had with Mr Mulligan I was by no means certain that I'd made the right decision to stay with him when Gold Cup morning dawned in the converted barn. Both of Martin Pipe's runners, Challenger du Luc and Cyborgo, were better fancied in the betting and Mr Mulligan was a 20–1 shot without many takers. My first two rides of the day, Pomme Secret in the Triumph Hurdle and Pridwell in the Stayers' Hurdle, didn't raise much hope of my improving on my opening-day score of two. When I sat down to contemplate the Gold Cup, having given my tack to Noel Chance after weighing out, I turned to Graham Bradley: 'If this horse runs like he works, we'll be tailed off.'

Noel admitted later that he didn't fancy the horse and recalled, 'I didn't have a lot of confidence and I didn't know what to expect. Even though he was now firing again, I just couldn't get that Newbury gallop out of my mind.'

Neither could I, but the paddock before a massive race like the Gold Cup is no place for negative thoughts. I knew that when he had looked so impressive as a novice in winning the Reynoldstown at Ascot he had gone a good gallop and kept on relentlessly.

Noel didn't give me any detailed instructions, just said, 'Be handy, he won't win from behind and he's brave.'

Just about the one thing I was certain of was that Mr Mulligan would stay. I popped him out of the gate and got a good position just behind the pack as Dublin Flyer and Brendan Powell led. Dublin Flyer was a fine front-running chaser, but as he had got older he had become much more effective at shorter distances than the Gold Cup trip of three and a quarter miles.

Mr Mulligan's jumping was good most of the time and it had been down to me when I decked him in the King George. However, he had made a bad mistake early in the Sun Alliance Chase the previous season. He could take some organizing if things were going wrong at a fence, so I made sure he had plenty of room and got a good view of his fences early on. After a circuit I moved him into the action and he was travelling nicely when we jumped past Dublin Flyer at the water jump for the second time, half-way down the back straight.

The previous year's winner, Imperial Call, started 4–1 favourite and was ridden once again by my boyhood hero Conor O'Dwyer. Unfortunately for Conor and trainer Fergie Sutherland, Imperial Call had encountered the same interrupted build-up as Mr Mulligan. Sadly for the Irish, while Mr Mulligan was putting his troubles behind him, Imperial Call's were still mounting. As Mr Mulligan advanced, Imperial Call retreated, and after a mistake at the seventeenth he was tailed off when Conor pulled him up after the next.

Meanwhile Richard Dunwoody had been trying to conserve every ounce of One Man's dubious stamina. Over the last thirty years or more there has been no better jockey than Richard at holding on to a doubtful stayer and nursing him home. He was well aware that Cheltenham offers no hiding place and began to move the grey closer from the sixteenth. When Mr Mulligan reached the fourth last I began to feel confident. He was travelling comfortably and I thought, I haven't asked him yet, I haven't pressed the button. There's plenty left. He gave the fence a hefty clout, but Mr Mulligan had to be a good horse to be going so well and I knew it would take something very good to come past him from here.

One Man made his bid on the home turn and moved into second place, but there was no way he was going to get to us. In a role-reversal of Kempton on Boxing Day, this time it was him running on empty.

In a race of such importance you can leave nothing to chance: although I'd been squeezing Mr Mulligan on the downhill run to three out, I fired him up going into the last two fences. It would take a super-horse to get to me and there was no Pegasus in this field. As One Man capitulated to finish an exhausted sixth it was old Barton Bank who stayed on to take second, but there was only one winner. Mr Mulligan by nine lengths.

I punched the air with my right hand and bellowed as I crossed the line, '*Yesssss!*' All the frustrations of the previous three weeks spilled out. Not in my most outrageous fantasies could I have seen myself winning the Champion Hurdle and the Gold Cup in the same season – only my third as a jump jockey. I was joining the most élite club. Only three other jockeys had managed it: Aubrey Brabazon did it twice with the same two horses in 1949 and 1950, Hatton's Grace and Cottage Rake; the legendary Fred Winter achieved it in 1961 on Eborneezer and Saffron Tartan; and in 1995 Norman Williamson won both on Alderbrook and Master Oats.

The grin didn't move from Noel's face from when I met him on the walk across the paddock to when we reached the unsaddling enclosure. I couldn't believe how lucky I was – but also I couldn't help thinking how hard the sport can be. For the third time in as many years Adrian Maguire had missed the Festival. This time it was because his arm had been shattered at Leicester in late February. He had been dealt some rotten hands of late.

With all the attention that surrounds the Gold Cup the race planners show sense in running the Foxhunters' Chase as the following race. That day there was plenty of time for presentation and a visit to the Queen Mother's private box. It was a wonderfully calm oasis in a frantic spell of activity and one I will always remember. It was clear to me that she loved jump racing and it is one of my regrets that I did not ride a winner in her light blue and buff striped colours.

I thought I had a third winner when Elzoba, trained by Martin, still held the lead going to the last in the Grand Annual Chase. But that wily devil Graham Bradley caught me at the last on another tricky old customer in Uncle Ernie. I was third on Or Royal in the Cathcart Chase, which was enough for me to win the award for top rider at the meeting for the second year in succession. My sixteen rides had yielded three wins, three seconds and two thirds with total prize money of just over £364,000. Now it was time to party.

Just about the only downside of the Cheltenham Festival is getting away from the course, and by far the worst traffic problems come on Gold Cup day. Several years earlier Brad and some of the senior riders decided to wind down and let the traffic clear before they left the course. The drink of preference was champagne and word gradually spread that the place to be at the end of that day was the jockeys' changing room. Whenever anyone called in, they usually stayed until closing time, and that could be any time. It was part of the tradition that the jockeys who had won the Champion Hurdle and the Gold Cup would provide the champagne and I was more than happy to pay out twice.

Brad, who has a good head for figures – or he did before the party – reckoned twenty cases of champagne were ferried into the changing room after racing that day. At the final count I paid for fifteen, although not a drop passed my lips. I was on top of the world. Unfortunately there's no such thing as vintage Diet Coke. If there had been I'd have settled for a case of it.

Brad, who had led home Michael Dickinson's famous first five on Bregawn in the 1983 Gold Cup, didn't try to hide his delight at my success and kept reminding me of the first day we'd met at Galway in 1994. To Conor O'Dwyer, who'd been with him that day, he said, 'I told you the lad would be all right, didn't I?'

Later Brad recalled bumping into Martin Pipe, who was enjoying the banter. Although Challenger du Luc and Cyborgo hadn't fired in the Gold Cup, he was really pleased for me. As the evening wore on, Brad was getting steadily refreshed, and shuddered later when he was reminded of his conversation with Martin who inquired where all the booze was coming from. 'Your jockey's bought most of it. Don't you think it's about time you bought a case?'

Martin smiled and turned to his wife, Carol, who carried the cash, and bought his twelve bottles. It was one of those nights and it finally began to wind down at around ten. Noel Chance and Michael Worcester had taken the restaurant at the Queen's Arms, East Garston, just outside Lambourn. It is still one of my favourite haunts and was then run by a very good friend of mine, Tom Butterfield. I would have liked to join them but, as the only sober member of our party, I was transporting everyone.

We walked out into the chill night air and it was spooky. Like an empty football ground, a racecourse with no people is strange. The lights from the weighing room illuminated the paddock and it was possible to see the silhouette of the winners' enclosure over to the right. Six hours earlier the place had been bursting with people cheering me as I enjoyed the finest moment of my career. Now they'd scattered to the four corners of the country, but they would always remember the day Mulligan and McCoy won the Gold Cup. I looked around for a few seconds and felt as high as a kite. I got into the car with Brad and his wife Amanda, and Conor and Audrey O'Dwyer. We tried looking for a restaurant for dinner but time was running out. Brad had the answer – like me he is a man of simple tastes on the food front. 'I'd like a pizza,' he said.

We found a Pizza Express, sat at a plastic-topped table and went through the card. Afterwards the night was still young and the Gas Club in Cheltenham has seen some incredible nights after success at the track, none wilder than when Richard Guest won the 1989 Champion Hurdle on Beech Road for my old boss Toby Balding.

Guesty is now rightly acknowledged as a horse master – he prepared and rode Red Marauder to win the 2001 Grand National. Back in the late eighties he was top of the handicap when it came to partying. After the 50–1 victory of Beech Road he began celebrating at the top of the club and kept the party going for twenty-four hours, ending up in the basement. 'It cost me five grand and I don't regret a penny,' he said at the time. He didn't ride for the next eleven days. But I had to be at Folkestone the next day.

We were late to bed at the converted barn, and although I'm

not the greatest riser in the morning, Graham Bradley is in a different league again. He had been, in his own words, 'upside-down drunk' a few hours earlier. At least it was only lack of sleep that left me muzzy-headed when the alarm went off at nine thirty. Brad took some rousing and, although jockeys aren't allowed to bet, I would have put a fair few quid on him throwing a 'sickie'. His only ride of the day was in the first at two o'clock, a lowly claiming hurdle, but the ride was for Charlie Brooks, then training in Upper Lambourn, with whom Brad had forged a loyal working partnership. He crawled out of bed, made it to my car and slept away the two-and-a-half-hour journey.

Unfortunately there was no happy ending for either of us: Brad faded with his mount, Whispering Dawn, approaching the last and finished fifth, and the nearest I got on four rides was third, but I was still buzzing from Cheltenham and the thought that I had Make A Stand and Mr Mulligan for the future. How wrong I was.

Cheltenham was the last time I won on Mr Mulligan. Next season I rode him on his first start when he finished second to Gales Cavalier over an inadequate two miles five furlongs at Wincanton. With my commitments to Martin Pipe strengthening, I went to Cheltenham on 15 November and rode a double for the stable. Richard Dunwoody rode Mr Mulligan to win unimpressively at 6–1 on in a five-runner chase at Ayr, the last time he was seen in public. An old tendon injury recurred and Michael Worcester decided to retire him. Some eighteen months later, when he was turned out in a field, Mr Mulligan received a nasty kick. He was badly disabled and had to be put down. A sad end.

Although Make A Stand finished lame in his next race at Liverpool, I was full of anticipation for renewing the partnership. Unfortunately, I didn't make the date due to a bizarre medical mix-up.

9. Doctor's Disorder

When I stepped off Mr Mulligan at Cheltenham I couldn't have believed I wouldn't ride another winner in Britain for nearly a month. After drawing blank at both Folkestone and Uttoxeter I went to Ireland for the Leopardstown meeting on Sunday. It was for just one ride, Clifdon Fog in the Harcourt Handicap Hurdle, but it was an engagement that meant a lot: it was for Jim Bolger.

Although I had not fallen out with Jim over my decision to leave for England he had waited until 11 January 1997 before he felt the need to employ me again, when I finished seventeenth on Clifdon Fog in the Ladbroke. My previous ride for him had been Gallardini, ninth at the Curragh on 25 June 1994.

Clifdon Fog was a strongly fancied 7–4 favourite and it was like old times when I stepped into the parade ring and Jim was there with the instructions. They weren't elaborate – just give the horse a chance early and come with a steady run. Apart from a couple of mistakes there were no real worries, but I was up against Ireland's top man, Charlie Swan, at the last. I didn't give him a chance to get past me and left him and Kilcoo Boy behind, winning by an all-out two lengths. The last winner I'd ridden for Jim was also over hurdles, Nordic Sensation at Tipperary on 26 May 1994. It seemed like a lifetime ago yet it was less than three years.

I had no rides in England the next day, and I'd gone four days and eight rides without success when I set out for two mounts at Uttoxeter on Tuesday, 18 March. I should have stayed in bed.

I was back on side with Paul Nicholls now and he provided the first ride of the day, Lansdowne, in the handicap hurdle. It was the second one, supplied by Martin Pipe, who caused the problems. I'll not forget Strong Tel for a long time.

He'd been good as gold on his two previous starts that season, finishing third under Richard Hughes in a bumper at Chepstow, then running third for David Walsh in a fair novice hurdle at Newbury. Perhaps I just got him on a bad day, but we didn't get past the first hurdle. I'd like to be more specific but I can't. All I can recall is Strong Tel approaching the flight and a split second later the white plastic wing coming towards me. After that, nothing: I'd been knocked out and I don't know for how long. I managed to walk to the ambulance and made my way into the first-aid room without assistance and waited to be examined by the young racecourse doctor, Andrew Toman.

When a jockey gets a bang on the head and loses consciousness it is vital that his mental state is assessed quickly to make certain he isn't going to be a danger to himself or anyone else. The cross-examination isn't very demanding but it quickly reveals concussion.

'How many fingers am I holding up?'

I didn't need to squint. 'Three.' You can't fake that one if you've got double vision, and if your brain isn't working it's not going to remind you that there aren't six fingers on one hand.

'What racecourse are you at?'

'Uttoxeter.'

'Fine. Now tell me how many rides you've had today.'

'Two.'

'And where do you live?'

'Weyhill Gardens.'

The doctor seemed happy enough and I had no further rides that day. I knew that because I'd been unconscious I would get a red entry in my medical book. Dr Toman signed me off for ten days. That was a blow: I'd miss eight racing days as a Sunday and Good Friday fell within the suspension. However, it could have been worse and at least I'd be back for the busy Easter programme. I was right – it could have been worse. A few days later it was.

I felt well enough the morning after the fall to ride out two lots for Toby Balding, but on Thursday I received a call from Dr Michael Turner, the Jockey Club chief medical officer. He explained that he had received the paperwork concerning the Uttoxeter accident and there was a problem with it. There was no such suspension as ten days. It was either seven or twenty-one. He thought it might be best if he came down to see me the following day.

Dr Turner has said subsequently that he was 'shaking like a leaf' as he pressed the doorbell. Well, the feeling was mutual.

He came straight to the point and explained that the doctor at Uttoxeter had made a serious mistake and that 'the system does not appear to have served you very well'. Dr Turner had seen a video of my fall and it was clear that I had been out cold for nearly three minutes. 'I'm afraid there's no doubt about it, you've got to be stood down for twenty-one days.'

Although my brain was crystal clear I struggled to take it in. I wanted to know how the ten days had come about. Dr Turner didn't know but said the rule was quite specific: up to one minute unconsciousness, it was seven days, anything over and it was a mandatory twenty-one.

'So, this course doctor makes a mistake, lets me drive my car home down three motorways and now you say I'm not fit to ride? I've ridden out for Toby Balding since the fall and not had a bother on me.' I felt as though Dr Turner had whacked me in the guts and kept asking him to explain how such a cock-up could happen. He was very understanding but said he didn't know.

There was no point in ranting – it solves nothing – but frustration engulfed me. It wasn't just the Easter programme I was going to miss: I'd be out of the Grand National meeting too. Deep down I knew that the rule is put in place to protect jockeys from themselves: in the days before safety measures were brought in some brave men were knocked silly. Not that I was in any mood to appreciate *that*. I had thought I might have a chance of becoming only the second man to win the Champion Hurdle, the Gold Cup and the Grand National in the same season. The only man to do it was Tommy Cullinan in 1930.

But that didn't matter now. I'd have to take it on the chin and be thankful that I was far enough ahead of Jamie Osborne in the jockeys' championship not to be too concerned about losing my title. However, the three weeks off certainly cost me more than ten winners, which would have seen me hit two hundred for the first time.

I broke the monotony with a short break in Dubai and I was back in plenty of time for the National. Luckily I got a call from the BBC to join their team. At least if I couldn't ride at the meeting I'd feel part of the action. It was also likely that I would not have had a particularly fancied ride in the big one: Martin Pipe's two runners Evangelica and Mugoni Beach had little chance – not that I got much satisfaction from that.

Still, it was good to be at the National and I travelled up with Graham Bradley and booked in at the Adelphi Hotel. It was here, after racing on the Thursday night, that I first met two lads with whom I was going to enjoy a lot of success and fun. When we got back to the bar I could see John Titley chatting to a group of footballers.

Titley, who won the National in 1995 on Jenny Pitman's Royal Athlete, is rightly looked upon as a legend in our game. He is revered as the friend of the famous and there's more than a hint of truth in the story that when he was talking to Eddie Irvine, the Formula One driver, in a fashionable Dublin club someone asked, 'Who's that with Titley?'

Brad and I joined the group, which was largely made up of Liverpool players, the Anfield Hombres, who were mad keen on racing and owned a horse in partnership in training with Michael Meagher at Ormskirk in Lancashire. It was named Another Horse and wasn't particularly good. Those involved included Neil Ruddock, Jamie Redknapp, Rob Jones, Phil Babb and Jason McAteer. However, two were much keener than the rest: the English internationals Steve McManaman and Robbie Fowler.

There is a crossover in sport in which one group of athletes gets real pleasure from the company of another. These boys loved their racing and I like nothing better than to relax either watching or playing football. It wasn't long before Brad, myself and the rest of the boys were deep in conversation. Steve and Robbie made it clear they wanted to up their stake in ownership. It so happened that Brad was considering branching out in the bloodstock business and had found a relatively untapped market for value: Germany. He had begun riding there and had noticed how tough the home side were when top-class horses from overseas challenged for the Group races. No one had thought of buying the older horses and running them over hurdles in Britain, and Brad reckoned it might be a good opening. The boys were interested and eventually had the kind of success that most people can only dream about. Better still, Brad and I were a big part of it, boosted by the talent of Martin Pipe.

But that was in the future, and the next night both Brad and I were feeling miserable. I'd missed two winners, on Cyborgo in the three-mile novices' chase, and Cadougold, in the two-and-a-half-mile handicap hurdle. There was nothing for either of us to salvage from the following day. Although neither of Martin's National runners had a realistic chance, I would be missing Make A Stand, who would start 7–4 favourite for the £40,000 Martell Aintree Hurdle.

It was far worse for Brad, though. He thought the world of Suny Bay, who would start second favourite for the National but would be ridden by Jamie Osborne. Brad is one of the best-natured men I know but he grudged Jamie that ride and had begged the horse's owner, Andrew Cohen, to let him have it. Brad rode the majority of the horses trained by Suny Bay's trainer, Charlie Brooks, but this season there was no retainer offered as Mr Cohen reckoned Brad was an unlucky jockey for him. Mr Cohen is not alone in being superstitious: plenty of owners before and after him have thought that certain riders are jinxed.

None of this was any consolation to Brad: he was on Lo Stregone, who had a chance but not the kind of chance Suny Bay had. As we talked, Brad gave me the impression that if Suny Bay won he would consider packing up. From a selfish viewpoint I did not want this to happen. From the year of my first championship, Brad and I had become good mates. We travelled everywhere together, and although he was nudging thirty-seven he'd looked after himself and had relatively few miles on the clock. I wanted him to go on for ever.

On National morning we made our way to the track, but it's not a place I like to be when I'm not working. I got absolutely no satisfaction from seeing Make A Stand finish third, but six minutes before that race was off the nearby Fazakerley Hospital received a chilling call. Someone using a recognized IRA codeword said that a bomb had been planted on the racecourse. Barely three minutes later the police control centre at Marsh Lane, Bootle, received the same coded message.

I was in the weighing room making idle conversation and geeing the boys up, telling them not to go too fast. Each year the senior steward gives us the same pep talk about being sensible, which is well meant but usually brings barely stifled giggles. Then, at three fifteen, the clerk of the course, Charles Barnet, strode in and told us that the racecourse was being evacuated and that everyone was to leave the weighing room, taking only a coat with them.

Some of the lads were taking their time, joking and generally treating the whole thing as, at best, an inconvenience, at worst a sick joke that would be exposed. People felt everything would be back to normal in half an hour. Not me.

I had been brought up outside Belfast but from an early age I had witnessed the carnage that a bomb can bring. You never forget things you've seen when you're a kid, and I'd seen charred and blown-out buildings. I knew that if a bomb were to explode in such a densely populated area the result would be too terrible to contemplate.

A couple of the boys were grumbling, so I said to them, in measured tones, 'Look, this is not the sort of thing you take for granted. I'm definitely not. In fact, I'm getting out to the centre of the course bloody quickly.' They took my lead. Not long after there was another scare, at Uttoxeter, and I took that seriously too.

Brad and I met up on the far side of the course. He was typically optimistic: 'This'll be over in an hour.'

For once I didn't share his view. 'Don't be so sure.'

Attempting to break the boredom, we went for a cup of tea – what else, when there's the chance of a bomb going off? – at an RSPCA post. After that we got talking to a couple of policemen.

They made us welcome in the back of their car and said they were members of the armed-response unit. They told us that there had been three controlled explosions but no bombs had yet been found. They became quite chatty and showed us an impressive array of weaponry, one piece of which, they assured us, could take someone's head off at a mile. They also said that the car we were sitting in was reinforced to withstand a mine going off under it. Brad was ecstatic. 'That's a bit of luck. If there's any bombs going off, we've got the best seats in the house!'

Brad has always been a quick thinker and he was on his toes when the announcement was made cancelling the remainder of the day. All the boys who had been riding were standing about in their breeches and silks with just an overcoat from their 'civilian' wardrobe. All money and, more important, mobile phones had been left in the weighing room.

'Have you got your mobile?'

'Yep.'

Bradders rubbed his hands together. 'Looks like we'll be staying over tonight and so will a lot of other people. Get on to the Adelphi a bit quick and book some rooms. There'll be plenty of takers. We could be here for Sunday night as well.'

He was right. The authorities soon announced that the National would be run at five o'clock on Monday as a one-off race with free admittance.

Brad was right about rooms being at a premium. Nearly twenty thousand cars were impounded until Sunday morning and there wasn't a spare bed in Liverpool. I booked three rooms, and God only knows how many slept in them over the two nights. Another jockey, David Walsh, had twelve sleeping on his floor and the hotel let people sleep in the ballroom. There was also a shortage of ready cash: most of the lads had left their money with their valets and couldn't track them down. Brad had left a roll of eight hundred pounds with his valet, so I had the dubious honour of being his personal banker for forty-eight hours. It was just as well I'd come armed with plenty of readies and my Gold Card.

One thing we didn't have to pay for was tickets to the Liverpool—

Coventry game on Sunday. Steve and Robbie organized those, although they were less than happy with the surprise 2–1 defeat. After the game we teamed up with quite a few of the players. They couldn't believe the way some of our lads were getting stuck into the drink before riding the next day. It was one hell of a party and at one stage we were joined by Martine McCutcheon, who has since gone on to tremendous success on stage but was then headlining on *EastEnders*. I assured anyone who asked that this was normal procedure for some of the lads. There wouldn't be a bother on them, especially as there was only one race the following day and that was at the civilized hour of five o'clock. Sure enough, the following lunchtime the sauna was crammed as the excesses of the previous night steamed out of their system. Brad was in the thick of the action having to get down to ten stone four, but I knew this was a National with an edge for him.

I tried telling him that he had a chance of winning himself on Lo Stregone. He would not have it, and he was right. Lo Stregone was never a contender and was tailed off when Brad pulled him up before the fourth last. I watched with mixed emotions as Suny Bay appeared to be travelling well going to the fourth last. Then, just when the horse couldn't afford a mistake, he made a bad one, and after that he was never going to hold Lord Gyllene. As Suny Bay trailed in twenty-five lengths second I knew I'd have my friend around for another season or two: as the horse hadn't won, he wouldn't want to pack up. What eventful years they were going to be for both of us.

Lord Gyllene's win was the biggest success in the career of Tony Dobbin, one of the good guys and a fine rider who, like Richard Dunwoody, the Flat jockeys John Reid, Ray Cochrane and myself, comes from Northern Ireland. He was probably pumped up on adrenaline when he said, in his post-race interview, 'I'm embarrassed. It is shameful and it makes you ashamed to say you come from Ireland after Saturday's bomb scare wrecked so many people's day out. It never should have happened. Never.'

Not me. I'm very proud of being from Ireland. You cannot be ashamed because of the actions of a very small minority.

It was typical of Martin that he wanted to put me straight back on a winner at Chepstow on 9 April and provided four short-priced favourites in as many rides. Three were second and one third, with no excuses. The trouble with days like that is the anticipation. The media build up the fact that you are coming back on four favourites and the public expect you to win on at least a couple. So by the time the final race arrived and I'd drawn a blank I was not in the best frame of mind. As is often the case, the horse that you feel is least likely to win comes good. Diamond Hall, trained by Karl Burke, ran away with the bumper and put me back on course. Losing my grip on the championship had never been a worry: despite having the best season of his career, Jamie Osborne had only managed ten winners while I was out of action.

However, my time out had caused one potentially tricky situation to arise. One of the rides I'd won on earlier in the season, Courbaril, had run the best race of his jumping career when finishing a length and a quarter second to the smart ex-Flat racer Sanmartino in the Grade Two novice hurdle at Aintree. Norman Williamson had ridden him and Dave Roberts acted as his agent.

I was on my way to Exeter, where I would ride four winners for Martin, when the phone rang. I was dozing but when I recognized Dave's number I answered.

'Pipe's office have been on and Courbaril's owner, Richard Green, wants to keep Norman on the horse at Cheltenham tomorrow,' he told me.

I wasn't happy and Dave understood why. If I was going to be Martin's stable jockey I reckoned I should be first choice for any ride. I saw this as more than just another winning ride I might miss: it was a matter of principle. If I let it pass unchallenged it might set a precedent for the future. I phoned the office at Pond House.

I got through to Gail, who has headed Martin's secretarial team for a long time and is known by the press as 'Boycott' in honour of the ex-England opening batsman's ability to stop nearly everything getting through.

Gail said that Martin was staying with Peter Scudamore for the two-day Cheltenham meeting.

'Well, you'd better get him to ring me.'

Not long after, Martin was in touch.

'The owner thinks Norman got on well with the horse and wants him to stay on it.'

I could see Martin's problem but it wasn't mine. I don't mind such arrangements being made if I decide to get off a horse in preference to another and the horse I've deserted wins. In that case it's only right that the owner wants to keep the same rider. But this wasn't my fault. I'd suffered concussion coming off one of Martin's horses and I'd won on Courbaril twice earlier in the season. I didn't hold back. 'That's all very well, but listen here, now. As far as I'm concerned, you and your owner can stick Courbaril as far as you can. As from today I will be riding for you on a freelance basis, which certainly won't be every day. As far as I'm concerned we're finished. I'm riding five horses for you today and when I get off the last of them that's it. As for being your stable jockey, it's finished.'

I hadn't raised my voice. In such situations I never do.

I've come to learn that Martin Pipe is the most loyal trainer any jockey could wish to ride for and he is not a man who looks for an argument. He tried to pacify me. 'There's no need to be like that.'

I thought there was, and I would not be talked round. I pressed the cancel button and the call ended abruptly.

There was no question in my mind that I had made the right stand and, as I ploughed on down the M5 to Exeter races, I became even more convinced of it.

Within ten minutes Dave was back on the line anxious to know the outcome. I told him what had been said. 'With all due respect, Dave, no one is going to walk over me or take me for granted. He either wants me to ride them all or he doesn't.' Dave could see the problems I was creating but understood.

'Yeah, you're right.'

Another quarter of an hour dragged by and I began to contemplate what it might be like out there on my own as a freelance with someone else on the Pipe runners and me having to fight him off to defend my championship the following season. Sure, it would be hard but nothing worth having comes easy.

Then the phone chirped into life. It was Martin and, if I'm honest, I was pleased to hear his voice. 'I've spoken to the owner and that's OK. You ride the horse tomorrow.'

I'm no great card player, but after that I might have considered taking up poker. All I could say was, ungraciously, 'That wasn't very hard, was it?'

I rode four winners for Martin at Exeter that afternoon and if you thought I felt any extra pressure when I got the leg up on Courbaril at Cheltenham the next day you'd be wrong. Starting 11–4 favourite, Courbaril hit a bit of a flat spot two out, having been up with the pace. I wound him up to challenge The Toiseach, ridden by Jamie Osborne, at the final flight and didn't leave him alone all the way up the run-in. I didn't want to risk any unpleasant post-race conversations and we won by two lengths with nothing to spare.

Although I didn't realize it at the time, the cancellation of the Grand National almost certainly played a big part in my winning the Scottish equivalent. Paul Nicholls saw that Belmont King had fretted over the disruption at the National. Some horses had been evacuated to nearby Haydock Park while the Aintree stables were searched by the Bomb Squad, and Belmont had worried a large amount of weight off his huge frame. Paul had to make a difficult decision. The National had been Belmont King's target all season but there was no point in running him below par in the most gruelling race in the British jumping calendar.

It was a massive disappointment to Belmont King's owner, Mrs Billie Bond. The then seventy-six-year-old suffered from the debilitating lung condition emphysema and seldom moved far from her home in Truro, Cornwall. For that reason, when she commissioned Paul to buy her a horse it had to be good enough to run in big races that were televised on Saturdays. The private deal struck with Belmont King's Irish owner/trainer Simon Lambert had been a sound one.

Ironically, Mrs Bond had made the long journey to Aintree then had to suffer the disappointment of his withdrawal on the day. There is, however, no doubt in my mind that, in his wasted condition and on faster ground than he likes, Belmont King would not have got anywhere near Lord Gyllene. I am equally certain that the decision eased his path to the Scottish equivalent: he went there a fresh horse in peak condition, physically and mentally.

I knew Belmont King inside out and Paul didn't give me any orders at Ayr except 'You know him, please yourself.'

The strapping nine-year-old looked in superb condition. I set out to make all and could hear the curses and bellows from behind as the opposition blundered round over the strength-sapping four miles one furlong. My only real worry came when Belmont King's concentration went and he ploughed through the twentieth fence. He was tired at the last and clouted it, but luckily nothing was travelling any better behind. I had to be hard on him all the way to the line, but he never lacked courage and saw off Samlee and Norman Williamson by a length and a half.

Unfortunately, the journey to Scotland was beyond Mrs Bond, but she revelled in the televised action and went through the full range of emotions, all helped along by a drop of good whisky.

One of the first men forward to congratulate me was Paul Barber, and Paul Nicholls was relieved when I came back to unsaddle: he had been criticized in some quarters for not running at Aintree but had now been proved right in some style.

There was only one big chase of the season left, the Whitbread Gold Cup at Sandown on 26 April, and I had a great chance of winning it on Flyer's Nap for Robert Alner. Unfortunately for me Robert had two others entered. One was Bishops Hall, Charlie Swan's mount but the least fancied of the trio, and the wayward but useful Harwell Lad, who would give me a headache. Flyer's Nap went into the race on the back of winning the National Hunt Handicap Chase at the Cheltenham Festival and was fully entitled to start the 4–1 joint favourite with Barton Bank.

The amateur rider Rupert Nuttall knew the quirky Harwell Lad well, and, unfortunately for me, he got a particularly sweet tune out of the eight-year-old that day. When Harwell Lad took over three out, I thought I had him covered and moved Flyer's Nap up to challenge. Rupert kicked his mount in the ribs and this was definitely a going day. They went a length up and I knew they wouldn't stop up the stiff Sandown hill. I needed Flyer's Nap to live up to his name at the last and land running. It didn't happen. He crashed through the final fence, losing all rhythm and power, and as I looked up I could see the red and white colours of Harwell Lad leaving us behind. We might not have won in any case but we wouldn't have been beaten by four lengths without that blunder.

Aside from winning big races, the one feat that a jockey really wants to perform is to go through the card. The man in the street knows that Frankie Dettori won all seven races at Ascot in 1996, even if he can't name one of his big-race winners. To put this in perspective, no jump jockey has ever managed it on a six-race card, although Ivor Antony rode the winner of all races on a five-race programme at Pembroke Hunt in 1906. I hope another Anthony finally manages to do it – and on far less exalted ground than Frankie at Ascot. I came close to winning all six races at Uttoxeter on 26 May with just five days of the season remaining.

In theory, going through the card that day was never an option because I didn't have a ride in the fifth race, but my first four rides were all favourites. I took the first, the maiden chase on Glamanglitz, for Paul Dalton, making all and never seeing another horse. Strike-A-Pose, trained by Bernard Llewellyn, nearly lost the selling hurdle with a mistake at the last but recovered. It wouldn't have been a normal day if Martin Pipe hadn't been involved, and wins three and four came from him. Doualago was an easy winner of the three-and-a-quarter mile handicap chase and again I won in splendid isolation on Northern Starlight in the two-mile handicap hurdle. And that's where the run should have stopped, because I didn't have a ride in the fifth, the novices' handicap chase.

Then one of my former lodgers, Peter Henley, tried to come to my rescue. Peter was down to ride Hangover for Richard Lee in the race but contrived to make sure he got caught in traffic. He phoned through to the course to let them know he wouldn't be there, but not before he had given me a ring and told me to make sure I was with Hangover's trainer, Richard Lee, when he got the news. I was. Unfortunately, Peter's fine show of friendship did not have the desired ending. I knew I had a great chance of winning the last race, the novice hurdle on Nordic Breeze for Martin, so I put everything I'd got into Hangover. I got him to the front at the tenth fence but he was spent when we were headed two out and had no chance when blundering through the last. And, yes, Nordic Breeze did win the last, to make it five out of six. I've reached most of my goals, but that one still eludes me.

The injury to my shoulder and the twenty-one days out with concussion had put the brakes on any chance of beating Peter Scudamore's record of 221 winners in a season, which he had logged up in 1988–9. Without the injury I'd have been in line for the earliest 150, too. It wasn't something that bothered me and if someone had told me the previous June that I'd win the Gold Cup and the Champion Hurdle I would have willingly settled for that.

In fact, the big Cheltenham double saw the first, and to date the only, official celebration party to mark my winning the championship. The company that was handling my business away from the racecourse at that time was RBI Promotions. The two principal men involved were Cameron McMillan and the ex-jockey Ronnie Beggan, a product of the Dickinson academy when Brad was learning his trade. Ronnie, who rode Oregon Trail to win the Arkle Chase in 1986, was one of the first to see the niche market for putting racing on the corporate-entertainment circuit and has since branched out into many other sports.

They managed to get the party sponsored and it was a wonderful night, held in the grandstand at Newbury racecourse. My ma and dad came over. In fact, with the exception of my brother and sisters and Billy Rock, who couldn't make it, everyone who meant something to me was there. Dave Roberts, seldom out of bed after nine thirty, came along to see me cut a cake and raise a glass of Diet Coke in thanks to all those who had helped me.

Dad, as usual, took it in his stride, but Ma, as mothers do, had to brush tears from her eyes. I'm sure she must have been remembering times past when she had wept with frustration at my pig-headedness. Both of them deserved to enjoy my success every bit as much as I did.

10. Vive la France!

To this day I have never signed a contract with Martin Pipe. As with a marriage, a piece of paper is no guarantee that you will stay together. Mutual trust and understanding, however, go a long way to making sure that you do.

We had overcome the molehills that might have grown into mountains, and at the start of the 1997–8 season we each knew how the other was ticking. It was the first time I began a campaign with the full might of Martin Pipe behind me.

As an indication of my commitment to Martin's yard I decided to move up the property ladder and nearer to his base – handy for schooling mornings. It was hardly a major upheaval, just down the A303 to Amesbury, but it made sense on two fronts. I was earning well and the time was right to invest more in property, so I moved into a grander house. In some papers it was loosely described as a mansion, and while it wasn't that it had plenty of room for one single man.

It was a lovely house with a massive garden. They say that everyone is entitled to one folly and this led me to mine. I decided the only thing missing from my dream home was a swimming-pool. A big hole was duly dug and the light blue concrete liner was put in place, with mosaic trim followed by the pumps and filtration units. I think I used it twice, although my friends had a ball!

In fact, the move was the wrong one. I found out that Martin only needed me early in the season or when there was something special going on before a big meeting. Otherwise he was relaxed about my appearances on the schooling ground and was happy to tie them in when I was riding at Taunton, Exeter or Newton Abbot.

Being out on a geographical limb had certain disadvantages and I was always driving to the races on my own. There are times when solitude is nice but equally a bit of company can make a journey seem shorter and lighten the driving too. Despite the pool, I didn't stay long in Amesbury.

Martin had his team fired up from the start, with the less-talented horses ready to collect at the minor meetings, and once he found his stride in August I couldn't stop riding winners. At one point, I had fourteen winners from twenty-one rides, which was phenomenal. For the month of August it was twenty-six wins from sixty-six rides, but with Martin's assistance it's always possible to rack up a total like that. When he decides that the race planning and conditions are right he can have a strike rate of over 50 per cent in a week. As the days got colder we seemed to get hotter, and on 5 November at Newton Abbot I rode a double for Martin in the first two races on the card. In the second, Sam Rockett gave me the fastest ever 100 winners. Now, you could rightly argue that the seasons had changed when I beat Peter Scudamore's quickest century by thirty days the previous year, but there was no debating the cutting of my own record: like Peter I was Pipe-powered, but I had done it sixteen days quicker than the previous season. While records are there to be broken, they aren't at the top of my list of priorities and I only began to think about them when they become a possibility.

However, my momentum didn't show any sign of slowing down, although it was a case of quantity rather than quality – not that it concerned me: when winners are totalled they aren't broken down into categories. They all count. The only two graded races I won before December were both on the smart but wayward hurdler Pridwell, which was ironic as he landed me in a heap of trouble with the stewards later in the season.

There was another quality winner the following month when up-and-coming two-mile novice chaser Direct Route won the Henry VIII Chase at Sandown on 6 December. He was trained by Howard Johnson up in Crook, Co. Durham, and it was another indication that things were going my way. Although it was accepted that I was Martin Pipe's first jockey it hadn't put other trainers off using me. And it was a further outside ride that gave me another 'fastest'.

When the former champion jockey Jonjo O'Neill gave me the easy winning ride on Jymjam Johnny in the Bodfari Stud Handicap Chase at Bangor-on-Dee on 17 December it was my 150th winner of the season. I had taken another of Scu's records, this time by fifty-one days.

There was nowhere near the present volume of racing when Jonjo won his first title in 1977–8 but he did it with a new record number of winners, 149. That magnificent score stayed intact until Scu, with Martin's help, smashed it with 221 winners in 1988–9. With such a fantastic springboard from the first half of the season, I began to think I might grab that record too, but everything would have to run for me – not just the horses. First, I had to stay free of serious injury: any replay of the twenty-one days off with concussion would make it nearly impossible. There was the risk of suspensions: the harder I tried, the greater the chance of breaking the rules. Last, there was the one thing over which I had no control: the weather.

The dice rolled my way. I was on a dream ticket. The momentum never ceased and once I'd passed 150 then Scu's quickest 200 was under siege. Often, these career milestones are reached at small tracks, but I chose a major Saturday to make the fastest double century in jumping: *Racing Post* Chase day at Kempton. It's also often the case that a jockey or trainer going for a record gets stuck for an uncomfortably long time on one short of the total, but not this time. I hit 199 on Supermick, trained by Martin, at Wincanton on 26 February. Nine rides later I reached 200 on Fataliste in the *Voice* Newspaper Adonis Juvenile Hurdle – yet another Martin Pipe production. The fact that it had taken me fifty-eight days less than Scu didn't mean much to me. The media hyped the whole thing up, but the only aspect that concerned me was retaining the championship and beating Scu's all-time record of 221. Now, that would be worthwhile. More immediately, I was concerned about the big race that followed, the *Racing Post* Chase.

I was riding Challenger du Luc for Martin, and he had developed into one of the most frustrating horses I was ever to ride. No matter how clever I thought I was, Challenger always had the drop on me. In previous seasons, when ridden by other jockeys, he had won the Cathcart Chase and the Murphy's Gold Cup, both at Cheltenham. So far that season he had finished second in the Murphy's in November before being beaten by a head at Newbury when he allowed Callisoe Bay back in the last strides. However, he saved his most audacious escape from the winners' enclosure for one of the biggest races of the season: the King George VI Chase at Kempton on Boxing Day. At 16–1 only one horse started at bigger odds in the eight-runner field, but Martin had him sweet as a nut. I knew from Newbury that I would have to arrive as late as possible and all the way round I had a tight hold of him, letting him think he'd got the better of me in the hope that he would also think he was better than a classy field headed by One Man.

One by one the opposition dropped away and we had the measure of a tiring One Man and the one-paced Grand National winner Rough Quest from the third last. See More Business hit the fence hard and still I hadn't let go of Challenger's reins. It was the same at the next fence, and come the last I was as certain as I could be that the race in which I'd decked Mr Mulligan a year previously was mine for the taking. Not even Challenger du Luc could get out of this.

How wrong can you be?

Challenger flew the fence to land running upsides See More Business, who was getting a thorough workout from Andrew Thornton and didn't seem to have a great deal left. Then it happened. Challenger du Luc put his head up, would not go by and allowed See More Business to win by two lengths. I was gutted, Martin Pipe was gutted and both of us felt sorry for the horse's owner, David Johnson. Fortunately, David has one of the best temperaments of any owner I have ridden for: he took it on the chin with a rueful smile.

Challenger du Luc rightly started 10–1 favourite for the John Bull Chase at Wincanton in mid-February. He looked different class but found yet another escape route, this time by falling when cruising at the cross fence four out. Now you can understand why I had things on my mind other than the 200th winner I had just ridden when I had Challenger du Luc to contend with in a £30,000 chase.

Again, it was jumping that sealed our fate. Going to the tenth fence we were tracking the leaders on the rails. Suddenly the field packed over and we were squeezed on to the rail, which made Challenger du Luc lose his footing. He was never happy after that. I moved him on to the heels of the leaders at the fourteenth, but he hit the next hard and I had to use him more than I wanted in order to stay close at the fourth last. After that he wouldn't have it and all but came down at the next, eventually finishing tailed off in fourth behind Super Tactics. He still hadn't finished with me, and I suppose I should have known better than to ride him in the Grand National. He fell at the first.

Not many horses have got the better of me but Challenger du Luc did. He raced on for the next three seasons and never won another race.

Fortunately, things were going to get much better for David Johnson, but he still has a soft spot for Challenger du Luc. Reflecting on the gelding, he said, 'He may have been a heartbreaker at times, but when he was younger he landed some decent punts for us. He cost me fifty grand and won over £200,000 in prize money and he was the one who gave me the taste for French-breds.'

David has been one of the backbone owners at Pond House Stables since he first arrived in the 1991–2 season. Born in East Ham, London, he was hooked on racing as a schoolboy, punting sixpence each way. Now the managing director of a finance company in Watford, his gambles have become legendary but it wasn't always that way. He says, 'When I got older I had an account with Coral's and I knew I must be doing badly because they kept inviting me to functions. One day at Newmarket I was in their box with one of their directors, Malcolm Palmer, and I was introduced to Robert Williams, who trained in Newmarket. I was with a few friends and we bought a couple of two-year-olds, Café Noir and Pinstripe, who both won. Then six of us decided to put four grand in each and we bought Mister Majestic for twenty-four thousand guineas. He won the Group One two-year-old race at Newmarket, the Middle Park Stakes in 1986 despite being the rank outsider at 33–1. We sold him later for £200,000, which was very good business that many years ago. My mates took their money and ran but I kept buying horses.

'The reason I went towards jumping is that I like to have a bet. With Robert, we'd take one up to Catterick to have a punt only to come up against a Maktoum horse or one of Sheikh Mohammed's and it was impossible to beat those guys. I began to think it might be a bit easier over jumps.'

He recalled the path to Pond House, which would make him leading jumping owner in 1998. 'I bumped into Peter Scudamore at Sandown. He said I should try jumping and that I should put one with Martin Pipe, who I didn't know from Adam. Scu arranged for me to go to see Martin and I decided to send him a filly I'd claimed on the Flat who was winning races for me called Beebob. She won first time out. Martin being Martin said that he'd just got a French horse. He asked whether I was interested and told me it would win first time out, too.

'He was called As Du Trefle and cost thirty grand. We went to Leicester and he absolutely bolted up. That was January 1993 and I really had the flavour after that. The business was going well and I must have been doing all right with the punting because I began to get my accounts closed.'

David Johnson was just beginning to build a full head of steam. When the 1998 Cheltenham Festival arrived he hit the jackpot and the bookmakers for six.

No matter how many winners you ride in a season, there is no substitute for riding top-quality horses. As Cheltenham approached I knew, deep down, that I was going to struggle in the two major races. Pridwell had ability but not enough to trouble Istabraq in the Champion Hurdle. As for the Gold Cup, it was wide open but Cyborgo needed to show considerable improvement to be in at the finish. Indeed he made an impact in the race but for all the wrong reasons.

On the plus side, as Martin Pipe's jockey I had nearly a full book of rides. Of the seventeen races I was eligible to ride in I failed to get a ride in only one, the Mildmay Of Flete Chase on the middle day. Of those sixteen rides only three were for outside stables, which underlines the strength of Martin's operation. And despite Cheltenham being the most competitive three days' jumping of the year only one of my rides supplied by Martin started at longer odds than 10–1. Five started favourite. Cheltenham definitely looked good and when the bookmakers opened their betting on the leading rider at the meeting I was entitled to be favourite. I didn't realize how great it was going to get.

I followed Graham Bradley's lead and took a house for the week. It was only a short drive from the track and I needed some extra space as my sister Anne-Marie and her husband Brian McCormack were over for their first taste of Cheltenham. I loved having my sister around and she knew me so well that I didn't have to put on an act of being happy all the time. She knew what a single-minded devil I'd been as a kid and it was hardly likely I would have changed, especially with the three most important days of my season looming.

Brian plays Gaelic football for Derry and is a fit man who knows all about nutrition. His only complaint whenever he stayed with me was that there was never any food in the house. I told him that if it wasn't there, I couldn't eat it. After that they brought supplies with them.

I don't like idle conversation on the way to any meeting, let alone Cheltenham, and they knew I was immersed in my own thoughts as we got through the early race traffic. I seem to leave earlier each year but I'd rather be three hours early than three minutes late. It's important to get your mind right when there's so much at stake.

John Dunlop, the leading Flat trainer, had booked me for Wahiba Sands in the first, the Citroën Supreme Novices' Hurdle, but despite starting third favourite he was a beaten horse when he blundered at the last and finished fifteenth. Several years on Wahiba Sands made a much bigger impression when he joined Martin Pipe. While no one likes losing, I had to be pleased with the result. Graham Bradley, now in the twilight of his career, gave the gallant mare French Ballerina the ride of his life to beat Ireland's 'good thing', His Song. It was a massive win for Brad fifteen years on from his Cheltenham Gold Cup victory on Bregawn.

Cheltenham is one of the hardest places to take a novice chaser. The fences come quickly, sometimes on the turn, and at undulating places, which can catch out experienced chasers, let alone novices. Martin's preparation of Champleve to land a massive gamble for David Johnson in the Guinness Arkle Novices' Chase was remarkable.

Like so many of David's best horses, Champleve came from France and the plan was to go for novice hurdles. He'd won only once in seven starts over hurdles for Jean Lesbordes, and he'd started his British career well enough by easily winning two moderate novice events at Newton Abbot and Chepstow. But Martin needed to know whether he was good enough to win either of the novice hurdles at Cheltenham. He found out when Champleve was unable to dominate at Sandown and weakened to finish nearly twenty lengths third to Lord Jim.

There was no point kidding anyone and I said to Martin: 'He'll not win a Cheltenham hurdle race on that.'

One of the reasons David Johnson has the majority of his horses with Martin Pipe and keeps them there is that he knows that every angle will be covered to get it right. All options have to be considered and Martin came up with one. He likes buying horses from France for several reasons, not least because he thinks they are athletic and taught to jump fences early. Champleve had never jumped a fence in public, but Martin saw a golden window opening for the Arkle that would give David the best-value gamble of his life.

David likes recalling it now: 'At the time Champleve was making his chase début at Lingfield I had Cyfor Malta, who was 5–1 favourite for the Arkle. Martin said to me that he thought Cyfor would get two miles five and why not have a crack at the Cathcart? No one had even thought of Champleve for the Arkle. So I asked the bookmakers what price Cyfor Malta was for the Arkle, and when they told me, I had a grand on. Then I asked what price

Champleve was. He was 33–1, so I had a couple of grand on. I backed him to take a quarter of a million out.'

Martin was well aware of another point in their favour. The weight-for-age allowances were heavily in favour of the young horses. Champleve, a five-year-old, would receive a whopping eight pounds from any older horse and three pounds from any older mares in the race. All he had to do was jump.

Jonothan Lower, the headmaster of the schooling ground at Pond House Stables, set about teaching Champleve to do just that and when he made his fencing début at Lingfield on 6 February he knew exactly what to do. It might not have been the greatest chase run but part of my job is to know when a horse is good. Champleve was certainly that and the Cheltenham fences wouldn't be a bother to win. Martin makes it no secret that he likes a bet but it is always owners first, and after the Lingfield win and my assessment he advised David Johnson to lump on for the Arkle. No five-year-old had won the race since Soloning, trained by Fred Winter in 1970.

It was important to get some more public experience into Champleve and five days later we made all over two miles at Ascot, easily beating the smart Doncaster winner Classy Lad, trained by Nicky Henderson. David had certainly got himself a bet.

There's always an air of expectancy in the paddock at Cheltenham but there was more of an edge before the Arkle. David has always been a fair and easy man to ride for, and over the years he has become more knowledgeable: he knows the opposition as well as his own horse. We knew that there were plenty of horses of similar ability to Champleve and, while there's no such thing as a bad race at Cheltenham, this wasn't the strongest Arkle ever ran. The bookmakers had the same opinion, making Kadastrof the 11–2 favourite in a field of sixteen. Champleve was short on experience and would need a bit of luck but he wasn't 33–1, he was now 13–2 third favourite.

David stood back as Martin legged me up. We were playing for a big pot. 'Best of luck,' he called.

We were going to need it.

Champleve was a free-going horse. There was no point in

disappointing him and I was never far off the leaders before sending him on at the seventh. His inexperience almost blew the operation when he smashed through the third last, but at that stage he was still full of running and recovered his balance.

Champleve was going well enough for me to press for home with two fences remaining and we were clear going into the last, with Richard Dunwoody flat to the boards on Hill Society, apparently getting nowhere. David must have been able to smell his winnings, but that big Cheltenham hill began to look like the bloody Matterhorn as I drove Champleve up it. The horse had given me plenty and was now running on empty. Suddenly, David could see victory turning to defeat. Dunwoody knew we had nothing left. He threw everything at us in the last fifty yards and when we hit the line Champleve was down to an extended trot. Pessimism overcame me and I thought we were beaten. The bookmakers thought so, too, and went 10–1 on about Hill Society. Richard wouldn't commit himself as we walked back to the winners' enclosure and it was simply a matter of waiting.

'I think we're beat,' I said, steering Champleve into second place.

David was consoling himself that at least he had the each-way part of the bet to collect, and everyone knew that, whatever happened, we'd been involved in one of the tightest finishes seen at Cheltenham for many a year. I told David that, win, lose or draw, his horse had run the race of his life for one with so little experience of jumping fences in public.

There was still no announcement as I walked back to the weighing room, and the longer it went on, the more hope it gave me. I thought we were beaten, but maybe we weren't.

It was nearly fifteen minutes before the announcement came and David went through the full rush of emotions. Someone said to him that it must be terrible, what he was putting himself through. He wouldn't have it. 'I've had a great bet and whatever happens I've got an 8–1 winner with the quarter odds each way for the place bet.'

Then he received a call that raised his spirits a little: 'I was sure we were second, but my mobile rang and it was someone I consider quite a good judge. He thought we had won and did I want an even five grand with Hill Society? I certainly did! I was delighted to lose five grand if it meant Champleve would be the winner. I was standing next to Martin's wife, Carol, and I said, "I think we've got a chance here, this could be a dead heat." '

I had changed into Pridwell's colours for the Champion Hurdle when the speakers in the changing room fizzed into life. There was an added air of suspense. Hill Society was number six and Champleve sixteen. For a heart-pumping split second both parties would think they had won. 'First, number sixteen, Champleve, second number six, Hill Society.'

I was elated: there had been more to it for me than landing a gamble by the narrowest of margins. I had beaten one of my idols, Richard Dunwoody. He was as good as they get, the man whose exploits I'd sneak out to listen to on the telephone when I was a kid at Bolger's. And I'd got him.

I probably derived as much pleasure from beating Richard that day as I had any single close finish before or since. It gave me immense satisfaction, and over the next few days I discovered just how much I had got to him. He hardly said more than two words to me for the rest of the meeting and I understood why. It had killed him inside, and it would have killed me exactly the same. It happens to me now and it doesn't get any easier. I'm everyone's target, a bit like a gunfighter: everyone wants to take you and sometimes they do.

Although Richard has retired I reckon he still thinks about it when we meet. If I bring it up he swings straight back with 'What about Eskimo Nell? I did you on Chief's Song that day at Sandown.' He did, too, in the 1995 William Hill Handicap Hurdle. That time Richard was in front and I failed to get him by a whisker. Don't let anyone tell you it's only elephants that never forget.

With the Arkle in the bag, Pridwell took over my thoughts for the Champion Hurdle. Unfortunately he was never up to the class of Istabraq and did well to finish fourth.

Luv-U-Frank came down four from home in the William Hill National Hunt Handicap Chase and there was only one ride left for the first day. Having already had one pressure ride in Champleve I now thought I faced another in Unsinkable Boxer. This was yet another master-stroke from Martin Pipe.

Martin had already virtually rebuilt Carvill's Hill for owner Paul Green in the 1991–2 season and when Mr Green's stepson, Nick Walker, retired from training in 1997 Martin was sent Unsinkable Boxer. The improvement was quite fantastic and the horse hardly came off the bit as I won three races on him. The first was a moderate novice handicap at Plumpton in December off an official rating of only 94. Martin began planning for Cheltenham and continued to nurture that handicap mark, running him in two further novice events, which he won head in chest.

When it was time for the Cheltenham entries he made one for each of the novice hurdles, but although the horse was good enough to have justified an option in the Stayers' Hurdle he decided not to make it. That might have told the handicapper too much. Unsinkable Boxer was allotted a mark of 128, the equivalent of ten stone twelve in one of the hardest handicap hurdles of the season, the Unicoin Homes Gold Card Handicap Hurdle. On the face of it, the handicapper had done more than enough, raising Unsinkable Boxer thirty-four pounds. Martin knew better – and so did the punters, who sent him off 5–2 favourite. Only one other horse had started as short for the race since its inception and that was Forgive 'N' Forget in 1983 – and he went on to win a Cheltenham Gold Cup!

Paul Green had been keen to go for either of the novice races but Martin was adamant: it had to be the handicap, even though it wasn't worth so much. In his mind it was the easiest option. I wasn't so sure.

As he came to collect my saddle from the weighing room I asked him about the race. 'How do you think I should ride him?'

Martin is never one for small-talk. 'Just ride him like you've always done.'

'That's fine, except that I've been riding him like a good horse and it's only been in novice hurdles at Plumpton, Fontwell and Doncaster. I'll be dropping him out last.'

'That doesn't matter, do that and pass them when you like.'

I wasn't sure how to take him. 'But I've been riding him like he's a machine.'

Martin looked straight at me with a half-quizzical look. 'You ride him just like that. He *is* a machine.' I half smiled, but Martin wanted to make sure I'd got the message. 'This is the biggest certainty to set foot on Cheltenham racecourse.'

That was some call in a twenty-four-runner handicap over three and a quarter miles, especially as the furthest he'd travelled in a race for us was three miles.

If anything, Unsinkable Boxer was running too keen, but I didn't change my plan, and as the field passed the stands and headed out for the final circuit I was disputing last place with Brad, who was riding Ivor's Flutter. The difference was, Brad stayed there. I gave Unsinkable Boxer a squeeze at the middle hurdle down the back straight and he passed five in mid-air. I still didn't know where to put him because I was going so well running from the top of the hill with about six furlongs ahead. With two hurdles left I had to let him go and I knew Martin was right: this *was* the biggest certainty to have set foot on Cheltenham racecourse. I was so buzzed up after jumping the last that, with a hundred yards of the race to go, I waved my whip in the air to encourage the punters to cheer. They didn't miss a beat. Clearly Martin wasn't the only one who thought I was on a certainty.

However, as I waited with Martin and Paul Green to mount the podium for our trophies I got a surprising reaction from the owner. 'I think we ran in the wrong race. He would have won the Stayers'.'

I wasn't best pleased and began to seethe inwardly. I had to say something. 'I think it's great to have a Cheltenham winner and I think you should enjoy it. Have you had one before?'

Martin, ever the diplomat, grabbed my arm, yanked it hard and whispered, through clenched teeth, 'Leave it!'

I drew a blank on the middle day, although two horses ran their hearts out for second place. Paul Green's Torboy was runner-up in the Royal & Sun Alliance Novices' Hurdle behind the spectacular winner French Holly. Or Royal, winner of the previous year's Arkle, was no match for One Man in the Queen Mother Champion Chase but probably put in the best performance of his life to go down by four lengths. He was never the same after that season.

The third day could not have begun worse but ultimately it signalled that my luck was in. My first ride of the day was Rainbow Frontier, who was having his first run for Martin in the Élite Racing Club Triumph Hurdle after being bought from Aidan O'Brien's stable. The horse was well fancied but a bit too impetuous. We were in front at the third but Rainbow Frontier took off a stride too soon at the next flight. He recovered from that but wasn't so lucky at the fifth and came down, leaving the field to trample over me. I got to my feet, feeling for any lumps that shouldn't be there. Yep, everything was working and where it should have been. I knew the aches would come later.

Hopefully I'd have the ideal remedy: a couple of winners.

Despite three tricky handicaps on the card, I felt sure I'd get at least one winner, and although Martin didn't train it, I had him to thank for being aboard Edredon Bleu in the Grand Annual Handicap Chase.

I wouldn't have been on the horse without an accident to Jim Culloty that sidelined him for the gelding's previous start at Sandown. In Jim's absence we won with me easing down from fifty yards out. Edredon Bleu had jumped those tricky fences brilliantly and I loved him. Jim was only starting to establish himself at the yard of Henrietta Knight, who trained Edredon Bleu, so I kept the ride. In fact, he would not have been fit anyway as he smashed his collar-bone at Huntingdon on the opening day of Cheltenham. When Martin had been sorting out his Cheltenham arrangements in late February I told him I'd never sat on a better handicapped chaser than this fellow. What's more, I'd have been surprised if Henrietta hadn't got more to play with. I told Martin that I'd like to ride him: 'It's going to be impossible for anything to beat him.'

Now, this might have been a tricky situation. Although I wasn't retained, I was riding all of Martin's horses. He had a couple lined

up for the Grand Annual and the likely runner was Indian Jockey,
who hadn't won since 1 November at Ascot when ridden by Chris
Maude. The horse was weighted up to the hilt and had to give
Edredon Bleu a pound. Martin said he didn't mind, so I was on
board one of the best chasers I have ever ridden.

Although Edredon doesn't have to make the running these days,
he loved to blaze away when he was younger and Cheltenham was
no different. Starting 7–2 favourite, Edredon Bleu was clear from
the sixth and made his only serious error when he clouted the
fourth last. He was tiring going to the last and hung to the left as I
drove him for the line, but he never looked likely to stop and had
three and a half lengths in hand of Tidebrook at the finish. This
was only the start of a magnificent Cheltenham record for Edredon
Bleu.

When we returned to the weighing room, news filtered through
that made us all uncomfortably aware that this sport sometimes
shows no pity. Adrian Maguire had won his first Cheltenham race
as a young amateur on Omerta for Martin Pipe in the Kim Muir
Chase of 1991, and took the Gold Cup on Toby Balding's Cool
Ground in 1992. Since then the meeting had been a nightmare
for him. Due to the death of his mother and injuries he had missed
the last three Festivals. Now he was in the first-aid room with a
broken collar-bone after Zabadi gave him a horrendous fall at the
third.

Cyfor Malta was next up, and I was attempting to give David
Johnson his second winner of the meeting in the Cathcart Chase.
There was no shortage of confidence even though the horse had
been beaten on his previous start at Sandown and hadn't won
over two miles five furlongs. Like Champleve, Cyfor Malta was a
precocious French five-year-old who was well able to handle
himself over fences. Having won two chases for Bernard Secly, he
won his English début at Sandown in January before being beaten
by Jack Doyle on his second attempt over the course. He jumped
markedly left on both his Sandown runs and we knew he'd be
much better going that way round at Cheltenham. Martin had
exploited the fact that steeplechasers were maturing much quicker

in France, and Cyfor Malta was attempting to become the first five-year-old to win the Cathcart since 1951, when Semeur won for the legendary Fulke Walwyn.

Cyfor Malta needed to be ridden with more restraint than my two previous chase winners, and there's no better feeling than spinning round Cheltenham, stalking the leaders in a good-class chase and knowing you can pick them off when you want to. It was like that with Cyfor Malta. I let him make steady progress in his own time and we arrived on the heels of the leaders two out. I quickened him upsides Dr Leunt and Richard Dunwoody at the last, and pushed him ahead soon after. There was no need for the camera this time: Cyfor Malta strode on to win by three and a half lengths. He hadn't stopped improving, and the next stop was Liverpool.

A large part of Martin Pipe's success is down to planning. As a clever person once said, 'Failing to prepare is preparing to fail.' No one can ever accuse Martin of that and he had plotted Blowing Wind up to win a big bonus for Peter Deal, who was still living the dream of Make A Stand's Champion Hurdle win the previous year. Martin told him early in the New Year that he might just have another Cheltenham winner for him, although there would also be something valuable to aim at on the way. Blowing Wind was yet another with the French connection but was not straightforward to place. He had won a hurdle race at Auteuil, which meant he had to run three times to qualify for a handicap mark. He was outclassed in the Knights Royal Hurdle at Ascot in December and never featured under automatic top weight in the Teal And Green Hurdle at the same course in January.

The last run to get a handicap mark was in the Champion Hurdle Trial at Haydock on 24 January, where Blowing Wind was outclassed and finished just over twenty lengths third to the highly regarded Dato Star. The problem from a handicapping standpoint was that Blowing Wind finished only a length behind the 1996 Champion Hurdle winner Collier Bay, who was rated 165, while the prolific Relkeel, rated 160, was twenty lengths further back in fourth. To make things look even worse, due to the race conditions and the higher prize money in France, Blowing Wind had raced off level weights with Relkeel and conceded three pounds to Collier Bay.

Later that night Peter Deal received a call from another of his trainers, David Nicholson: the Duke was chortling. 'I can see your plan and you've blown it.'

Peter kept up the *craic*. 'Why? Just because we've beaten Relkeel? He must have had a bad day and the handicapper's not going to take any notice of that.'

Peter still remembers David Nicholson's parting shot: 'Relkeel was on song. You'll be rated 150.'

Peter was adamant. 'The horse has been run fairly and openly to get handicapped. I think we'll get 130.'

He was spot on. Blowing Wind made his handicap début under a top weight of eleven stone ten in the Sunderlands Imperial Cup at Sandown on 14 March, having been gambled on in the ante-post market from 10–1 to 5–1 favourite. I was able to take my time and never had a bother, taking him ahead soon after the last to win by a very easy four lengths.

Now Martin was after the same £50,000 bonus that the sponsors Sunderlands were offering for any horse that could win their Sandown race and go on to win at Cheltenham. He had done it five years earlier with Olympian, and in the pre-bonus days Floyd for David Elsworth and Moody Man for Philip Hobbs had also followed their Imperial Cup wins by landing the County Hurdle. A seven-pound penalty took Blowing Wind's weight for the Vincent O'Brien County Hurdle to eleven stone eight. We had to put considerably more effort into landing the £27,000 first prize and the £50,000 bonus, but it proved well worth it.

Despite the massive field of twenty-seven we started 15–8 favourite and I had to wait out the back. But I was on a horse tuned to the minute and was able to put him where I wanted. Running down the hill to the second last I made my move and was upside going to the last, where Paul Carberry, my old friend from Jim Bolger's, was waiting for me on Advocat.

It wasn't nice to see him. I wound Blowing Wind up and

we soon had a length lead, which we were never in danger of surrendering. At the line it had extended to a length and three-quarters.

Victory in the Festival finale meant that once again I ended as leading jockey at the meeting. This time the total of five victories meant much more: only two jockeys had managed it before, Fred Winter in 1959 and Jamie Osborne in 1992. I was in excellent company.

The only black spot over a fine three days had come in the Gold Cup, and once again it involved Martin, Cyborgo, Paul Nicholls and Paul Barber. There were big expectations for See More Business, who started 11−2 second favourite under Timmy Murphy. I was riding Cyborgo, the horse who had caused such bad feeling between Nicholls, Barber and myself. Both Timmy and I were in touch with the leaders at the sixth, but the race still hadn't started as we approached the next fence, turning out of the back straight.

Suddenly I felt Cyborgo lose his action and go badly lame. In those situations a jockey can only think of his horse. I had to get him out of the race as quickly as I could.

I called out and pulled him sharply to the right. Unfortunately Timmy was too far back and couldn't hear me. He simply could not get out of my way as I ran Cyborgo off the course. Both See More Business and Martin's other runner, Indian Tracker, were carried past the wing and were out of the biggest race of the Festival.

No one said it was intentional − how could it have been? − but both Paul Nicholls and Paul Barber were extremely upset and disappointed. Nothing was ever said to me, but there were heated words afterwards between Paul Nicholls and Martin. There has been tension between them ever since. To this day neither talks about it, but I am happy to have ridden winners for Messrs Nicholls and Barber since.

I said earlier that reaching the fastest totals means little to me but I was keen to beat Peter Scudamore's record total of 221 winners in a jumping season. I needed five winners once Cheltenham had finished and, unusually in such cases, I didn't have any long losing runs to build up pressure in the media. Six days and fifteen rides after Cheltenham I reached 222 winners for the season on Petite Risk in the juvenile novice hurdle at Ludlow.

This was the climax of something that had grown relentlessly since I'd started riding in England, just over four years earlier. Scu's feats inevitably became a target the more championships I won, especially as I had the same man behind me in Martin Pipe.

The aim was always winners, and winners at the big meetings, but when I got past Scu that day at Ludlow it was a huge personal milestone.

I was on a massive high when I returned to the weighing room. When I was presented with a bottle of champagne I sprayed anyone within ten feet of me. Well, I wouldn't be drinking it, would I? In the picture that appeared on the front of the following day's *Racing Post* I looked like a kid at his birthday party with every present he'd wanted.

It was probably the first time it occurred to me that others thought I was good at my job. The person who gave the most balanced opinion on me that day was Peter Scudamore. He said, 'I always thought my record would be beaten but I never thought it would be beaten quite so easily. But then, I never thought there would be summer jumping either! I have always had the greatest respect for what John Francome did and Richard Dunwoody is still doing, but this fellow could set standards that no one will ever match. It would be wrong to say he's the best jockey ever, but nobody has ever ridden better, or most likely ever will.'

I felt humble when past champion jockeys lavished praise on me in the following day's papers. When such legends as Tommy Stack describe you as a 'super-talent' it's hard to take in that they're talking about you. And Jonjo O'Neill said I was 'brave as a lion'. A very nice tribute, but the same applies to all the lads who have gone before or since. Ron Barry reckoned I had 'no nerves at all'. Maybe I'm just a good actor. I'm sure that when my time's past, I'll be wheeled out to say the same about a youngster who has cut through my records.

Toby Balding observed, 'I think the keynote to his success was his natural ability allied to tremendous dedication. He would ride in every single race if he could.'

Toby has subsequently compared me with a former champion jockey of the sixties, Josh Gifford: 'The more I look at AP the more I'm inclined to compare him to Josh Gifford except that he's stronger. They both go by the same theory that there isn't a horse born that wants to fall. Most falls are human-induced. McCoy bears comparison with Lester Piggott, you can't copy him.'

Perhaps the tribute I valued most that day came from the man whose faith in me never wavered. Billy Rock had broken out a bottle of champagne to celebrate my success. I enjoyed listening to him recall the good old days, which seemed a lifetime ago, but were only twelve years in the past. 'He wasn't too keen on school. In fact, he used to sign himself in and come straight to my place. I used to pick him up in all sorts of weather out on a country road in mid-Antrim and sometimes he would dump himself in my car like a drowned rat . . . I looked upon him as a son.'

Billy knew me and my family well and he was right when he said, 'Today is a very special one and time for a major celebration but, funnily enough, the last man to be letting his hair down will be Anthony's father, Peadar. He's a very quiet person and will take things easily, but the importance will not be lost on him.'

It wasn't. When I called Ma and Dad later that day they were very proud of what I had achieved. It was the easiest thing in the world to tell them that without their help and understanding it would not have happened. I also was quick to point out that without Martin Pipe neither I nor Scu would have reached such totals. Not that there was any chance of resting on my laurels. It wasn't long before the bookmakers were pricing up odds on me riding 300 winners that season. Dave Roberts put that one into perspective: 'It's a long shot and near-on impossible.'

Despite the plaudits, I continued to assess what I was doing. When I had started riding in England I had shortened the length of my stirrup leathers by six holes. At the beginning of that record-breaking season I had pulled them up another couple of notches because I felt that I still looked rather big on a horse. By riding that bit shorter I could bring myself down lower into the saddle and get hold of the horse better. You can't stand still in any sport.

Of course there was a trap around the corner, and it was sprung by the Aintree stewards.

It is natural that when a jockey is censured by the stewards he feels hard done by: whether it is for trying too hard or not hard enough, you feel that there is no pleasing some people. But at the Grand National meeting of 1998 I reckon that I gave Pridwell the best ride I have ever given a horse, before or since, when he won the Grade One Martell Aintree Hurdle.

However, far from being ecstatic at winning the £50,000 first prize, I received a double slap in the face that led me to re-evaluate my outlook on riding, which had been evolving since I was a kid. The meeting couldn't have got off to a better start. Fataliste, who took me to the fastest 200 winners, made all in the first race of the three days, the Seagram Top Novices' Hurdle. Although Champleve was still feeling the effects of his Cheltenham exertions and finished only third in the Sandeman Maghull Novices' Chase he owed no one a penny – not that David Johnson had to wait long to get into the winners' enclosure.

Cyfor Malta definitely wasn't marking time. The momentum of his Cheltenham success carried on to Liverpool where he struck another blow for the youngsters by producing a truly breathtaking display over the National fences in the John Hughes Chase.

It was a credit to the horse that Martin thought he was good enough to run over such a tricky course aged only five. What was more, with a weight rise of seven pounds for his win at Cheltenham, Cyfor Malta carried eleven stone eleven, which meant he gave weight to all but four of his twenty-one rivals. It didn't matter: he displayed the arrogance of youth that April day and gave me one of the most memorable rides of my career.

To put his feat into perspective you must understand that no five-year-old had ever won the John Hughes, once known as the Topham Trophy. No trainer had even bothered to enter a horse of that age since 1953. It's as well horses can't read.

Cyfor Malta always had a tendency to jump left-handed so it was a plus that he was going that way round at Aintree. But his biggest asset was pure class: he was in another league compared to anything else over that two miles six furlongs. It was just a matter of making sure he got round and there was never a bother on that score. He was a natural: never missed a beat, never touched a fence. I was never far off the leaders and let him get a good look at those tricky fences, which he was viewing for the first time. The one aspect over which I had no control was where we raced. With his tendency to go left Cyfor wanted to be tight on the inside. Even at Becher's Brook, where you want to be out in the middle of the course because the drop on the landing side is less steep, he wouldn't have it. We took the steepest landing on the inside and he never checked his stride. The biggest bonus came at the Canal Turn, which is a sharp dog-leg left immediately after you jump. Cyfor Malta took this tricky manoeuvre like it was a U-turn. Some horses can lose thirty yards or more by going straight on before getting the bend right. We actually made ground.

In all his races, I always delayed my challenge until the last fence and I knew I could take Ballyline, ridden by Brendan Powell, whenever I wanted. The final jump was soon enough to make our move and I hardly had to shake the reins at Cyfor Malta for him to quicken ahead soon after touching down. I will be surprised if I ever get a better ride over the course.

The next season's Grand National is usually put up as the logical step for the winner but not for Cyfor Malta at that stage. The minimum age limit was set at seven, having been raised from six in 1987. However, the ease of Cyfor Malta's win made the Jockey Club rethink, and lower the minimum age back to six in 1999.

Unfortunately it was of no use to Cyfor Malta, who would not see that season through because of serious injury.

The winners kept flowing on Friday. Mouse Morris provided my third win of the meeting with Boss Doyle in the Mumm Mildmay Novices' Chase, while Unsinkable Boxer retained his Cheltenham form to run away with the Belle Époque Sefton Novices' Hurdle. However, this was a day that was marred for everyone present by the death of One Man, whose glittering career came to a cruel end with a fatal fall in the Mumm Melling Chase won by Opera Hat.

As usual for the National meeting I was staying with Graham Bradley, this time at the Moat House. The following day would be a big one for him. He had got the ride back on last year's National second, Suny Bay, and he thought the world of him. Brad was convinced it was his big chance to add the National to his Gold Cup and Champion Hurdle successes. In any event Suny Bay was a brave second, trying to give a massive twenty-three pounds to Earth Summit. It was a heroic performance, which sent Brad home almost as happy as if he'd won the race.

So, with so much at stake, he decided to have a quiet Friday night. I was only too pleased to oblige.

I would be lying if I said I had thoughts of causing Brad any trouble on Challenger du Luc, although there was always a chance that such a quirky customer might take an interest when confronted with such a unique circuit. In the build-up to the race, Martin's son David was quoted as saying, 'We'll know after the second fence whether he loves or loathes the place.' Some chance – we fell at the first! However, I am the first to admit that I didn't go out for the race in my usual focused style. In fact, I was steaming with indignation.

Pridwell had been a reformed character from the start of the season. In fact, as it progressed, the most respected of racing publications, *Timeform*, withdrew the squiggle from his hurdle rating that denotes a horse who is ungenuine. In a typically quirky attempt to explain his rehabilitation, Martin Pipe had said that it might have helped that the girl who looked after him, Donna, had got married. However, there was no escaping the fact that Pridwell had a mountain to climb in the Martell Aintree Hurdle. He was up against the new Champion Hurdler Istabraq, who had beaten him by just over fourteen lengths at Cheltenham, and would go on to become a triple champion and one of the greatest hurdlers of all time.

The conditions were desperate enough to test the enthusiasm of any horse, let alone one with Pridwell's suspect nature. But the race was over half a mile further than the Champion and the one major factor in his favour was his proven ability to win over three miles. Although Istabraq had won over two and a half, he would never have been involved in a slog like this.

Although it was only two and a half weeks since the Champion Hurdle, Martin had kept Pridwell at his peak. I told him my plan was straightforward: 'We'll have to make sure we stay and Istabraq doesn't.'

At Cheltenham Pridwell had lost ground at the start and, while that hadn't cost him that race, it might well cost this one, which would be run in a bog. He jumped off fine and was happy to track the leaders, so I decided to turn the screw four from home and sent him past Collier Bay.

Charlie Swan on Istabraq was biding his time and swept through to challenge at the second last, where the Champion's speed should have been decisive. Fortunately for us, he gave the flight a whack, which meant he had to use vital energy to take the lead at the last. Many thought that was game over for Pridwell, but he was like a lion that afternoon.

I got down tight into him and drove him with every ounce of energy I possessed, using my whip in rhythm and never losing vital balance. Gradually we started to haul the champ back as the heavy ground began to sap him. Twenty-five yards from the line we retook him and Pridwell stayed on gallantly for a head win that will go down in the record books as the best and most significant of his career.

Martin was delighted and met me as we walked back to the unsaddling enclosure. 'Great ride, great ride,' was all he said. I thought both horse and jockey had done well for each other. When I got back to the changing room Brad gave me a pat on the back and just said, 'You gave him a peach.'

Then I got a call from the stewards' secretary to say the stewards were holding an inquiry into my use of the whip.

Surely they weren't going to do me for excessive use? I understood it was a sensitive time, with animal-welfare groups voicing concern about the whip. What could they have seen that I'd done wrong?

It wasn't long before I found out. I gave my evidence to the panel of three stewards. I explained that he was quirky, that he sometimes had his own ideas about how the game should be played and that they didn't always coincide with mine. At those times I had to persuade him that I was right. I also pointed out that I had to keep him happy through a race or he'd pack up work for the day quicker than any shop steward. For that reason I hadn't given him a smack with the whip until after the last – and even that was a last resort after I'd done everything right to make sure we won.

I was asked to wait outside while they deliberated. When I came back in the chairman gave the verdict. I had been found guilty of using my whip with excessive frequency and I'd be suspended for four days.

I might have said, 'That's a joke,' but I can't fully remember because I was livid. In the last furlong and a half I had known I would have to be strong on him, but I do not believe for one second that Pridwell would have tried as hard as he did if he felt he was being bullied or harshly treated.

I walked back into the changing room absolutely gutted, and felt it was right to appeal to Jockey Club headquarters in Portman Square, London. Why shouldn't I?

I said to Brad, 'I think that's the best ride I've ever given a horse.' Looking back, even though I've evolved since, I still don't think I've bettered it.

Timeform's Chasers and Hurdlers of 1997–8 summed the situation up better than I could possibly ever hope to. It said: 'It seems perverse to taint the memory of this stirring race by even giving the briefest mention here to the subsequent treatment by the stewards, interpreting the rule-book to the letter, of winning jockey Tony McCoy, who had, quite simply, ridden like a man inspired.'

When my appeal was heard by the disciplinary committee a week later they did not have those words to hand. I doubt it would have made the slightest difference. They clearly thought I was wasting my time and theirs, and added two more days to my suspension for launching a frivolous appeal.

Unfortunately, this was only the beginning of a nightmare with the stewards over my use of the whip. Things would only get worse next season.

So far as this one was concerned I would put my friendship with Brad under pressure, but only for a short time.

As Richard Hughes was required to ride on the Flat, Mouse Morris gave me the ride on His Song in the Country Pride Champion Novices' Hurdle on the opening day of the Punchestown Festival on 28 April. This set up a rematch with his Cheltenham conqueror French Ballerina, who would again be ridden by Brad.

As usual, we travelled together and as part of a thank-you for winning the Citroën Supreme Novices' at Cheltenham, owner John Magnier had given Brad the use of his house at the K Club in Kildare. I was included in the party. The trouble was, I had a plan to spoil that party when we got to the races. I reckoned I knew how to beat French Ballerina.

At Punchestown the ground was desperately heavy, and she wasn't very big whereas His Song was huge. I started off running in the middle of the course but I knew Brad would have French Ballerina on the rail, just as he had at Cheltenham. He soon had company: I gradually moved His Song over towards her and we were racing together from four flights out. Then I let my fellow lean on top of her and squeeze her up to give her something she might not like. You could not have got water between us. We were that tight and, no matter what Brad did, he couldn't get French Ballerina away because they were pinned on that rail – there had been seven lengths between the pair at Cheltenham, where Brad had kicked off the final bend. This time we had been stride for stride and, with the ground and the extra attentions of His Song, French Ballerina could never get clear. We finally nailed her in the dying strides and as we pulled up Brad called me every bastard he could lay his tongue to. He didn't leave me out back in the changing room: 'I even let you stay in the effing house!'

After the last race he'd quietened down, and we left the course together. He had always been an admirer of what he sees as skilful tactics and gamesmanship – he'd used plenty in his time – and I was soon forgiven.

The impetuosity of youth still clung to me as I approached my third championship and I took the ride on Merry Gale for Jim Dreaper in the Marlborough Cup, a cross-country race at Barbury Castle, not far from Marlborough in Wiltshire. Many of the jumps were timber poles and the ground that Sunday, 24 May, was bone hard. I made contact with it early in the race when Merry Gale turned over and was thankful when the medics put the plastic mask over my nose and mouth, freeing me from pain.

I was rushed to Princess Margaret Hospital, Swindon, and the pain came flooding back as I was X-rayed from all angles. This time I was relatively lucky, although I had fractured two vertebrae and had taken a severe hammering in the process. Rest was the pre-scribed remedy and for once I was only too happy to take it. The season was all but over. With 150 of my 253 winners coming from Martin Pipe, I was 133 clear of my nearest rival in the championship, Richard Johnson.

The lure of sun and golf in Spain looked like a great aid to recuperation but there was just one problem. On 8 May at Stratford I had been riding Amlah for Philip Hobbs and got the better of a terrific duel with Norman Williamson on Stately Home by a length and a quarter. The stewards said we had both used the whip too freely and suspended us for three days. Like a motorist, I was logging up unwanted points on my licence. I knew a problem was lurking and it returned with some force next season.

11. Whipping Up a Storm

Racing is the only sport I know in which you can be suspended for winning. It is something I feel exceptionally strongly about, and throughout the 1998–9 season I thought the authorities had a special agenda for me.

In 1996 the Jockey Club had brought in a totting-up system for riding offences, which was fairer than the old system: under that, if a jockey was suspended three times within a calendar year he was automatically referred to Portman Square, where he would be handed a lengthy suspension. It didn't matter if the three suspensions were of a relatively minor nature, the end result would be the same. Now a rider would not be sent on to Jockey Club headquarters until he had been suspended for more than fifteen days. After that, it would be a minimum of a fourteen-day ban before starting again with a clean licence.

The alarm should have sounded when I was suspended for four days following my winning ride on Pridwell at Aintree, and was then handed another two days by the Jockey Club. Then I picked up another three days on Amlah at Stratford on 8 May, taking my running tally to nine. At that stage I was on 246 winners and any faint hope I had had of beating Sir Gordon Richards' record of 269 winners in a season went out of the window. The distant dream was finally laid to rest with my fall from Merry Gale.

I should have realized that the whip was now a hot potato as far as the Jockey Club were concerned and, in fairness to them, they had made me aware of their concerns. They were worried that the RSPCA, through public opinion, would bring about its abolition. Also, there was a chance that if the Jockey Club did not exercise its authority in the matter a jockey might find himself prosecuted for cruelty by the RSPCA. They saw me as one of the sport's figure-heads and, in an effort to get things right, I had met with stewards'

secretary Paul Barton before racing at Newbury in January to talk
through what was and was not acceptable where the whip was
concerned. I found it easy to talk with Paul, who had ridden plenty
of winners as a professional and understood the problems jockeys
faced. I told him it was difficult to change something that I felt
came naturally but I would do my best. Clearly that hadn't been
good enough in the matter of Pridwell.

I started back for the new season at Stratford on 26 June, managing two winners from three rides. All went well until Stratford
again on 15 August, where I was beaten by a neck on Ozzie
Jones in the three-mile handicap chase and picked up two days'
suspension because I was too liberal with the whip. It was made
clear to me that the Jockey Club were watching me when Christopher Hall, chairman of the disciplinary committee, took me aside
for an informal chat. He was extremely open and I appreciated the
time and concern he showed on my behalf. He explained the club's
view: 'You are the champion, every youngster in the land who
aspires to be a jump jockey will be modelling themselves on
you. Therefore it is important that you are the right kind of
model.'

I said I would do my best and set out with good intentions.
Unfortunately, they didn't last long and the next day at Newton
Abbot events turned nasty.

I was riding Coy Debutante for Martin Pipe in the last race, a
bumper. The filly would have won her previous race at the course
but we were hampered and brought down on the home turn. She
was a well-backed favourite for this second outing but wasn't very
good and finished eight lengths third. Although I didn't feel I had
been over-hard on her, the stewards called it differently and gave
me four days for using the whip 'with excessive force'. To rub salt
into the wound, they added that they considered I had been too
hard on a horse who was only four years old. That was rubbish.
On the Flat, horses often have their hardest season in their classic
year when they are only three.

Although it was the last race on the card the press realized there
would be a good story. When I came out of the stewards' room I

gave them plenty of copy for the following day's papers. At that moment I felt sick to death of the sport. What was more, I didn't try to disguise it: 'I feel like giving the whole game up and going off and playing golf. I've been done so many times for excessive force it's just a joke. I'm very, very annoyed about the whole thing. They told me it was because the horse was a four-year-old and I was too hard on it. Too hard on it? What am I meant to do, just sit there? You may as well get girls to ride the horses. They don't seem to get done.'

Things were getting serious. I had now been suspended for fifteen days. One more infringement would see me sent on to Portman Square before the season was out of first gear.

I had more to say: 'I might as well get another ban and take October off, because if I get one later in the season it could rule me out of a big race or a big meeting and that would make me even happier! Every time they've suspended me it's for excessive force, except at Stratford, which was for unreasonable frequency. I'm in a no-win situation and I'm not happy about it.'

Malcolm Wallace, the Jockey Club's director of regulation, went on record as saying that 'The message Christopher Hall was trying to make obviously didn't sink in.' He added, 'I invited Tony to come to Portman Square, just as Frankie Dettori did when he was having trouble with the whip, for a session to look at his style and look at the rules with a view to helping him. As yet he has not taken up the offer.'

There wasn't a doubt in anyone's mind that I'd be arriving at Portman Square sooner rather than later.

Martin Pipe came in with wholehearted support, which I really needed. The day after the Newton Abbot ban he said, 'He did nothing wrong in my eyes or those of the owner. There is not a mark on Coy Debutante. The stewards are doing racing an injustice by banning someone like Tony McCoy for nothing except trying. I don't know what he has done wrong. All the punters love McCoy because he tries and he only hits horses that are responding. That is the key point. If a horse is not responding he puts the whip down.'

In hindsight I would probably have been better off getting a couple of days at this relatively unimportant time of the year. Had I done so, I would have copped my two weeks, then started with a clean slate and begun the totting-up procedure all over again.

I spoke to Martin about it and he said publicly, 'The fact that Tony could even think about deliberately getting one more ban to trigger a long suspension now, rather than later in the season, proves that the rules are wrong. To penalize someone for trying can't be right.'

I've always tried to play fair and decided not to manufacture a suspension, so I didn't fall foul of the stewards again until 9 November at Fontwell. Quite simply, it could hardly have come at a worse time outside the Cheltenham Festival or Aintree. The season proper was in full swing and, to make things even more galling, I was helping the authorities by riding with a new foam-covered whip, which was deemed to be less strenuous on horses.

Bamapour, trained by Martin, was no superstar. That said, he was 2–1 second favourite for the claiming hurdle and I had a duty to the horse's connections and the betting public. Bamapour was a horse who knew a trick or two himself and I caught him and the opposition out when kicking clear, three flights from home. Had I waited we would have been beaten; as it was I had to be firm with Bamapour to make sure he held on to his advantage. From being ten lengths clear on the home turn we had just three-quarters of a length to spare over Keep Me In Mind at the line.

It was my seventieth win of the season, and although it was a modest race, I get real pleasure out of stealing races through tactics and perseverance. This was one of them, and by using the prototype foam-cushioned whip I didn't see how I could have broken any rules. A call to the stewards' room shattered that illusion.

I stated my case but the stewards were set. Despite using a whip designed not to hurt a horse I had used it, according to them, too frequently. I was now to be dealt with in a fresh hearing at a higher court at Portman Square, where the punishment would be at least fourteen days and possibly more. I hadn't felt such a sense of injustice since I started race-riding and I think it is worth repeating the comments from the British Horseracing Board's official form book concerning my ride on Bamapour.

This was a brilliant performance from McCoy to get the gelding home in front, only for him to incur the displeasure of the stewards and receive a referral to Portman Square over his use of the whip. There is no doubt he was strong on the Flat but the transgression appeared marginal, and he was using the new foam-covered whip which the stewards appeared not to have taken into consideration. McCoy is one of the most talented National Hunt jockeys ever to have graced the scene and to watch him ride is a sight to marvel at. However, with the Rules as they are and in the present climate, he may find it necessary to modify his whip style in order to avoid the wrath of the stewards.

This was my fifth breach of the whip guidelines within twelve months and stewards' secretary Jeremy Ker explained why I was in hot water again: I had hit Bamapour nine times from the last hurdle and 'The first five were forceful.'

On reflection, the cushioned whip wasn't helping me. I felt that I had to bring it down harder to get a response from the horse and explained that I tended to look more forceful when using it. This wasn't the approach the Jockey Club wanted and Malcolm Wallace said, 'The purpose of these whips is not to get jockeys to hit horses harder. The whip is constructed in such a way that it is less likely than the standard whip to injure a horse.'

I can still remember how frustrated I was as I left Fontwell that day. Nowadays I would handle myself differently, but back then I spoke from the heart without, perhaps, letting my brain engage. I said, 'It is a bit embarrassing, really, because I thought I was brilliant on the horse.' It wasn't meant to sound arrogant but that's how it came out and such comments would not have won me many friends at Portman Square. I continued, 'I am not going to go half-way up the run-in, whether it be a claiming hurdle or a Champion Hurdle, and ask myself, "If I don't hit it once more I am going to get beat so do I put my stick down or do I give it another smack?" The only answer is to give it another smack. I certainly don't think I was guilty of using brute force. I am not going to change my whip style and this doesn't put pressure on me to do so; I am just going to have to take my days and get on with it.'

Looking back, I wasn't thinking clearly. The one point I would make now and should have made then is that there isn't a jockey riding who does not have love and respect for horses. It's that affection which makes us want to be jockeys in the first place.

More immediately, I was due at Portman Square to learn my punishment and, like someone who had been found guilty of a civil crime returning for sentencing, I was preparing myself for the worst. The previous season Timmy Murphy had been suspended for twenty days with ten more to be activated if he broke the rules again in the following twelve months. Tom Jenks had been handed twenty-two with five deferred. The date was set for 16 November, a week after the Fontwell incident. I was certain I was looking at three weeks at least, which would rule out the rest of November and part of December. During the following seven days it gnawed at me, sometimes consciously, sometimes not. I was carrying a real sense of injustice and that wasn't the right thing to do. I didn't understand what I was doing wrong and both Martin and I felt I was being victimized.

What I should have been thinking was how I could operate effectively within the rules of the sport. I also had an obligation to those who looked on me as a role model. Even in the relatively short time that I had been involved in racing the game was changing. Being seen to be hard on horses was no longer acceptable, and although I didn't want to admit it at the time, the authorities were right. If I didn't change I'd have to change my job – become a holiday rep.

I wasn't good company that week before the hearing. Slowly, the world just seemed to close in on me until I felt under siege. Fortunately, I can be single-minded to the point of bloody-minded, so I focused on the first major handicap chase of the season. The race in question was the Murphy's Gold Cup over two miles five furlongs at Cheltenham the following Saturday and I was back aboard the ever-improving Cyfor Malta.

There was also another problem bubbling below the surface. By his own high standards, Martin wasn't firing on all cylinders. During the two weeks before the Murphy's in the previous season he had produced sixteen winners from fifty-one runners. This time there had been just four from twenty-two. There had been some pressure lifted when Tamarindo won the amateurs' handicap chase under Ashley Farrant, the first race on the opening day of the meeting. He was our first chase winner for two months. The media put forward various theories, including one about problems with one of the gallops, but Martin said nothing and knew the winners would come. As usual, he was right.

Cyfor Malta had been a well-backed favourite ever since the weights came out for the Murphy's, despite having been raised ten pounds for his impressive win in the John Hughes Chase at Liverpool the previous season. I might have been like a bear with a sore head when I was off a horse but nothing mattered apart from winning once Martin legged me up. Hopefully, I wouldn't need the whip.

On the face of it the statistics were against Cyfor Malta, as no five-year-old had won the race since it was first run in 1960. Despite his youth he was an easy horse to ride, so I tucked him in behind the leaders and had a good view of Graham Bradley taking a heavy fall at the eighth when leading on the previous year's winner Senor El Betrutti. Two fences later I pushed Cyfor Malta ahead and turned the screw on the opposition by going clear on the downhill run to the third last. We had the race in safe keeping from that point and, although he began to idle up the hill, there was never a chance that Simply Dashing would reach us.

A few yards from the line I stood up in the saddle, looked over to the stands and thrust my arm in the air. It was a heady mixture of pent-up frustration and elation. Some observers reckoned I hadn't seen the late rally of Lorcan Wyer on Simply Dashing and was lucky not to get caught – I can assure you I was well aware of it. However, the elation didn't last long and when I was led back towards the winners' enclosure I found it impossible to show any sign of happiness. Two days later I'd be facing the disciplinary committee and I felt everything was against me. A smile never crossed my lips.

I finally cracked when we walked into the winners' enclosure and before I dismounted I raised my whip and threw it into the crowd. A racegoer kindly handed it back to Derek Thompson, the *Channel Four Racing* presenter, and he gave it back to me while I was being interviewed. I hadn't expected to see it again and was a bit sheepish. 'Ah! The whip,' was all I said. When I was pressed as to why I had thrown it into the crowd, I wouldn't answer. I had now cooled down and realized my spontaneous gesture might yet land me in more trouble.

The stewards were unaware of my indiscretion and when it was pointed out to the senior steward's secretary, Patrick Hibbert-Foy, he said, 'We were not aware of the incident until after racing, but I do not condone it and I will be looking at the video of the incident.' It could have landed me in even more hot water, but the stewards were understanding and Mr Hibbert-Foy called me out of the changing room and gave me an unofficial warning. He said the stewards understood the pressure I was under and that on this occasion nothing would be done. However, if I made such a gesture again I could expect to be in trouble. Nothing further was said on the subject and I was thankful for that.

I was thankful, too, that Graham Bradley escaped serious injury. We'd thought he had fractured his pelvis but he was discharged from hospital and rode the following day. In the future he would deputize for me on several occasions, for example, when I could not attend the awards dinner at Cheltenham after racing on the Saturday night of the Murphy's. This was always because I had a light weight to do on the Sunday card, but this year was different. I received the champion jockey's award from Jack Dowdeswell, the oldest living champion, who won his title in 1946–7. Mr Dowdeswell was a grand advertisement for the life of a jump jockey and, despite having had his collar-bones removed so that they didn't break when he fell, he looked extremely well. His presence was a timely reminder of how much the sport had moved on in half a century. His winning total was fifty-eight and came in the same season that Sir Gordon Richards achieved the all-time record of 269 winners in a season on the Flat. I may have ridden nearly two hundred winners more than Mr Dowdeswell to register a new record for jumping winners in a season, but I was certain that each one of his fifty-eight was as hard fought as any of mine.

I managed a winner on Sunday, on Capenwray for Jeff King in the Food Brokers' Handicap Chase, but immediately the meeting finished my mind centred on the Jockey Club inquiry the following day.

Through either self-delusion or pig-headedness I still could not accept that I had been in the wrong and I was fortunate on two counts. First, Graham Bradley was a fine horseman and jockey, as well as being my friend. We travelled to the races together most days and he knew the torment I was going through. When I discussed the matter with him he was adamant that I would have to change. A few years earlier, in 1994, he had given career-saving advice to Adrian Maguire when he, too, had been found guilty of whip abuse. Brad took exactly the same line with me as he had with Adrian: 'Listen here, Wee Anthony, you can't keep breaking the rules. The Jockey Club are like the police. If you keep driving at one hundred miles an hour down the motorway every day you are going to get caught. If you keep on doing it the court will take your licence away. That's what'll happen with your jockey's licence if you don't ride within the rules. They aren't going to change. You have to.'

Deep down I knew Brad was right.

The second count on which I was fortunate was the press coverage. It was possible I would be handed a twenty-eight-day suspension and I was very lucky to receive a good and constructive assessment in the media, particularly from the trade's paper, the *Racing Post*. In a page-one opinion piece on the day of my hearing, Brough Scott gave a balanced view of the impending case and my plight. He wrote:

Time for cool heads and common sense. For racing's sake, don't let's make more of a drama out of the crisis that is Tony McCoy . . . To be near Tony McCoy after he won the Murphy's on Saturday was to see someone perilously close to a nervous breakdown. This was no footballer blaming the ref to avoid a suspension. This was a champion who believes he is doomed, who genuinely cannot understand what is going on over his use of the whip.

For if the Jockey Club sticks to its letter of the law when McCoy faces the Disciplinary Committee today it will put on the heavy face, tell him that it is quite unacceptable to break the whip rules five times in a year, hand out a hefty suspension, and then wash its hands while headline-writers gorge on versions of 'Champ lashed for whip sin'. The whole whip furore will break out again. Our racing will have yet another day of shame.

. . . The facts are that British racing has put horse welfare higher on its agenda than have any of the other major racing territories. A lot of work and argument and diplomacy has taken place to make this something of which all parts of the parish should be rightly proud. And it is something that gives the Jockey Club a big opportunity today.

For, at the end of its deliberations, it should be able to say that all the effort has been for the good of everyone: owners, trainers, punters, race fans alike. It should acknowledge the very considerable progress which has been made, not least by the man sat in front of it.

If Tony McCoy really were a heedless butcher he should have no hiding place. But, while an implacably committed competitor, he is both polite and responsible.

. . . But, in this case, it should use common sense to pull our greatest asset back from the brink, where his own unbelievable efforts have taken him. It should show that this is the game with the heart . . .

The article was lengthy and well judged and it gave me heart as I read and reread it on the journey to Portman Square, accompanied by Michael Caulfield who holds the Jockeys' Association together. But I was convinced I would get a month out.

I was happy to be proved wrong and came away with a fourteen-day suspension. Four days would be added to that if I broke the rules again within six months. I took the view that there was no point in trying to defend the indefensible and that the Jockey Club were doing everything within their power to make the whip user-friendly. I admitted that I had broken the rules at Fontwell but was fortunate that Christopher Hall chaired the inquiry.

Mr Hall had gone out of his way to talk to me informally and impress on me just how vital it was that I got things right. He also knew that I had tried hard to adapt and that I was genuinely confused and frustrated. I am sure this is why I was treated with relative leniency, but there were certain conditions to go along with my suspension. I would undergo further tuition with Paul Barton and also attend the British Racing School at Newmarket for a day.

I would have done anything to get things right and said so as I left Jockey Club headquarters. 'It was a very fair hearing and hopefully this will be the last you will see of me at Portman Square for a while. I will come back as keen to win as ever, hopefully without committing any breaches of the rules. I will do my best to keep within the guidelines.'

The suspension cost me dear financially. In the corresponding period over the previous three years I had steadily won more prize money, moving up from £50,381 in 1995 to £67,169 the following year to £94,789 in 1997. I was due back on 4 December but would miss the Hennessy Gold Cup at Newbury, which was the intended target for Cyfor Malta. He didn't make it either, having met with a slight setback in training, and in the event I would have been second on David Johnson's Eudipe, who was ridden by Timmy Murphy and was no match for the exciting Teeton Mill.

I took a holiday in Dubai and put everything out of my mind concerning racing, but when I returned I was determined to get the whip problem sorted out. It was a bit of a media circus when I arrived at Newmarket on Monday 30 November, but the three-hour session I had with Paul Barton and Robert Sidebottom, the school instructor, was private. The point was made that this was a coaching session and not me going back to school as the papers liked to put it. In turn, I made it clear that I wanted to get my whip action and its application right.

I worked out on the mechanical horse but it just wasn't me. I had to go through it and try, but I never thought I was going to learn much from it. I was made aware of the three problem areas. The first was frequency, the second was the degree of force, and the third was where the blows landed.

The suggestion was made that I was bringing my whip from above my head and that I should in future bring it round from my side. That would ensure that I would be hitting the horse on the quarters and not on the rib or stifle.

When I spoke to the media afterwards I did my best to be positive and said, 'The instruction was very good and will be beneficial. If it keeps me within the guidelines then it's got to be worth knowing. I don't want anyone to think that I'm trying to hit horses too hard, because I'm not. It's something I've been doing through adrenaline and trying to win. Hopefully, when I change the way it all looks it'll be as effective as it was before.'

However, I knew this was going to cause some serious overhauling and explained, 'It'll definitely take time and it's something I can't immediately think of as soon as I return to riding. I've got to try to win my races first.'

I think Robert Sidebottom thought he would be able to change the way I rode fundamentally. That was impossible. The way he wanted me to use the whip would, in my view, have meant I would be hitting the horse out of rhythm. When you've taught yourself to ride from a young age, as I had, there is no one who can get you to do it differently. It's like a golfer who teaches himself a particular swing when he's young: he can't change it later in life – it's all about rhythm.

I did try what the authorities asked but I couldn't do it. As I had thought, the whip problems did not go away overnight. I was banned for two days at Sandown in January. Eudipe was something of an under-achiever and I had been driving him hard from six furlongs out in the Anthony Mildmay Peter Cazalet Memorial Chase. A mistake at the last by Glitter Isle gave us a chance and I grabbed it, getting the horse home by a hard-fought length. The stewards kept the inquiry going until after racing and came to the conclusion I had hit the horse in the wrong place, behind the ribs and before the hindquarter. The two-day ban triggered the four that had been deferred and I was off for six days. Some bright spark asked if I was going to appeal. 'Six days is enough. The last time I appealed I got more days. I don't want any more so no thanks.'

It is an uncomfortable fact that no matter how badly off you think you are, there is always someone in a worse situation. I never set too much store by statements like that, but the previous day Graham Bradley was arrested in a dawn raid by the Serious Crime Squad and taken to Charing Cross Police Station. When Dave Roberts told me a couple of hours later, what little colour I had in my face drained out.

It was almost a year since the first batch of arrests on alleged race fixing, which had seen Jamie Osborne, Leighton Aspell and Dean Gallagher rounded up. One by one they had been released, but not before racing had been dragged through the front pages under lurid headlines. More were sure to follow now, and my mate was going to be making them. Brad, with the former trainer-turned-TV pundit Charlie Brooks, had been arrested over the running of a horse called Man Mood, whom Brad had pulled up in a two-horse race at Warwick on 5 November 1996 when the horse began choking. The top Flat jockey Ray Cochrane was also arrested at the same time.

It was a sombre weighing room at Ludlow that day and no one was in a joking mood. I rode two winners but couldn't wait to get away and hear news of Brad. The press kept asking for my view and I told them, with total honesty, that I had no doubt concerning my friend's innocence. I did not tell them that I was shortly to begin lodging with Brad and his future wife Amanda.

I hadn't been happy living at Amesbury. The house was fine but it was in the wrong place because I wasn't required to school at Martin's, unless I was due to race in the West Country, and that had been the main reason I'd moved there. I decided to move back to civilization and found some houses under construction at Baydon, just outside Lambourn. The only problem was that they wouldn't be ready for months and I had already had a good offer for the Amesbury house. As soon as I mentioned it to Brad he offered me the spare room at Sparsholt.

Brad has always been looked on as the bad boy of racing ever since he committed the jockey's cardinal sin: he was caught placing a bet at Cartmel in August 1982. From that low point he progressed to being one of the great stylists of jump racing and a man who revelled in the big arenas, like Cheltenham and Liverpool. However, the authorities always kept their eye on him and to many this latest episode was his final comeuppance.

With a conspiracy charge hanging over him there were plenty who questioned the wisdom of me staying under his roof. It never once entered my head not to. I had only to look back to the pat on the shoulder when I needed it as a kid after Richard Dunwoody beat me by a short head on Havin' A Ball at Galway in 1994. There had been plenty more help too, particularly over the previous three months when I was in bits because of what I perceived as persecution over the whip. Of course I was moving in. We were good for each other.

Brad appreciated my show of solidarity and when his mind was not on the charges laid against him he acted as my whip coach. We watched video after video of me riding a finish, then him riding a finish, just as I had done at the British Racing School, except this time I had the master taking me through the moves. We were like a couple of kids going through the motions with the whip, but what he was imparting to me made sense.

I helped him, too. Despite my public face, which I am sometimes told makes Lester Piggott look jovial, I have a dry sense of humour and I could pick Brad up when he was down. His partner Amanda, always known as Bob, was a rock for him too. He admitted later that the faith we showed in him had kept him going during the black days.

However, private shows of solidarity are not enough and I made it my business to be at his side whenever possible. The day after he was bailed was the day of the Mildmay Cazalet at Sandown and Brad rode a winner on Luke Warm at Warwick. He went on riding winners and by 10 March there was still no evidence offered against him. He fully expected the charges to be dropped when he was recalled to Charing Cross, but he was bailed again until 13 April. Later in the day both Ray Cochrane and Dean Gallagher were released with all charges dropped. Brad was mortified and became paranoid that his car was bugged with a tracking device and that his mobile phone calls were being monitored.

It was painful to watch Brad torturing himself at home, away from the public gaze. One plus point was that his whip clinic had worked and I'd stayed free of trouble until I was handed four days for hitting Majadou unnecessarily when we were clear from the last in the Mildmay of Flete at Cheltenham. It annoyed me but had to be put in the right context: the runaway success of Hors La Loi III gave me two at the Festival but Mick FitzGerald took the riding honours with four, including a fully justified win for See More Business in the Gold Cup.

As 13 April arrived even Brad's unquenchable spirit was flagging. The strain was grinding him down and then he received another massive blow. Charlie Brooks was released with all charges dropped, but Brad was charged with stopping Man Mood.

We talked long into the night.

'I'm telling you, Wee Anthony, that this cannot come to court. There isn't a shred of evidence against me. I know that, because I haven't done anything wrong!'

The next day he was granted bail of £15,000 and was due to appear again on 9 June.

That night I did my best to raise his spirits but it was no easy job. The following day he had just one ride, Country Star at Cheltenham, and he had convinced himself it would be his last.

He was due to see the stewards of the Jockey Club the following day and knew that now he had been charged they would certainly take away his licence. 'Even though I know I'm innocent it could take two years for this case to come to court. By the time that's over I'll be too old to come back.'

I drove Brad and Bob to Cheltenham that day and made sure I was photographed arriving with him and that I was with him when he came out for what might be his last ride. The rest of the lads made a path for him to the paddock and I don't think any of us ever wanted more to see one of our own win a race.

It was therefore typical of Brad's luck at that time that Country Star was going like a winner when he fell four out and was put down. Brad said goodbye to everyone, convinced that he would never come back to Cheltenham as a jockey. There weren't many laughs on the home journey.

He was right about the outcome of his appearance at Portman Square the next day: his licence was duly withdrawn.

It seemed strange leaving the house to go racing each day without Brad, but life goes on. When I got back at night we'd go through the videos of that afternoon's racing but it was a hard time.

The season finished on 31 May and the final winner could not have been better. Auetaler was the first horse Brad had bought for our friends from Liverpool FC, Robbie Fowler and Steve McManaman. His long odds-on win in the two-mile novice hurdle at Uttoxeter was his fourth of the season and the most welcome. It gave me my fourth title, although with a depleted total of 186 winners, my lowest since I first won the championship.

There was no jump racing on 7 June and we were drinking tea and planning a round of golf when the phone rang. Brad answered it. After a few seconds his face creased and he ran round the room screaming. It was his solicitor, Paul Rexstrew: all charges had been dropped through insufficient evidence. It was a wonderful moment.

My new house at Baydon had been ready for some time but I could not have left Brad's house until he had been cleared. How would that have looked? Now I could walk away knowing we had both been good for each other.

I thought I had just about got the whip sorted out. Naturally, I was annoyed by a two-day suspension at Taunton on the Monday of Cheltenham week and the four-day ban on Majadou at Cheltenham, but overall I felt I was getting things right and didn't get another suspension all season.

However, there's never room for complacency in this profession and the following August I found myself spinning from one side of the rule book to the other. Now, I am the first to agree that there have been times when I thought I should have been done and wasn't, and vice versa. So when I was done for four days at Bangor for unreasonable force, then handed three days for easing a beaten horse at Worcester the following day I didn't know where I was heading.

I had a real sense of injustice over my win on Picasso's Heritage at Bangor. She had never won a race before and I hit her four times. I asked the stewards' secretary how the stewards knew I had been too hard and was told the filly had been marked. Luckily for me there is always a camera in Martin Pipe's horse-box so that pictures of injuries can be taken on the spot.

I asked the veterinary officer if it would be all right to take pictures of the marks.

'There aren't any marks.'

I went back to the stewards' secretary. 'The vet says there aren't any marks on that filly, so why have I been suspended?'

There was a switch of emphasis: 'It doesn't matter if she was marked or not. You hit her too hard.'

That was that, then. No point in wasting breath.

The next day was a double stint, involving just one ride at Worcester in the first race, Galix, before making the long journey across country to Market Rasen in Lincolnshire for two rides at the evening meeting. I should have left the day shift alone.

Galix, trained by Martin, started 9–4 favourite for the selling hurdle, but after being up with the pace and leading briefly she began to weaken after the third last. She was legless when she made a mistake at the last and I virtually pulled her up on the Flat so that she didn't finish distressed. We were beaten around forty-seven lengths, but the stewards' secretary said I hadn't ridden out to get the best possible placing because two horses had passed me on the run-in. I was handed three days off and although they would not count in my whip total the meter was running towards another lengthy suspension just as the season was beginning to build.

But it wasn't all doom because I felt, at last, that I was getting the situation under control. I didn't fall foul of the stewards until seven months later. Over time, I had begun to incorporate the changes that Brad had recommended during my stay. He encouraged me to use my whip in the backhand position when I began to push a horse. This meant that my hand was completely around the handle with the flap pointing downwards. The opposite, when the whip is in the forehand position, means that the flap is pointing forwards or up. This induces a wider arc, leaving the possibility the whip will land in the wrong place.

On reflection I put those whip problems down to exuberance and ignorance. Since I first began riding I had had a fear of getting beaten in a finish, and people saying I wasn't strong enough when it mattered. I had got it into my head that whether I was tactically good or not, I would be as strong as I could in rhythm with a horse. It had just snowballed. I'd got to a stage where I couldn't accept being beaten. It was partly excusable when I was young. Back then I didn't always know that I would get another chance on the horse, but as I grew older and more established it was inexcusable.

No one knows how hard I worked to get the whip right, but I was and am conscious that young riders will copy me. I often watch old videos and think how moderate I looked as a conditional. Even when I won the Gold Cup and Champion Hurdle there was still a lot to work on.

It is vital that a jockey keeps analysing what he does and why. Now I consider I'm much tidier than I was in performances of that time: I wasn't getting behind horses as much as I should have done and wasn't as tight as I could have been.

It's also a fact that you get physically stronger and much more aware tactically. You get to know the tracks better the more you ride them and where to save a vital length. It's the same when the going changes: you have to adapt, change tactics and use your brain. No jockey is going to get to the top by brute force alone.

Martin Pipe had retained the trainers' championship in 1998–9 but it was mighty close. Paul Nicholls had sent out See More Business to win the Cheltenham Gold Cup and gain some consolation for his acrimonious exit the previous year. He also won the Queen Mother Champion Chase with Call Equiname, and when the Scottish National meeting came round in April Paul looked certain to take the championship with a £96,000 prize money lead over Martin. The bookmakers stopped betting on the outcome, but it is at times like this that Martin Pipe is most dangerous.

Martin scoured the *Programme Book* for races that fitted those horses still in work and on the penultimate day of the season, the May Bank Holiday, he made 124 entries – twenty-two in one race! He ended up with twenty-six runners in eighteen races over six meetings and completed an eight-timer at accumulative odds of 10,460–1. It was a close-run thing, but Martin came away with his ninth and most hard-won championship.

On the jockey front I was reminded that the breaking of records isn't my exclusive province. Thanks to Paul Nicholls, Joe Tizzard beat my previous best by winning the conditional jockeys' championship with ninety-one.

12. The Crying Game

My problems with the whip weren't quite a thing of the past but it wasn't until Leicester on 16 February that I was up before the stewards again. It was seven months since my last infringement and this time I got two days for excessive use of the whip on Ciara's Prince, trained by Jonjo O'Neill. I was just three winners short of beating my own record for the fastest double century. That would come two days later when Mr Cool won the opening novice hurdle at Sandown. This time I'd done it ten days earlier.

However, I had set a record that meant more to me at Cheltenham on 11 December, two months earlier, when Majadou, trained by Martin Pipe, jumped like a buck and made all to win the Wragge & Co. Handicap Chase. This followed a first race win on Martin's Heros Fatal and gave me a career total of 1,000 winners in England and Ireland.

As the media closed in on me during the preceding week, I couldn't ride a winner for love or money. Having lost fancied rides when Ayr was abandoned on the Monday, I was beaten on a 2–9 shot at Fontwell, then whacked my head when Bramblehill Duke refused at the last. I got a dose of flu before Leicester on the Wednesday, so I gave up after one ride and went home to bed.

I still felt rough when I turned up at Ludlow the next day and was beaten on two more odds-on shots. When Miss Fara won at Cheltenham on the Friday I breathed a sigh of relief. You know winners will come but, no matter how many you ride, self-doubt can creep into your mind. The following day Majadou put me into the record books and I felt proud to become the fifth jockey to have achieved the feat. I was by far the youngest and had done it in little over half the time it took Peter Scudamore. When I looked back later that night it seemed like a lifetime.

The two-day ban after Ciara's Prince was frustrating because it proved costly and highlighted how, in racing justice, the punishment does not fit the crime. It goes without saying that if I had known the outcome I wouldn't have ridden the horse, but Jonjo had been holding on for two weeks, changing entries, so I could ride. I knew the horse was a little monkey and Jonjo had refitted blinkers, but the gelding was far from happy and I was at him throughout the final circuit. Although we managed to win by eleven lengths, I never felt at any stage that I could ease up.

However, the stewards reckoned I had been too severe. Their secretary, Geoffrey Forster, explained later, 'The stewards considered that McCoy had made contact with his stick twenty times in the final circuit.' A circuit at Leicester is over a mile and a half long. He continued, 'The stewards realized that it was a difficult animal, but they considered that McCoy's use of the whip was just beyond the level of acceptability, and imposed the minimum penalty.'

That minimum penalty had maximum effect and I kept my mouth in check when questioned by the press: 'I don't want to make any comment about it – it just wouldn't be a good idea.' But I was fuming: I didn't think I had broken the rules at any stage during the race. If I had thought that, I would have put the whip down: I certainly wouldn't have risked being ruled out of the big pre-Cheltenham meeting at Kempton on 25 and 26 February, where I was due to ride Gloria Victis in the £43,000 Racing Post Handicap Chase. I honestly thought I had won a race I should have lost. What was more, Jonjo was over the moon about the ride – and he knows more about horses than any panel of stewards you care to mention.

Believe me when I tell you that in cases like this the money is secondary. Yes, it's nice and we all need it, but that's not why you become a jump jockey. No one can tell me that the lads who scrape a living working in a yard and riding three winners a season are doing it for the financial benefits.

Gloria Victis was the best staying novice chaser I had ever sat on and I didn't want to watch someone else winning on him. The way was open for him to go right to the top. He was another of

Martin's good buys from France, but the improvement he showed when moving to Pond House was exceptional.

He had been bought by one of Martin's staunchest owners, Terry Neill, having been placed in two runs over hurdles and one over fences. Once he'd been through a thorough processing at Pond House Martin soon realized that he had bought something special. There was no point running him at a small track: this was a horse going places and Martin chose the Fulke Walwyn Chase over two and a half miles at Newbury on 27 November, the race that kicked off the Hennessy Cognac Gold Cup card. Although I didn't have a ride in the big one I did ride two other good-class winners for Martin that day, on the moody staying hurdler Deano's Beeno and the novice hurdler Far Cry. But it was Gloria Victis who etched himself on my memory after making all and beating the favourite Windross by fourteen lengths.

Two horses who were well beaten that day went on to underline the value of the race. Later in the season fourth-placed Beau won the Reynoldstown Chase, the Great Yorkshire Chase and the Whitbread Gold Cup. Gingembre, who was fifth, won the Future Champion Novices' Chase at Ayr and would return there the following season to take the Scottish National. Neither saw which way Gloria Victis went once I kicked him clear from the seventh and, despite a tendency to jump right and a blunder at the eleventh, he sailed home.

When you ride as Martin Pipe's first jockey there are certain responsibilities you must undertake and one of the most important is doing a report on each horse you ride for the yard. This started when Peter Scudamore was riding for him: he would give Martin a written assessment of a horse and what might be achievable in the future. Before Scu arrived, Martin did the reports himself: 'What jockeys told me after a race I'd put on tape and have it transcribed. It's impossible to remember everything. All the little things are important.'

Of Scu, Martin said, 'He knew what was going on in a race and would be able to tell you about other horses – this one made a noise two out, that one blew up three out. The winner beat us and

. This can be a dirty game.

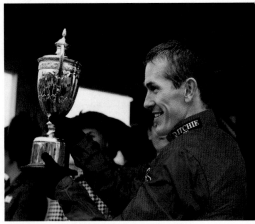

31. Holding the Thomas Pink/Murphy's Gold Cup after winning it for the third time following the success of Shooting Light in 2001.

30. Riding the fastest 100 in a season. Present Bleu wins the claiming hurdle at Plumpton, 17 September 2001.

32. Trying to turn victory into defeat. I'm almost unseated at the last on Westender in the Rehabilitation of Racehorses Handicap Hurdle at Cheltenham, November 2001.

33. Walking back past the stands after the blunder on Westender, and I can't bear to look at the replay on the big screen.

34. On days like this I'd pay to do the job. Taking the final open ditch on Shooting Light in the Tote Silver Cup Chase on 22 December 2001, the day I rode five out of six winners at Ascot.

35. A day I'd rather forget. Bow Strada fires me into the ground at the last in the novice hurdle at Newbury, 9 January 2002.

36. I know what a boxer feels like when he's trying to beat the count. Feeling the effects of the fall from Bow Strada – but things got worse.

37. (right) The padding and plaster cover the stitches that followed the third and final fall of that bad day at Newbury when Baclama buried me at the seventh fence.

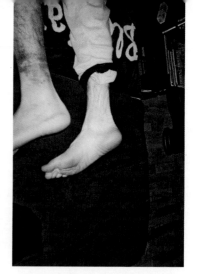

38. Bum deal. The massive haematoma which resulted from a real kicking at the feet of Image De Marque II at Kempton Park, 29 January 2001.

39. Unlucky break. My left ankle is badly swollen after I'd broken two bones in it twisting awkwardly playing football.

40. Thinking it through.

41. (*right*) The only bright spot in a miserable 2002 Cheltenham Festival. Royal Auclair clears the last to win the Cathcart Chase.

42. Going out for the Champion Hurdle on Valiramix. I honestly thought he could become one of the hurdling greats. His death hung over the rest of the season.

43. The smile on my face says it all. I've just equalled Sir Gordon Richards's record of 269 winners in a season on Shepherds Rest in the Barford Handicap Chase at Warwick.

44. Valfonic has earned himself a place in racing history by becoming my 270th winner of the season in the Leek Wooton Novices Handicap Hurdle, Warwick, 2 April 2002.

45. As good as it gets. Spraying the crowd Grand Prix-style after beating Sir Gordon Richards's 1947 record number of winners in a season.

46. I'm behind you, Tiger. Relaxing on the golf course — a lot safer than playing football.

47. Getting the hump at Ascot. I don't think Lawrence of Arabia has got much to worry about, but how many winners did he ride in a season?

48. The perfect end to a wonderful season. Bounce Back romps home in the Attheraces Gold Cup, the last big race of the season at Sandown Park, 27 April 2002.

49. Receiving the Belfast Telegraph Sportsman of the Year award for the second time from my fellow countryman, the top flat jockey John Reid, himself a previous winner of the award.

50. No one laughs louder at Luke Harvey's jokes than Luke himself. On stage at the annual Lesters Awards in London with my former weighing-room colleague turned television presenter.

51. Celebrating winning the title for the first time. Dad is handling it well but it is a bit too much for Ma!

52. The clan McCoy assembled for the wedding of my sister Anne-Marie to Brian McCormack. From left to right, Ma, Colm, Brian, me, Anne-Marie, Peadar, Jane (*front*), Kelly, Roisin. Ma was looking forward to the celebrations more than having her

54. Never kiss strange men. My godchild Seaneen, daughter of brother Colm, looks none too sure about kissing the Godfather.

53. With my long-term girlfriend Chanelle.

56. Caught with my trousers down at Kempton thanks to Image De Marque II. This shot did the rounds on the internet.

55. Classified, who won six out of seven in my record-breaking season.

57. Putting Best Mate through his paces on Henrietta Knight's gallops. I should have won the King George VI Chase on him and he justified my conviction in the Cheltenham Gold Cup – but I wasn't on him.

was only half fit, so you don't want to take that on again. That way you knew about your own horse and the opposition for another day. Take all these things into account and they might make you a winner next time.'

All the lads who ride regularly for the yard do the reports, but Scu was always the one held up as the prime example: 'I've got some very good reports from Scu that I've kept and might publish one day. He could ride one in August and say, "This one's a bit special." Later, when it had run up a sequence of winning seven from seven I'd be happy to tell him he was spot on.'

What Martin didn't appreciate was that it might have been a bit easier for Scu than me to put his thoughts down on paper. He was educated to a high academic standard and, as you know, I wasn't too special at the three Rs, unless they were Riding, Racing and the Racecourse.

I might not have been that good to begin with and Martin observed: 'You say you ride a lot of yaks but then all the yaks win! You said you were riding a yak in the Gold Cup but it still won.' Just imagine what he'd have said if he had trained Mr Mulligan.

However, I soon accepted that reports were part and parcel of the job and when I get home in the evening it is one of the first things I do. I'm lucky that in January 2000 I took on Gee Armytage as my personal assistant: she writes them out as I dictate them. I couldn't operate without Gee organizing my diary. Dave Roberts handles the rides but Gee arranges everything else.

Because of the pressures of the job, plus keeping my weight down, it is difficult for me to have a long-term relationship with a woman. I have tried but it isn't fair to either of us. Gee knows that. She was one of the most successful women jump jockeys ever and, thanks to Gee A's win in the 1987 Mildmay of Flete, remains the only one to have won as a professional at the Cheltenham Festival.

When she arrives in the morning I'm often sweating in the bath and I never want to talk to anyone while I'm doing that. Time is usually tight and we keep our exchanges to a minimum. When I get back at night we get down to answering letters and requests. This is something I have always taken seriously: If I can help a good cause I will. I have been granted a good life and career, and it is the least I can do.

Then it's the reports. Martin says I'm getting better and I don't think I underestimated the potential of Gloria Victis, although I was guarded in my assessment. 'Moved to post very well and was good in the race. Went a good gallop and stayed, going well.' My recommendations were: 'Obviously better right-handed, could go back to two miles.'

Because of the pace he showed over two and a half miles we dropped him down to two for the Grade Two Henry VIII Novices' Chase at Sandown a week later. The distance proved too short and the race might have come a bit soon after Newbury, but Gloria Victis still ran well, leading to the second last until passed by the specialist two-miler Decoupage. He won by an impressive five lengths as Gloria Victis failed by only a head to hold Wakeel for second. My report read: 'Went a good gallop, just stayed on one pace from three out. Definitely needs further. Might want blinkers.'

Martin now moved the horse up to three miles for one of the most important staying novice chases of the season, the Grade One Feltham Novices' Chase at Kempton's Christmas meeting.

He went off the 2–1 favourite and the pace was quick. It wasn't until the tenth that I sent him on and despite clouting the fourteenth nothing could get near us from four out. He won by an easy eighteen lengths from Zafarabad. Perhaps the most significant aspect of his win was the time: despite winning easily Gloria Victis clocked a marginally faster time than the Gold Cup winner See More Business achieved in the following King George VI Chase.

When the year turned he would be six, three years younger than See More Business. The chasing world was now at Gloria Victis's feet and my report was short but very sweet: 'Jumped well, went a good gallop. Very impressive.' Not many horses get that.

Martin has always favoured making the most of the relatively lenient handicap marks that can be handed to novice hurdlers and chasers. Providing they are clever enough to look after themselves he will pitch them into valuable but competitive handicaps.

He had no doubts about sending Gloria Victis for the *Racing Post*

Chase. In this first handicap he was allotted a rating of 151. Martin wasn't complaining – and neither was I, until that two-day ban put me on the sidelines.

Directly Martin knew I'd be out of action he went through to Dave Roberts and secured Richard Johnson for the ride. I spoke to Dickie about Gloria Victis and said I thought he was a Gold Cup horse, although I didn't know if it would be this year. I knew right enough that I'd be back on the horse at Cheltenham in whichever race was chosen, but it didn't ease my frustration, so I went to Madrid for a couple of days with Graham Bradley to visit Steve McManaman.

My friendship with Steve and Robbie Fowler had grown since that first encounter after the postponed Grand National. Brad had bought some good horses at bargain prices from Germany for the lads, including Auetaler, a decent handicap hurdler, and their latest star, Seebald. Our relative work commitments meant we didn't meet that often but I spoke to them three or four times a week. When Steve found out I would be kicking my heels for a few days, he invited Brad and me out and I couldn't wait to go: I wouldn't have to look at Gloria Victis winning. What was more, Steve's club, Real Madrid, were due to play Barcelona that weekend. It would be a massive game in La Liga, and we'd have two of the best seats in the Bernebau.

I could see why Steve had settled into the Spanish lifestyle. In Spain everything happens later in the day. The match, which kicked off considerably later in the evening than an English fixture, went the right way with Real beating their arch-rivals. I'm much better at night than in the morning and it suited me fine that we didn't sit down to eat at a nearby restaurant until after eleven. Then it was off to a club where we met up with some of the other players. The only problem was that they couldn't understand us and vice versa. It didn't matter and we had a cracking night. I got into bed at around three thirty and slept like a baby.

I returned on Monday and that evening settled down to watch the racing I'd missed. I don't know what Dickie Johnson put in his report to Martin, or even if he did one, but what I saw was a truly brilliant performance by Gloria Victis. He was giving weight to all twelve opponents yet none of them, including the following season's Grand National winner Red Marauder, could get near him. Dickie let him quicken clear from the thirteenth fence and he ran home an easy ten-length winner over Marlborough, who received sixteen pounds and would go on to frank the form by beating Beau in the William Hill National Hunt Handicap Chase at Cheltenham the following month.

It gradually dawned on me that I'd missed something really special as I watched the replay again and again, analysing a performance that was impossible to fault. Still, I could console myself that, barring injury, I'd be on him at Cheltenham. And on that evidence he would be a penalty kick in the Royal & Sun Alliance Novices' Chase.

With just two and a half weeks to Cheltenham, it turned out that it wasn't going to be quite so straightforward. The Monday after the Kempton stroll, the *Racing Post* produced a front page with the headline 'Go for it, Martin. Why Pipe's sensational *Racing Post* Chase winner Gloria Victis must take his chance in the Gold Cup.'

Senior writer Alastair Down wrote a lengthy article on why Gloria Victis should run in the Gold Cup. He finished, 'Go for it, Martin. In twelve months' time the Chinese could be here, your brain may finally have been curdled from mobile-phone abuse and I could be pushing up the snowdrops. Run the thing. You want to see it, I want to see it – everyone wants to see it.'

But there was still the concern about the horse's tendency to jump right, and although the British Horseracing Board handicapper, Phil Smith, raised Gloria Victis fifteen pounds for his Kempton win it left him with eleven pounds to find with the best staying chaser and reigning Cheltenham Gold Cup winner See More Business.

Dickie was in no doubt about the horse's potential and said, 'He's a very, very good horse – definitely the best I've ridden this season and probably the best I've ever ridden. To win the race like that was incredible. If he runs in the Gold Cup he'll give See More Business a run for his money.'

There was another angle. I'd been offered the ride on Looks Like Trouble in the Gold Cup. His trainer, Noel Chance, had trained my 1997 winner Mr Mulligan and was casting around for a rider after sacking Norman Williamson in controversial circumstances.

Norman, a good friend of mine, had ridden Looks Like Trouble to win the Grade Two Pillar Chase at Cheltenham on 29 January by a distance. Subsequently, Noel and Looks Like Trouble's owner, Tim Collins, said they weren't happy with Norman's riding of the horse in the King George VI Chase at Kempton on Boxing Day, when he was pulled up. It was a sickener for Norman who had felt he had done the best thing for the horse when he wasn't travelling on the soft ground.

Knowing both parties well, I stayed out of things. When the ride was offered I told Noel I would ride Looks Like Trouble, providing Gloria Victis went for the Sun Alliance. The racing media focused on the pluses and minuses of running a six-year-old in the Gold Cup. I simply said I was happy whichever race he ran in.

On Thursday 2 March, I was riding at Taunton, so I went early and called in at Martin's to discuss the running plans for Cheltenham. When it came to the Gold Cup it was between Martin and Terry. I said, 'I'll be happy to ride him in either race. It would be easier for me if he went for the Sun Alliance but I genuinely think he would win either.'

There was still no decision eleven days before the Gold Cup, when I went to Newbury on Sunday morning to put Looks Like Trouble through his paces in a two-mile gallop with the Kim Muir Chase entrant Stepaside Boy. Unlike the last time I had ridden work for Noel at Newbury before a Gold Cup, the disastrous Mr Mulligan gallop, this went smoothly. Looks Like Trouble swept away from his workmate and I told Noel and Tim that I'd ride if Gloria Victis wasn't in the field.

Crunch time came on 7 March. Terry Neill went to Pond House to make the big decision. They sat in front of Martin's multi-screen display and watched videos of all Gloria Victis's races in England. They tossed the options back and forth and finally decided on the big one. I was riding at Exeter that afternoon but Martin called me and told me of their decision. That was fine by me: I had every bit as much faith in Gloria Victis as they had.

There was the carrot of a £50,000 bonus on offer for winning both the *Racing Post* Chase and the Gold Cup, but this was a secondary consideration and Martin explained his and Terry's reasoning at the time: 'We came to the same decision. You might only get one chance at the Gold Cup, and Gloria Victis is very fit and well. He's improving and deserves to take his chance. It's always a worry when a horse hasn't been to Cheltenham before, but that applies to any race he runs in at the meeting.'

This was a big call for Martin and his best chance of winning the Gold Cup. The nearest he'd been to it before was with Rushing Wild, who finished two lengths second to Jodami in 1993.

Terry's nerves were strung out. 'If he were a Flat horse we might have a year, but with a jumper you never know what might happen.'

Terry never spoke a truer word.

Noel and Tim Collins went searching for a jockey and decided Dickie Johnson was the right man. He had ridden Mr Mulligan in his novice season then lost him to me. The debt was about to be repaid in full.

When Cheltenham opened I had taken my pick of Martin's blanket entry and he and owner Peter Deal had let me off any obligations I felt towards riding Make A Stand in the Champion Hurdle. The old horse was having his first run since going lame at Aintree three years earlier and was a 33–1 chance, while Dermot Weld had asked me to ride second favourite Stage Affair.

That ride helped to make me favourite to be champion jockey at the meetings, but Istabraq never managed to give Charlie Swan an anxious moment as he powered to his third consecutive Champion Hurdle. At the end of the first day I didn't have a placed horse, let alone a winner. I travelled back to Baydon that evening and had a quiet supper with Norman Williamson at the Queen's Arms, East Garston. We'd both had a poor day and tried to convince ourselves that a better one might just be round the corner.

Norman duly won the first race on Wednesday, the Royal & Sun

Alliance Novices' Hurdle. Monsignor, trained by Mark Pitman, was regarded as a banker and couldn't be faulted. It was followed by the Queen Mother Champion Chase. This was the race above any other that I wanted to win, including the Gold Cup, the Champion Hurdle and the Grand National. I can recall all the great two-mile chasers. I'd even ridden one of them, Viking Flagship, but that had been at Aintree.

Two miles jumping fences at ferocious speed. It's all got to go right, no room for mistakes. You've got to have everything. It's the supreme test for a chaser and quite often produces the best race of the meeting. In Edredon Bleu I knew I had my ideal two-mile chaser. He'd become my ride two seasons earlier when we'd won the Grand Annual, before being beaten fair and square by Call Equiname, in the previous year's Champion Chase. In the current season he'd managed only one win, which came under Jim Culloty at Huntingdon when I was on duty at Ascot. However, at the Festival, the ground was riding very quick and those were his ideal conditions. I had complete faith in him. I didn't worry coming down the hill at Cheltenham flat out at thirty-eight miles an hour – it never occurred to me that this fella might not take off. If it was physically possible for him to stand off and jump he would.

I was right that the Queen Mother Champion Chase produced the best finish of Cheltenham 2000. With the ground riding so quick I sent Edredon ahead at the second and really turned up the pressure running down the hill to three out. This decision probably won us the race. It put the jumping of our two biggest opponents, Direct Route and Flagship Uberalles, under pressure and they were both sticky. Edredon finally shook off Flagship Uberalles at the last, but Norman fired Direct Route upsides and fifty yards after the fence they went a head up. Nine times out of ten that's the end at Cheltenham, but I knew Edredon Bleu would carry on giving. He didn't let me down.

With seventy-five yards remaining, the knot in Norman's reins unwound. At that precise moment Edredon battled alongside and the pair were locked for the final strides. I wasn't sure if we'd won but thought we might just have nicked it. Norman had his head down, but I honestly do not believe that the loosening of his reins made the difference to winning and losing. I must have watched the race twenty or more times since, including the head on, and both horses never changed their stride pattern.

The presentation by the Queen Mother was a wonderful bonus and I left the course in a considerably brighter mood than twenty-four hours earlier.

The front page of the *Racing Post* summed it up: 'Pure Gold.' It certainly looked the race that had everything: previous winner See More Business, the Festival regular Florida Pearl, bang-in-form Looks Like Trouble and the rising star Gloria Victis.

There's always apprehension before a big race but there was a little more this time because we were pitching in a precocious young horse with some seasoned older hands. Still, we weren't trying to achieve the impossible. The record books said that the legendary Golden Miller was only five when winning his first of five Gold Cups, and Fortina, Mont Tremblant and Mill House had all won Gold Cups at the same age as Gloria Victis, six. Dawn Run had managed to win the Gold Cup with just four chases behind her, two fewer than our lad.

I went through the handshaking and good lucks, and Gloria Victis stayed calm in the parade. Then, once the tape rose, he wanted to eat his fences. There was nothing I could do to stop him going right at them, but although it was a championship contest he didn't lose much ground and we held the advantage until the tenth when See More Business took over. By the thirteenth we had retaken the lead, and swinging down the hill after the fourth last I was more than happy. I felt that I'd gone pretty steady and we were always travelling comfortably, three or four lengths clear. I've looked at that video fifty or more times since and every one of the horses behind him looks stone cold. At that stage he was going to be the youngest Gold Cup winner since 1963. Then the dream turned black.

I began to push him and he didn't pick up as I thought he would, and that allowed the others to close up and press us going to the second last. I don't know to this day whether something went wrong with him in the previous five hundred yards. What I do know is that I don't agree with those who said he had come to the end of his tether. On reflection, it didn't look as though he would keep galloping the way he normally did after going so easily. That makes me think he might have been feeling something. The Gold Cup ends at the winning post and whether Gloria Victis would have won or not is something we will never know.

I was thrown clear as he crashed to the ground two from home. I didn't realize how badly he was injured until I picked myself up and saw that he was having trouble regaining his feet. In the background I could hear the commentary being drowned by the 50,000-plus crowd but it didn't register. I couldn't have cared who won – and I still don't: the fact that I could have been on the winner, Looks Like Trouble, never crosses my mind.

I was helped into the ambulance but I knew as I left that Gloria Victis was in a pretty bad way. I was just hoping he'd be saved.

The ambulance room is at the back of the weighing room and I hadn't been in there many minutes when Martin's son David came in. I knew it was bad news. He had tears in his eyes and was in bits. 'They've had to put him down.'

I pulled a plastic curtain around myself and sat alone on a bed. Then the tears came and I cried for fifteen minutes. Sometimes when a horse is killed it's difficult to know who the tears are for. Sometimes they are selfishly for yourself, at others for the owner, trainer or lad who has devoted part of his or her life to the horse. Sometimes it's the frustration of the races that wouldn't now be won. But this time I knew who I was crying for: it was Gloria Victis. Not only was he talented and special, he was a likeable horse who would do anything for you. He had one of those wonderful heads and you only had to look into his eye to know that he'd go all the way for you. If you had to go to war then you'd take that fellow with you. You tend to look differently at less talented horses. He wasn't the best-looking, but he was the perfect jumping racehorse. You looked at him and you could sense him telling you that he was up for it. 'Let's go!'

Terry Neill was in a state of shock and Martin was devastated. I

was in another place and another time. The frame of mind I
was in, I shouldn't have ridden in the next race. There was a
sixty-five-minute gap but I can't even remember what I said to
Martin before he gave me the leg up on Carandrew in the Grand
Annual Handicap Chase. I just went through the motions and fell
off the horse at the last ditch, the seventh. It wasn't that I didn't
care: I just couldn't see the point of it.

I stayed a short while at the party in the weighing room afterwards, but only because the traffic was so bad. I just wanted to get
home and see no one.

I was lucky that I was at Folkestone the next day. There was
hardly anyone there and no one was paying any attention to how
I was and what I was feeling.

I can only guess at the torment that Terry Neill and Martin went
through. The loss of Gloria Victis affected everyone at Pond House.
His stable was in the covered barn and Martin couldn't bring
himself to put another horse in it for nearly two months. He said
to me, 'Every time I go by that box I think of him. People don't
realize how we take it when we lose a horse. Good or bad, we
wash their eyes, nose and bum out every day. They do live for ever
with someone and you remember the boxes they were in. I'm
lucky that I can fill a box when we lose one – but you never forget.'

The death of Gloria Victis started one of the most heated and
personal exchanges ever seen in the letters column of the *Racing
Post*. The outpouring of bile on Martin, Terry, myself and Alastair
Down, who wrote the initial story begging for Gloria Victis to run
in the Gold Cup, seemed unending. At various times correspon-
dents spoke of 'the disgusting actions of the champion trainer'.
Another spoke of my public statements 'which influenced the
decision to send Gloria Victis to his death'. We were variously
described as 'greedy, impatient and inhumane'. Another considered
that Gloria Victis was 'a Christian thrown to the lions'.

I don't doubt that those letters were written from the heart, but
after reading a few I didn't bother any more. If people wanted to
vent their rage in public that was fine, but I didn't want to read
about it.

Fortunately, the editor Alan Byrne called a halt to the correspondence after a week.

My dismal record in the Grand National continued when I was unseated from Dark Stranger at the third, completing a miserable month for his owner Terry Neill. On a happier note, I confirmed that I could win over those unique fences by taking my second John Hughes Trophy in three years when Northern Starlight beat King's Cherry by a length and a quarter. The winner was the best advert for the saying 'Size doesn't matter.' He was very small for a chaser but as hard as they come. He ate those fences only six days after coming back from looking well beaten to win a valuable handicap chase at Ascot.

For the first time ever the season finished on a high note with the Whitbread Gold Cup meeting at Sandown. Although I came down at the fifteenth on Royal Predica in the big one, I rode my 245th and final winner of the season on Exit Swinger for Martin in the novices' handicap chase. It was a landmark season for Martin: he became the most successful trainer for the number of winners when he passed the 2,988 of Arthur Stephenson. It had taken the legendary 'WA' forty-six seasons, from 1946 to 1992. Martin had passed him in just twenty-five. He also continued his reign as champion trainer, with total prize money of £1,616,791 from 243 winners, plus placed horses. My total was eight off my personal best but there were too many poignant memories in that season for me ever to take winning the title for granted.

Graham Bradley decided to retire, despite my arguments that he was still riding as well, if not better, than ever. It was selfishness on my part: I wanted him travelling with me in the car, lightening those long winter journeys. But there was no chance. He'd had enough, and ours is no game to play half-heartedly. He decided to concentrate on buying good horses from abroad, principally for our great friends Steve McManaman and Robbie Fowler. Fortunately, the good times for the four of us were not far away.

Richard Dunwoody gave best to a recurring shoulder injury and retired. This also left a massive void. They didn't call him 'The Prince' for nothing.

The jockeys gathered at the Hilton Hotel later that year to honour the achievements of Brad, Woody and others like myself who had won Lesters awards through votes cast by our peers. However, I don't think Michael Caulfield of the Jockeys' Association could have summed up better two of the best jump jockeys ever when he said of Graham and Richard, 'When one was coming in from a night out, the other was getting up to ride out in the morning.' They were complete originals.

Much earlier in the season every jump jockey had been given the kind of wake-up call that sets you thinking how cruelly short your career or even your life can be. Scott Taylor had been making a success of his career in the north of England, but it ended abruptly when he fell on Te Akau Dan in a novice chase at Perth on 20 August. He was in intensive care for a long time and has shown courage that would make you weep despite being subsequently confined to a wheelchair.

Throughout the season there were many fund-raising activities and every jump jockey I know felt privileged to be involved, no matter where they were held. When people ask why we stick together the answer is a simple one: we have to look after our own because there, but for the grace of God, go I.

13. It's Not Only Lobsters Who Get Boiled

When I was a kid starting out at Jim Bolger's one of my heroes was the American ace Steve Cauthen. I was also a fan of Mick Kinane – I thought he had the best way of propelling a horse, pushing through with the whole of his body, right from the backbone. But it was Cauthen, the three times British Flat champion, whom I would subsequently find it easiest to identify with. Not for his dedication: Steve would as soon take in a West End show as a Windsor night meeting and that's never been my way – each to his own. However, Steve had a massive battle with his weight and towards the end of his career he needed a bit of notice to ride much below nine stone.

Once I had broken my leg and my weight shot up I had known life was never going to be normal, but when you decide to be a jockey you know that there is going to be plenty of self-denial. Usually there must also be self-inflicted physical and mental abuse along the way, some of which will stretch the mind like a guitar string until, without warning, it snaps. It's the weight. It's always there. You know you've got to fight it and there's no short-cut. Whatever you take in, you've got to work out or boil out.

It is a little-known fact, but one I'm proud of, that never in my career have I once put up any overweight. I'm not sure if many jockeys, apart from the natural lightweights, could say the same. But I have to pay a hefty price to keep that record intact to the extent that I suppress my natural bodyweight of eleven stone ten by at least seventeen pounds.

Diuretics are rightly banned, although they weren't when I was an apprentice and I used them just as the other riders did. However, the putting up of overweight has become a personal thing. It's nothing to do with Martin Pipe. He says he'd rather have me riding a shade heavy than not at all. With me it's a matter of principle: I'd rather not ride than put up two pounds overweight, then come home and have to watch a video of the horse getting beaten by a short head.

You can be sure that if I do ten stone it's for something special in a big handicap and for that reason I'll know well in advance. I don't need more than a week's notice but to do any lighter than ten stone four I need three days and for the minimum I gradually grind it down for a week so that I won't be dying on the day of the race. I begin by eating less and less and sweating in the bath in the morning, in the sauna at the track and again in the bath at night. I might nibble something at the races, then after the last sweat at night I'll probably have a biscuit or a piece of chocolate before I go to sleep. That way I know I'll wake up lighter in the morning than if I've had a meal.

On these wasting days I have a tough regime but it works. I drink a lot of tea with sugar, sometimes with as many as eight or ten spoonfuls. Depending on the weight, I might have a bit of chicken before, during or after racing. I'll eat it with a bit of mayonnaise but never bread and butter. Once I get home, I have some more ultra-sweet tea, get into the bath and nibble some chocolate or a biscuit.

Now, I know any dietitians reading this will be throwing up their hands in horror but I need the energy the sugar gives me to kick-start my sweating. It is no good getting into a bath knackered because you just won't sweat. If I get up at six in the morning and go straight into the bath I won't sweat: to sweat well you need to be wide awake.

When I'm not doing extremely light I might have toast with butter. At the races I'll have the sweet tea, and one of my tricks is to have it boiling hot. That way I don't drink it too quickly. Quite a few of the lads take Coke with ice into the sauna but I usually wait until half an hour after I've got out. Fortunately I never have the urge to eat before racing.

But no matter how firmly you believe you're on top of the weight it's there, like your shadow, and at the start of the 2000–01 season I was at a crisis point. What happened then turned my head inside out. For a few weeks I wondered if it was all worthwhile.

Like most problems in racing it started with a fall. The season was nearly three months old on 23 July when I rode Baron Allfours for John Pickering in the three-mile maiden chase at Southwell.

I'd been taking a few days off here and there, flying off for a bit of sun and golf when Martin didn't look like having many runners and my weight wasn't great. I'd got it down to ride at ten stone eight in the preceding race, but I don't remember much about the third on the card because Baron Allfours buried me at the sixth and I was unconscious for several minutes.

This time there was no argument from me about the mandatory twenty-one days' suspension for concussion. I decided to use the time to my advantage, have a holiday and live normally, sometimes having lunch *and* dinner in the evening. When I got back to looking at my weight I couldn't believe it when the dial on the scales spun round to eleven stone ten. That was the heaviest I've ever been, before or since, and it was a serious wake-up call. I found it easy enough to shift a stone in three days, but the rest just would not come off.

I came back at the scene of my departure, Southwell, on 14 August. My lightest ride was ten stone eleven on Suvertica, who won the novice hurdle for Martin but by then my weight was all over the place. I knew that, despite Martin's back-up, I would have to get down to a regular ten stone four or I could kiss my title goodbye. And make no mistake, even though I'd been champion since 1995–6 I loved my position – and still do. It was getting to me mentally and I decided that desperate times called for desperate measures. I decided bulimia was the answer.

This is self-induced vomiting and some Flat jockeys do it without a second thought. Often at American tracks there are toilets specifi- cally for the use of 'flippers', as they're called. I had done it when I was an apprentice and trying to do very light, but I was no good at it. Now I was older, though, I thought it might work.

People are revolted by the idea but, believe me, when you're desperate you'll resort to anything. I began to talk myself into it. I could have a good meal at night then go to the loo and get rid of it. This might seem bizarre to people who live outside a world where weight is everything but no one realizes the pleasure that chewing food and swallowing it can bring until you can't do it. The thought of a good breakfast is tempting but getting up in the morning and knowing that you are going to force yourself to be sick is as bad as knowing that the bath is waiting for you.

That didn't stop me giving it a go. There was only one problem. I couldn't get it to work. I tried it two or three times, stuck my fingers down my throat but I couldn't get the knack to flip it up. It just wouldn't happen, so there I was, head over the bowl with tears streaming from my eyes and nothing to show for it. Now I'm glad: it's a disease and if I'd got used to it I'm certain I'd have given in to it, and that over time it's much more damaging to your health than sweating.

So, there was no quick fix. The weight would have to be starved and sweated off, and when I am under those spartan conditions I am not good company. It's impossible to be happy when you're shifting six, seven or eight pounds over one night before you ride the next day. At those times, which are quite often, I just want to be on my own.

No matter how well-meaning the person might be I don't want anyone telling me that I shouldn't be doing it. And I don't like the idea that people might think I am attention-seeking because I am doing it. I don't need people telling me I look ill. I realize that. I look in the mirror and that doesn't lie. I know that sometimes my eyes have sunk back so far that there are healthier-looking corpses on a mortuary slab. But don't tell me about it. Never think for one minute that I would be doing it if I didn't think I should be. It's the life I've chosen and there are plenty more in the same boat.

Strangely enough, on the days when I've got down to nine stone eleven to be able to weigh out at ten stone I sometimes feel a heightened sense of awareness. I've ridden a lot of winners in that state.

Like all jockeys I have been through the diet fads. Like supermodels, if there's a wonder diet going we'll try it sooner or later.

Unfortunately, there's never been one that suits me. I like eating nice things – and if you cast your mind back to the beginning of this book that means out of the frying-pan or the roasting tin. Dietitians throw in the towel because I like steak, chips, the skin off roast chicken and the wings, quite often topped off with mayonnaise. I never feel guilty when I'm eating and I'm better off eating a little less of what I like than a wagon full of something I don't. You can only eat food that you don't like for a certain amount of time before it does your head in. I've been on them all from the Hay Diet to the Neutron Diet. That's the one where your blood is analysed and tells you what your body reacts to. When mine was tested it revealed I could eat fish but no dairy products. Although there was plenty of food it seemed dry and uninteresting. I did that about four years ago and although it didn't affect my riding I wasn't happy with it. If you want to keep doing a job you love and it means watching your weight year on year, you can only do it in your own way. I know that mine is a continual grind of sweating and fasting, there's no other way, but I would be lying if I said that it doesn't still get to me.

I had a long-term relationship with a wonderful girl, Chanelle Burke, but in the end it wasn't fair on her to be living under the same roof as me. When I'm in a bad mood, because of my weight or things not going well, it doesn't matter how hard someone tries to be nice to me. In the end I make them miserable.

We'd been going out, off and on, for about five years. Most of it was great but there were times when I made life so difficult for her. When I came back at night from racing she says she knew from the way I put my car keys down whether she should say hello or not. That's sad to be able to make someone so aware by such a small gesture. I made it impossible for Chanelle and there was only so much she would take and in the end she left.

When she did, I was absolutely gutted, but it was a symptom of the way the job was going: it was taking over and there seemed nothing I could do about it. If I'd had a bad day when I got home from racing I couldn't wait for the night to be over so I could get going the next day, ride two or three winners and make it better.

The trouble is, then you start to think, What if I don't ride two or three winners the next day? And it begins all over again, so you're not happy either way.

For a lovely twenty-four-year-old intelligent girl like Chanelle, it wasn't exactly a lot of fun. I don't know if things would change now because I don't know if I've achieved what I want to achieve. At the moment, there's always something else. But I do know that I want to marry eventually and have children. I don't want to be alone all my life. I still have plenty of people staying, but they're nearly always jockeys so they know exactly what it's like and just keep quiet. There are times when even my mother doesn't want to speak to me. She knows me better than anyone and when you get to the stage where your mother doesn't want to talk to you you know you're in trouble.

Ma and I speak nearly every day, and they're not short conversations. But she can sense how I am when I'm doing light, and we'll leave it a couple of days. The thought of that steaming bath every morning that I ride hangs over me like a black cloud. I look in the mirror and know that four pounds has got to be shifted from somewhere, yet no matter how hard I pinch myself I can't find a fold of flesh to see where it will come from. Sometimes I stand outside the bathroom door and can't put my hand on the handle. When I'm in, facing the bath, I stand there looking at it thinking, I don't want to get in there. Once or twice, when it's really bad, I've put my head in my hands and wept because I don't want to do it. At times like that I'd pay anything for someone else to do it for me.

I know that for the average person a lovely warm bath is a luxury to look forward to but for me it's torture. You test the temperature with your hand and the heat stings, but you know you've got to lower the most tender parts of your body into it or it's a waste of time. Once you're in, the scalding hot tap maintains the temperature. How the TV stands the steam in the bathroom is a mystery to me. It's usually around eight thirty a.m. that I ask myself why I'm doing it, and is it really worth it? The pain is mental and physical. My sympathy with lobsters is real.

The best thing to do is focus on the future. During my sweating time and travelling to the races I have no interest in speaking to anyone, unless it's the boss or Dave Roberts. That's business, and all I want is to be mentally right for the horses that afternoon. I try to get someone to drive me to the races because I sleep a lot: I get tired quite easily and I want to be alert when it matters most. It's vital that I'm switched on for the three or four hours a day that I'm doing my job. Thank God I don't have to contend with hangovers.

It's not until the day's racing is over that I can relax, and it goes without saying that if I've had a few winners then I'm a bit easier to talk to. Generally when five o'clock comes I'm happy to give people my time. Then it's back on the wheel.

It was nearly a month after I came back from the fall on Baron Allfours that I was able to ride as low as ten stone five and that was on Miss Tango for Martin at far-off Sedgefield. On 4 November at Wincanton I managed ten stone four for Seebald, owned by Steve McManaman and Robbie Fowler, and was second in the Élite Hurdle. Seven days later, at Cheltenham, I finally did ten stone again on Kaki Crazy in a valuable handicap chase. Like the rest of those light rides, he didn't win, but I'd kept my record intact: no overweight in the form book.

14. Getting the Needle

Perhaps more than any other sportsman, the jump jockey is going to be injured. That isn't meant to devalue the dangers in other sports, it is just that we are at risk in our profession for considerably longer than, say, a footballer. He may play two games a week, but no matter how busy he makes himself he is not going to be at the sharp end of the game for ninety minutes. Likewise rugby players.

Racing drivers and boxers take severe physical risks, but they don't do their job six or seven days a week. A jockey does, and no matter what grade of race you are in, the same risks apply with a minimum of eight hurdles or twelve fences to negotiate. Not that you will hear a complaint about it from any jump jockey because we know that it's simply part of the job. One of the first financial lessons you learn is that, whatever other payments you let slide, you always keep up with the private medical insurance: you know full well it's not a matter of 'if' you're going to need it but 'when'.

I've been very lucky in that area. Maybe I got my bad fortune out of the way early when I broke my leg as an apprentice. My boss Jim Bolger was sure I was putting myself at greater risk by going to England a year earlier than he thought fit. Maybe he was right that it was just good fortune that I didn't get broken up. The fact is, though, that while I've suffered concussion twice and received some good kickings after falls, my worst injuries might be best described as self-induced. It was only the foolhardiness of youth that saw me take the ride on Merry Gale in the Marlborough Cup cross-country race that resulted in me cracking my spine.

But half-way through the 2000–01 season I nearly wrecked my chance of a sixth championship and had to cheat nature for nearly two months – and all because I love to play football.

Every sportsman needs an outlet and when the weather is good there's nothing I like more than a round of golf. However, there's no chance of that in the winter, with the poor weather and short days. The early finishes at the track from November through to the middle of January mean that we get home at a reasonable time and a bunch of us play football in John Francome's well-lit covered school at Sheepdrove, high above Lambourn. Apart from John, there is a nucleus of twelve including jump jockeys Matt Bachelor, Sean Curran and Mick FitzGerald, trainer Martin Bosley, and Michael Caulfield of the Jockeys' Association. I make no apology for saying that it is one of the treats of my winter weeks. For that hour or so I can be who I want, providing he plays for Arsenal and scores goals. Thierry Henry it is!

It had been a hard drive back from Southwell on 24 January, no winners and the last race was at four ten. I made it back for seven thirty. Playing up front, as I tend to do, I was standing away from the action with my strike partner Curran. I turned to run upfield to get into the action, my trainer twisted under my heel and I went over on my left ankle. I heard a sharp snap and a ripping sound. My stomach jumped with nerves and I went cold. Sean fixed me with an anxious look and I stared at him. 'Did you hear that?'

His gaze didn't waver. 'Yep. Are you all right?'

'I don't think so.'

I knew I had done something bad because the pain had hit me.

I hobbled to the side, where there was a hosepipe, and took off the trainer. Then I knew I was in serious trouble. As Sean and I looked at it the ankle ballooned with most of the swelling on the outside.

We tried to convince ourselves that maybe it was best that it had swollen up, and perhaps that was a good sign. At that moment I'd have believed anything if it meant I hadn't damaged myself. Ice or very cold water is the usual recommendation for swelling and by the time John and the other lads came over I was directing a jet of water on to my throbbing ankle. My mind was racing at treble speed as I tried to think of an excuse as to why I had done such a bloody stupid thing. 'What can I say to people?'

No one was going to believe that I'd just turned over on it. What would Martin Pipe say? I kept thinking of how Jonothan Lower had broken his leg playing football.

There wasn't the slightest chance that I could make up a face-saving story that I had been kicked by a horse or I'd had a fall schooling: too many people had seen what happened. If I had done serious damage there was no way it could be kept quiet. A. P. McCoy, the dedicated champion, had been unprofessional and I wouldn't be able to wriggle out of it.

I hopped into John's house and tried to get hold of my physio, Rabbit Slattery, but I was bang out of luck: she wasn't at home and I couldn't make contact. Then I tried her mother, Mary Bromiley, one of the best human and equine physiotherapists in the country, who taught Rabbit. No luck. I was starting to panic.

John had an ultrasound machine, which is supposed to increase circulation and improve recovery in humans and horses. Neither of us had any idea if it would do any good but I strapped it on anyway.

After twenty minutes I tried to walk. I had to. No matter what, I had to walk out to my car and drive home. It wasn't too bad, providing I didn't put all my weight on it.

But John knew I wasn't right. 'You've got to go to Swindon and get that X-rayed.'

The stubborn cussedness that's been in me since I was a child kicked in as a defence mechanism against reality. 'I can't. Anyway, I don't want to know. I've got two good rides at Warwick tomorrow. Rodock's having his first run in a novice chase and McHattie will nearly win the three-mile handicap hurdle. I've got to ride them.'

John knew I was being a mug but didn't say anything: even though he'd been retired for a long time he hadn't forgotten how a jockey thinks.

I knew it would stiffen up overnight, and indeed it was extremely sore the next morning. It was time to call on the jump jockey's best friend in the medicine cabinet: the painkiller. Everyone has a brand they swear by, and I had been given some by an old fellow named Billy who used to use the Boot in Shipton Bellinger, which was my local when I lived at Weyhill. They were called co-codamol and if I couldn't exactly run through a wall with their help I knew I'd at least be able to hobble over it.

I managed to see our physio Rabbit Slattery before I went racing at Warwick. The diagnosis was what I'd expected. 'That's not good.'

The ankle was badly swollen and I was reasonably sure that I'd broken a couple of small bones. At least they were on the outside of the ankle: if they'd been anywhere else I'd have been history for a month, maybe more.

I got Rabbit to strap me up as thinly but as tightly as possible, providing support and protection. Luckily I have some riding boots that are loose round the ankle, which allows extra padding, and I pulled them on gingerly. Buoyed up by the painkillers I shuffled my way to the parade ring to ride Rambling Sam for Toby Balding in the first. He didn't say anything but must have been thinking quite a lot. The horse made a couple of bad mistakes and we came home in our own time, finishing last – but at least I knew my ankle would stand up to a jolt.

Martin wasn't at the races and was represented by Chester Barnes. I'd already spoken to Chester that morning. He's got a million contacts and the first thing he said to me was, 'Is it right that you've broken your ankle?'

I kept the truth to the minimum and said I'd just gone over on it. I'm not sure if he believed me when I hobbled up to ride Rodock in the next, but there weren't any complaints about my performance after we cantered in by three lengths.

Having won the handicap hurdle on McHattie, I convinced myself that everything was all right, but Rabbit, as befits the professional she is, had another look after racing. She insisted I had the ankle X-rayed. No chance. We reached a compromise. 'If it gets any worse I will. If it doesn't I'll keep going.'

A couple of days later a doctor friend of mine had a look at it. After feeling it and twisting it he told me what I already knew: 'There's a fair chance you've broken one small bone, if not two. You'd better get it X-rayed to make sure.'

'Just strap it up, Doc, and we'll see what happens.'

Thank heavens for doctor–patient confidentiality.

Four days later I was beginning to get used to the ache in my ankle. Then I got a whack on the other side, which balanced things up. It resulted in a picture of me with my breeches round my ankles talking on a mobile phone at Kempton's third last fence.

I was riding Image de Marque for David Johnson and Martin in a two-and-a-half-mile novices' handicap chase. Although he had run over fences in France this was his first attempt at English fences. Despite jumping left it wasn't until four out that he began to back-pedal, but all chance had gone when he buried me at the first in the home straight. I knew I'd had a bad smack and the horse kicked me hard on the right buttock as we went down. Just think what damage a human kick can do, then multiply it by four.

The green screens were put up around Image de Marque while he regained his feet, and in this relative privacy I dropped my breeches and inspected the damage to my bum. Then I borrowed a phone and called Martin. At that moment a quick-thinking paparazzo snapped me.

Once I had finished talking to Martin and twisted round to inspect the damage, all thoughts of my ankle disappeared as my buttock expanded before my eyes: a haematoma came up like a massive maroon balloon.

I got a lift back to the weighing room and as I walked in it got bigger and bigger. I didn't ride again that day and stuck a big bag of ice on it, but by the time I left to go home it was tight and extremely sore. By the time I went to bed the haematoma covered nearly all of my right buttock and I had to lie face down to sleep. The next morning I was in agony. I got a lift to the races and lay across the back seat on my left side. Fortunately the journey to Taunton is nearly all motorway and straight so I didn't move about much. I knew one thing for certain: the state my backside was in I wouldn't be able to get it near a saddle.

Fortunately for me Dr Philip Pritchard had a runner at the meeting. Dr Pritchard is a GP, trains successfully at Purton and still rides quite a few of his own horses. He's been an exceptionally good friend to many jockeys. He could see my problem and I asked him if he could bleed me.

Luckily, he had a large syringe, which he stuck into the bloated red mass. The loss of fluid reduced the size and pressure so that I could ride. I managed a treble, which would have been impossible without the doc's help. For some time afterwards I didn't know which was more painful: the bum or the ankle. For a while, the dispersing haematoma gave me more concern. As the fluid drained away, it travelled down my leg and got to my knee. There were a couple of worrying days when I could hardly bend it, but gradually it freed up. I'd pushed my luck and got away with it. Had the bang been anywhere near the ankle I would have been out, no doubt about it. I was sore in both areas for about a month but gradually the pain died down and I managed twenty winners.

Pain is something I'd rather ride through than sit around thinking about. Quite often painkillers and adrenaline keep you going, but eventually Nature tells you when to stop.

As for the football, I still can't wait to play on Wednesday nights. However, I'm extremely careful how I turn and I don't do any impressions of Patrick Vieira when I'm tackling.

I reached a hundred winners for the season when Scrahan Cross won a handicap chase at Carlisle on 6 November. The season was now boiling up nicely. And five days later the Thomas Pink Gold Cup provided the first big chase of the season and the first serious test of my judgement.

Martin had three confirmed runners for the big Cheltenham handicap, all having their first outings of the season but typically tuned up to win. I rejected the outsider Majadou, who ended up running well, and was left with the choice between Lady Cricket and Exit Swinger. I had won good races on both and at times like this the decision has to be mine alone. I can ask plenty of people for advice, including Martin, his son David and, of course, Dave Roberts, but the buck stops with me. I'd have to get down to ten stone four if I chose Exit Swinger, who had impressed me by winning on his British chasing début in a Sandown handicap on the final day of the previous season.

However, I kept remembering how good Lady Cricket had been in the early part of that season, and I had been told she was in great order at home. I chose her and didn't have much to worry about once we swept ahead after the fourth last. I lost a stirrup for a few strides when she faltered at the last, but even so we had ten lengths to spare over Exit Swinger and Dickie Johnson.

If the placings had finished in reverse I might have taken it a little better than a year earlier when I made the wrong choice between Copeland and Rodock in the £34,000 William Hill Handicap Hurdle at Sandown. When the entries came out five days before the race I asked Martin what was happening and he replied, 'Which one do you want to ride?'

'Either of them can win. Copeland's got a good weight, but Rodock's improved enough to win it with eleven stone ten.'

I was wrong. I chose Rodock, and David Casey, who had come over to ride for Oliver Sherwood and was lodging with me, took the ride on Copeland. The weight was a killer for Rodock: half-way down the back straight I knew he wasn't travelling, although he'd been running away when I got down to ten stone on his previous outing at Cheltenham. David took a narrow lead two out, but Rodock gave me the lot and we began to inch towards them up the Sandown hill. David took things easy in the last couple of strides and we flashed upsides, but I knew we had been beaten by a short head. I was absolutely burning up with anger because I'd been beaten by my stablemate, although I was happy enough for my lodger, who had been going through a poor run with Sherwood and would ultimately get the sack for being late.

But from a personal standpoint I was livid. Martin wasn't there and, in a bout of petulance, I hardly spoke to him for three weeks. I realize now how stupid that was and, fortunately, I'm considerably better about such things now: Martin has so many owners in the yard and they're all entitled to a crack at the big prizes. It's just up to me to be on the ball and pick right.

I got it right at the first big Ascot meeting in mid-November when Upgrade finished a long way in front of Blowing Wind in the First National Gold Cup and I came away from the two-day meeting with five winners. I also had a fantastic run of nine winners from sixteen rides at the end of November. As the season wore on, my worst enemy was injury, in the shape of the two broken bones in my ankle.

However, calamity hit the country, with serious repercussions for racing. On 21 February I tuned into Radio Five Live on the way back from Ludlow and heard that a case of foot-and-mouth disease, the first for twenty years, had been detected in an Essex abattoir. Those with long memories could remember the massive outbreak of 1967, when racing was stopped for several weeks. We in the sport held our breath. It wasn't long before we knew our fate. As the epidemic spread across the country the Jockey Club suspended racing for a week from 28 February. In fact, we didn't race again until 10 March at Sandown.

I had been brought up in a farming community, so I understood the hardship and anguish farmers were going through. Even though some in racing maintained there was no need for us to call a halt, the majority of us wanted to be seen to be doing something. Showing solidarity with the farmers, if you like. When you saw those pyres on the news and knew that the life's work of a family was being wrenched away from them, it didn't seem to matter missing a few winners. When it was all over we'd be back in the groove as though nothing had happened. For those farmers it would take years to build back up to what they had once had. Some never would, and I am glad we made the gesture of support.

Now that we faced a break it was sensible to turn it to an advantage. Dubai's sun, sea and golf courses looked the right way to charge up the batteries so a team of us, including Mick FitzGerald, Carl Llewellyn, David Casey and Graham Bradley, took up the option. When our minds swung back to business there was always Cheltenham to look forward to – or so we thought. Cases of foot-and-mouth bobbed up like mushrooms just outside the exclusion zone around the course, but the track stayed safe until the week before the Festival. Then someone discovered that sheep, which grazed on the course, had not been removed within the time required by the Ministry of Agriculture. That meant no Cheltenham. The cancellation was a real sickener.

People rightly call Cheltenham our yearly Olympics. Although the Grand National gets the nation's pulse racing on a Saturday afternoon in April, Cheltenham is where the exam results are published and you know if your horse has finished top in his class. No one would be named top of the class in 2001, and that included Istabraq, who would surely have won an unprecedented fourth Champion Hurdle.

It was also a close call as to whether the National would be run, though that was down to heavy rain, which produced the most desperate ground anyone could recall. I had a difficult judgement to make on the run-up to the race as Martin had ten runners, a quarter of the field. Ten days before, I was being asked which I would ride. Two days before, I still hadn't made up my mind although I had decided that I would not be on Moondigua, Kaki Crazy, Art Prince or Tresor de Mai. There was speculation that my choice would be between Dark Stranger, who had started 9–1 favourite but unseated me at the third a year earlier, You're Agoodun and Northern Starlight. In the end I went for the 50–1 outsider Blowing Wind.

Although he was unproven over anything like the distance of four and a half miles he was a relaxed horse who would switch himself off and conserve energy. Also, I knew he had class: three years earlier he had landed the Imperial Cup and County Hurdle double.

Almost as important as winning the race was a personal matter that ran deep. My five National rides had resulted in a dismal record that read, fell, pulled up, fell, fell, unseated. If I didn't win, the least I wanted to do was get round.

Some said that, because of the desperate ground, the race should not have been run. The bare facts back up their argument as only four of the forty runners completed the course after a loose horse took out ten of the field at the eighth, the Canal Turn. Personally, I felt it was right to run the race, even though any chance I had went when the riderless Edmond cannoned into us at the nineteenth. He knocked me out of the saddle and did the same to Ruby Walsh on the previous year's winner Papillon for good measure.

At that point Ruby and I knew we had no chance but, as we'd seen, anything could happen. We started looking for our horses. They hadn't gone very far, were standing huddled further down the fence with a few others.

Ruby and I just schooled round with no idea what was happening up front, but after the last it was time to say farewell to Ruby: 'Thanks for the company, I'll see you later.'

Ruby called back, 'Give me a wave on the run-in.'

Several seconds later I looked round. Ruby was now a long way behind so I gave him a wave.

There was nothing ahead of us on the long run-in, but we were still getting plenty of vocal support from the crowd. When we crossed the line I realized why: Red Marauder and Richard Guest had outlasted Smarty, ridden by Timmy Murphy, but after that McCoy and Walsh were the last men standing and Blowing Wind came in for the £55,000 third prize. We were one minute and forty-three seconds behind Red Marauder, but we still got paid!

However, if I never manage to ride a Grand National winner I will always consider this as the one I should have won. Blowing Wind went on to finish third again the following year in a better-class contest.

It's worth repeating that I felt the race had to be run. Yes, there were accidents caused by loose horses, but that can happen in any year and in any race. The best statistic to come out of the 2001 Grand National was that no horse was seriously injured. The loss of Cheltenham had ripped the heart out of the season and, although the British Horseracing Board tried their best, it was virtually impossible to salvage much from the wreckage.

The Whitbread Gold Cup meeting at Sandown, which finishes the season at the end of April, was upgraded into a Cheltenham consolation and, despite the rain-lashed ground, my trusty ally Edredon Bleu won the Championship Chase. The official form book made a comment about him that I have never seen before or since: 'Jumped brilliantly.' I couldn't argue with that and it won us the race. It bears saying again that he is my ideal two-mile chaser and he won the near-£50,000 prize through jumping and pure guts.

I set out to make all, but knew there was trouble when my old foe Ruby Walsh drove Fadalko up to challenge at the Pond Fence three from home. I kept digging into Edredon, trying to shake off Fadalko, but he wouldn't go away. At the last I could still see Ruby out of the corner of my eye and fired Edredon for one last leap. He was magnificent, and Fadalko matched him again. There was never more than half a head between us as we surged up the hill, but it was as though my boy knew which of the two winning posts at Sandown was the right one, and he put his head down on the line when it mattered most. There really didn't deserve to be a loser that day – I'm just pleased it wasn't us. He was my 191st winner of the season and there could not have been a more fitting one to sign off on. No fewer than 120 had come from Martin Pipe, which helped secure me a sixth championship. But Dickie Johnson had served me notice of his intentions: he rode in 114 more races than I did. Fortunately, I managed thirty more winners, despite my spells on the sidelines.

The Championship Hurdle, run as a Cheltenham consolation, lacked Istabraq, and Landing Light took advantage to run out a worthy winner under Mick FitzGerald. I was only third, yet the horse I rode that day gave me the distinct impression that he would be more than a handful for Istabraq and the rest of them come March 2002. I was falling in love with Valiramix. Little did I realize that love would turn to heartbreak at Cheltenham.

15. Searching for Sir Gordon

In the early days it was the Flat jockeys I idolized. The other lads called me Lester and eventually I got used to being nicknamed after a legend, even though he was coming to the end of a magnificent career. There were plenty of others for me to look up to, with Steve Cauthen, Willie Carson and, of course Mick Kinane. And my Ulster homeland had produced two Derby-winning jockeys of the eighties and nineties, Ray Cochrane and John Reid. It was easy for me to identify with all of them because I'd watched them ride on TV, heard them interviewed and felt as if I knew them, just a bit.

Before the mid-eighties the top jockeys had been only names to me – Joe Mercer, Scobie Breasley, Doug Smith and Sir Gordon Richards. Sir Gordon Richards. He might have been just a name, but as racing began to take me over I learned that he had done things no other rider had. He was the only jockey to be knighted, and finally won the Derby in the year the Queen was crowned. Most importantly of all, he was a man who stood for everything that was good and decent in racing. I was aware that he'd been champion Flat jockey more times than anyone else – but that was all. It never entered my head that I'd be mentioned in the same sentence as him.

There was another Gordon Richards that I knew a good bit more about, namely the man who trained at Penrith in Cumbria and had handled countless top-class chasers from the sixties, including the ill-fated but brilliant One Man and the 1984 Grand National winner Hallo Dandy. To avoid confusion, he called himself Gordon W. Richards.

But there was rightly only one Sir Gordon Richards and throughout the second half of the 2001–02 season I came to respect him all the more. In 1947 he had set a new record for the number of

winners in a season – 269 – but it was what he went through in
1933 that meant he would have understood what it was like for me
when I tried to take his record through the winter and spring of
2002.

The target for Sir Gordon in 1933 was a man with whom I had
much more in common, the riding legend of Victorian England,
Fred Archer. 'The Long Fellow' way before the name was applied
to Lester Piggott, Archer had to purge and starve himself mercilessly
to ride at a minimum eight stone six. That, coupled with the
tragedy of losing his brother, son and wife, broke his mind and he
shot himself on 8 November 1886. He had been champion jockey
thirteen times from 1874 to the year of his death, and in 1885 he
included four classics among a magnificent total of 246 winners
from 667 rides. Like me, Archer didn't take to schooling but it was
no hindrance. Also, when he was operating there was no telephone,
let alone an agent at the other end to book rides. All his engagements
were made by telegram or word-of-mouth.

He was described variously as highly strung, sensitive and melan-
cholic. It is easy to understand why. Sir Gordon wrote that the
season in which he beat Archer's record was the greatest of his
career but added:

I cannot honestly say it was the most enjoyable. It was so hectic a season
from so many points of view that, on looking back, I often wonder how
I got through it in one piece.

It was a tremendous satisfaction, of course, to beat the legendary Fred
Archer's record and it was heart-warming to find that apparently the
whole racing community – from the King himself to the humblest backers
– was every bit as pleased about it as I was. But it imposed a strain upon
me which I hope never to have to withstand again.

He penned those words after his retirement in 1955 and I know
exactly what he meant.

Sir Gordon's final total in 1933 was 259. He equalled the record
on the day that marked Archer's last ride and beat it on the
anniversary of his death. The winner that had taken him into the

record books was Golden King, winner of the Wavertree Selling Plate at Liverpool on 8 November. He was trained by Frank Hartigan, who operated from Weyhill, where I would turn up in the summer of 1994.

Sir Gordon's new record of 269 in 1947 didn't create anywhere near the stir of the first, although people were asking him the same questions that I get asked. He recalled, 'Some extraordinary people asked me – and quite seriously – if I ever got tired of winning! My answer was short.'

So is mine.

Sir Gordon had died before I came to England but I would love to have met him. John Francome got to know him well when the great man lived quietly in Kintbury, a village between Hungerford and Newbury, and says he was terrific company.

Apparently, there was one thing Sir Gordon considered more important than any other: he reckoned a good night's sleep was the best thing in the world for a jockey. I couldn't agree more, except that I might go to bed a bit later and lie in a bit longer than I should.

The introduction of summer jumping provided me with the base to make Sir Gordon's record a possibility. In some sections of the media it was seen as my likely target for the 1997–8 season when I managed my best ever score of 253 but suspensions and a couple of knocks towards the end put a stop to that.

At the start of any season, I never set myself any specific goal – except to win the championship. Achieve that and anything else will follow. It's all about winners. When I was an apprentice at Jim Bolger's I'd be happy with a ride a week, let alone a winner. But when they start to come you can't bear the thought of not getting enough. It must be like a miser hoarding money because he can't bear the thought of being without it. Believe me, winners are like that.

Keeping my title by the widest margin and taking as many of the big races as possible in the process was all that was in my mind when the 2001–02 season started. And when I walked away winnerless after three rides at Plumpton on 30 April I could not have foreseen that the season which started just twenty-four hours later would be the toughest but ultimately most satisfying one of my career.

May proved lively with thirty-six winners, as good a start as I could have wished for. Martin Pipe had kept some of the good-class horses going while the ground stayed safe and Seebald and Auetaler, owned by Robbie Fowler and Steve McManaman, won their novice chase débuts that month. There was still a dash of quality in early June when Westender won at Stratford after running out at Wincanton and, although I managed half my total of the previous month, I was on fifty-three and flying as July arrived.

A more relaxed atmosphere surrounds jumping at this time of the year. We are shuffled off to the back of the stage while the Flat takes over at Newmarket, Epsom and Royal Ascot, and we don't get a serious glance until late October, early November. That's fine by us – but don't think it's any less competitive or hard fought because we're out of the media eye. And, yes, it is more pleasant to be operating in decent weather, feeling the sun on your back – but sadly everything has a price and you bounce a few inches higher off the firmer ground when those inevitable falls come.

With the long seasons we now have, which loop one into the next, plus the coupling of afternoon and evening meetings, the subject of jockey burn-out is often brought up. I am the first to admit that there are times when I get tired and low, but I try to have a brief holiday when I feel the need rather than when the stewards think I'm due.

After drawing a blank at Stratford on 7 July I hopped on to a plane for Malaga with a few of the boys, including Graham Bradley, Mick FitzGerald and Carl Llewellyn. Plenty will think that four days isn't long enough but believe me when I tell you that after four days with these boys anyone would need to get home for a rest.

Sir Gordon evidently had his relaxation in the winter, curling on the ice at St Moritz. As we are party people when we're away, the only curling I want to do is in bed. Only a good round of golf can stir me. On breaks like this I put racing out of my thoughts and it doesn't edge its way back until I'm spinning down the M4 from Heathrow and the phone goes. Then I'm back in the real world.

Quite often it's hard to get winners in the summer months when fields cut up because of hard ground, and it's then that Martin comes into his own. So, too, does Dave Roberts. Martin has his less talented but able horses ready to win in their class and Dave is as careful as he can be that he doesn't put me on something that looks dangerous. In this game there's no point looking for trouble because it will find you on its own soon enough.

The system was working better than ever and, by the end of August, a treble for Martin at Uttoxeter had put me on ninety for the season. The run carried on and at Plumpton on 17 September I rode my hundredth winner of the season. Significantly it was by far my earliest. It came seven weeks sooner than my previous best on 5 November 1997, and while I was well aware that the season now started considerably earlier I had still managed it in two weeks fewer.

The ton came up with a typical armchair ride for Martin on Present Bleu in the claiming hurdle. I was delighted because I knew that, barring accidents, I'd be back riding over two hundred winners – I'd missed out the previous season, finishing on 191, due to the concussion and foot-and-mouth. At this stage 200 was as far as I was thinking, nothing more.

I meant it when I said in the press that I relished every ride and added, 'I'm very lucky. I have a great job – it's a great way to earn a living. I couldn't think of a job I'd want to do any more than the one I'm doing now.'

Sir Gordon's record never slipped into my thoughts. If it had I'd soon have brushed it aside, but the media and the bookmakers had different ideas. Two days after I'd hit the ton the Tote decided to drum up some business on my back and made me only a 4–5 chance to beat Sir Gordon. They also reckoned I was only 13–8 to ride 200 winners by 19 January. I looked at the story and tossed the paper to one side. It was easy for the men in suits to sit in their offices and offer odds on me breaking a record that had stood for fifty-five years: they didn't have to go out and do it. I did, and I didn't want to think about it. No one close to me mentioned it. Then on 23 October at Exeter I had the kind of reminder that every jump jockey gets – namely that no matter how good we are, only one fall separates you from any ambitions you might secretly harbour.

Dickie Johnson, my nearest pursuer and thirty-nine winners behind me in the championship, took a heavy fall from Ilico II at the fourth fence in the novice chase. He was brought back to the ambulance room in great pain and it was no surprise to hear that he'd broken his right leg. All you can do at times like that is offer your sincere wishes for a speedy recovery, then thank God it's not you being carried way.

Ironically, the first time someone mentioned the possibility of getting past Sir Gordon was when I was crossing the Severn Bridge on the way to Chepstow the day after Dickie's accident. Chepstow was the course where Sir Gordon had set yet another record that still hasn't been bettered in Britain. On 4 October, in the year he broke Archer's record, he rode all six winners on the card, having won the last race at Nottingham the previous day. That gave him seven consecutive winners, and on the second day of the Chepstow meeting he rode the first five, giving him an unbroken run of twelve. He was beaten by only a head and neck on his last ride. Afterwards he came out of the weighing room and sang for the crowd 'Little Man, You've Had A Busy Day'. Whatever else I might achieve, I'm not even going to think about topping that.

I was being driven by my co-author, Steve Taylor. Looking straight ahead, he said, 'You do realize that the media are going to start getting up your tail about the Gordon Richards record?'

I was dismissive. 'Nah. Can't see it happening, can you?'

'It's possible, but bloody difficult. I reckon you'll have to ride twenty-five winners a month between now and the end of April. That doesn't account for you getting banged up, suspended or some bad weather.'

'Looks hard, then, doesn't it?'

'It does.'

I didn't improve my score of 120 that day. With the season

beginning to boil up there were more important things to think about, in particular whether Martin Pipe had enough quality horses to challenge for the big Saturday races.

I had voiced my doubts to Martin after a schooling session in early September. Martin isn't someone who likes bullshit and I remember telling him that I didn't think he'd have been champion trainer the previous season if Cheltenham hadn't been stopped by foot-and-mouth. 'In my opinion we've only got one horse capable of challenging for the championship races and that's Valiramix. After that, we're struggling.'

I don't know which way he took my thoughts, but I got the feeling he set out to prove me wrong. And, with the benefit of hindsight, I was worrying about nothing. As the pressure mounted throughout the season Martin kept pulling out big-race winners, which had me shaking my head in disbelief.

Because of my association with Martin, other trainers tend to assume that I'm always riding out for him, which isn't the case. Quite often I'm tucked up in bed when the rest of the boys are schooling or riding work and I'm not arguing with that. I follow an open-house policy, which means anyone can take a bed for the night or, in the case of David Casey and Seamus Durack, months. Even the Flat lads Jamie Spencer and Shane Kelly get their heads down at my place, and when my friend from the north, Graham Lee, came down to ride work for John Gosden at Manton in the summer of 2001 he was a welcome visitor. The only house rule is, don't wake me up when you're leaving. I enjoy schooling and riding work, though: it's bred into me, and if I'm asked I'll always go. In fact, there's only one trainer in Lambourn I won't ride out for because I think he once took me for granted.

When I arrived he told me – didn't ask – to tack my horse up and take the droppings out of the box. Now don't get me wrong: I've got no problems with doing that if I'm asked politely or if the trainer is a bit understaffed. There's certainly nothing élitist about me and I can cite one time in the summer of 2001 when Richard Hughes and I rode out for our friend Sylvester Kirk in Upper Lambourn and not only mucked out a few but swept the yard too.

We might not have done a fantastic job but it was the thought that counted.

Towards the middle of October I received a call from Oliver Sherwood to see if I would school for him a couple of mornings a week before the season got really busy. Oliver's a good guy whose fortunes have taken a dive over the past five years since he lost his number-one rider Jamie Osborne through injury and then retirement. The arrangement worked well. I liked working with him and it got me motivated early in the day. It also provided me with the first of what became an uncomfortably long list of races in which defeat was almost snatched from the jaws of victory.

A couple of days after Chepstow I went to Fakenham on 26 October, principally to ride two for Oliver that had good chances. One pulled himself into the ground and was beaten, but the other, Tik-A-Tai, looked like hacking up as we came clear into the last fence of the novice chase. For a second I took my eye off the ball. The horse overjumped at the last and landed so steeply that he stumbled and knuckled over with his chest hitting the floor. A ten-length lead had evaporated to nothing. Luckily he didn't fall left or right but struggled to his feet, like a camel, with me sitting tighter than Lawrence of Arabia. It was a tribute to the courage of the horse that we got going again and managed to hold off Infrasonique by two lengths on the relatively short run-in. The form book said it was one of the recoveries of the season. If I'd been beaten it would have been one of the biggest embarrassments of the season. There would be a few more retrievals and I began to think that, with my luck running like this, anything was possible.

I was also well aware that in November racing would be even more competitive and I didn't want to miss anything. Jockeys are selfish and I'm no different. That meant Martin and I would have different ideas about where I should go. The first run-in came as November opened.

Jonjo O'Neill offered me the ride on Legal Right in the £29,000 Charlie Hall Chase at Wetherby on Saturday 3 November and I wanted to take it. I'd won on the horse two years earlier at Cheltenham and although he was delicate he still looked on the way up and would start favourite for the Charlie Hall. Martin wanted me to ride five on the same afternoon at Ascot and I didn't fancy one of them. I knew when I asked if I could ride Legal Right that he wanted me to go to Ascot. 'Do what you like, then,' was his reply. In other words, 'Do what you like, but if you get off mine you're really going to piss me off.' I nearly always know what he really means from the tone of his voice.

I wasn't happy. Cue for a sulk. By the time I headed north to ride at Wetherby on the Friday I still wanted to get off the Ascot rides. All the way up I whinged to Dave Roberts: 'What am I doing riding them yaks?'

I wasn't very talkative to Martin when I got to Ascot on Saturday, and when I'm like that he just leaves me to it. Sure enough, the first ride, Turkestan, won the novice hurdle by six lengths, giving Martin his fastest hundred: he was fourteen days ahead of his previous best, achieved a year earlier, and that had to be good news for me. But I was still thinking about Legal Right.

Three races into the Ascot card Martin pulled another masterstroke when You're Agoodun won the United House Handicap Chase. Then a spare ride for Mark Pitman, Father McCarten, won the novice chase. As I came back to the changing room the result of the Charlie Hall was flashed up. Legal Right started 2–1 favourite but hadn't finished in the first three behind Sackville and David Casey. As Jim Bolger would have said, 'You're some fool.'

Martin's wife, Carol, had another view. 'You're a spoiled little brat!' she told me. Well, I think that's what she said.

I did get to win on Legal Right the following month when the Tripleprint Gold Cup meeting at Cheltenham on 15 December was abandoned early in the morning because of frost. I'd got five fancied rides, including Shooting Light in the big chase, and Valiramix was due to make his reappearance in the Bula Hurdle. In those situations you've got to salvage what you can and Jonjo had told me I could ride Legal Right in the Tommy Whittle Chase at Haydock that afternoon. It meant that Liam Cooper lost out but I'm afraid that's part of the game. I made the journey with Mick FitzGerald, who jocked young David Dennis off Kingsmark in the race and the pair of us fought out the finish. It was tight but Legal Right got home by half a length.

A couple of days after the Ascot treble I rode four winners at Newton Abbot, three for Martin and one for Philip Hobbs on Ross Minster in the three-and-a-quarter-mile handicap chase. Ross Minster takes a fair bit of riding and I was at him from a long way out before getting him back in front two from home, winning all out by a length and a half.

I travelled back with Norman Williamson, who decided to put a different spin on my day. 'Hey, champ, you only have to point those Pipe horses and they win. You'll need plenty of those Ross Minster rides to clear your wind if you're going to do the record.'

It was after that four-timer that I went public: 'I'd be lying if I said it's not my aim to beat Sir Gordon's record.'

The Tote shortened the odds still further, making me an 8–13 chance from 4–5. I commented, 'That's not very brave of them. I'd better get my finger out. I'd love to break the record but I've got to keep healthy and keep my trainer happy – he might sack me.'

I don't think that ever crossed Martin's mind, although I wasn't the easiest to deal with throughout November. On the plus side, November also turned out to be the month that allowed me a cushion against a bad run or bad weather.

At this stage, my personal assistant Gee Armytage had set up a running total on the computer, which let her know exactly where I stood and how many winners I still needed. Dave Roberts had the same figures in place. We never talked about it. We all knew it was there but didn't want to jinx it. But November was an amazing month, topped off when Martin took the three-day Thomas Pink Gold meeting from 16 to 18 November by storm.

On the first day he legged me up on Manx Magic to win the novice chase, and on the main day, Saturday, he had three in the Thomas Pink Gold Cup. I had no doubts about choosing Shooting Light, who had been revitalized since transferring to the yard at the start of the season, and we took the £58,000 prize by a ready three lengths. However, early in the race I got things wrong. I squeezed him up to jump and he just put down with me. When he did it the second time I knew I couldn't fire him into his fences. I took him to the outside on the start of the second circuit and he began to find his rhythm. The more he got into the race the stronger he moved, and when you ride one of Martin's you know it will be 100 per cent fit.

There wasn't much wrong with his other runners, either: Exit Swinger and Cadougold finished third and fourth. It was Martin's fifth win in the race, following Beau Ranger, Challenger du Luc, Cyfor Malta and Lady Cricket. I'd ridden the last two. It was typical that he tried to hand me the compliment for 'a brilliant ride', but I couldn't accept that and said, 'The trainer sent this horse out to win a £20,000 handicap and then, seventeen days later and with a stone more on his back, he's won a race worth nearly £60,000. No matter who the horse and jockey are, for a trainer to do that there's only one word for it – genius.'

We also won the main supporting race on the card, the £27,000 Tote Bookmakers' Handicap Hurdle with It Takes Time, and made it four for the meeting when Image de Marque II won the novices' handicap hurdle.

On Sunday Martin was still on fire. Tarxien was a different class in the novice hurdle and Seebald put himself forward as one of the best two-mile novice chasers of the season when he easily beat Armaturk. The rapidly improving Westender, owned by the enthusiastic Matt Archer and Jean Broadhurst, was on a five-timer and started 11–8 favourite for the most valuable race of the day, the Rehabilitation of Racehorses' Handicap Hurdle worth £32,500. It should have been straightforward, and that's how it looked as I pushed Westender clear going to the last, but he caught the top of the hurdle and stumbled badly on landing. For a few precarious seconds, I looked like dropping out of the side door. But this was the season of lucky recoveries and Westender stayed under me. Brian Harding on The French Furze made the most of the blunder, yet Westender still had enough left to regain his stride and battle on up the hill to beat him by two lengths. The crowd gave me a tremendous reception, but as I walked back down the course I caught a glimpse of the replay on the big screen and saw what a mess we'd made of the last. I put my head in my hands and couldn't watch through embarrassment.

The haul over three days was seven, and I was looking forward to a night in the pub with the boys when I uncovered a disaster. Someone had stolen my mobile phone. I was beside myself with rage and all the gloss of riding seven winners was washed away. My mobile – or, more important, the SIM card in it – is my lifeline. I use it all the time. It's my phone directory with every important number stored – and despite what you might think about me being a racing junkie not all those are for business.

It was ironic that I'd been presented with a new mobile for winning a race at the meeting sponsored by Direct Answers. Why the hell couldn't the thief have lifted that? Everyone who mattered to me, professionally and socially, knew the mobile number and would be trying to make contact. Worse still, it would take a while to get the old number switched to a new phone. In a matter of ten minutes all the pleasure of riding those seven winners was gone and I was like a bear with a headache. It is at such times that Gee Armytage is worth far more than her weight in gold bars.

She had a contact at a mobile-phone company, In Touch, and took the phone I'd won to their Winchester base early on Monday morning. They pulled every string they had and switched my number to the new phone. Gee dashed up the A34 and met me at the Peartree Services at Oxford on my way to Leicester. I was connected to the real world again. Unfortunately, I'd lost all my stored numbers so between races that afternoon and on the journey home I punched in the numbers I needed.

There are times when my commitment to Martin means missing out and, much as I loved riding Edredon Bleu, I knew there was no chance that I could be with him on his seasonal comeback at Huntingdon on 24 November. I had to be at Ascot for Martin and all I could think of during the preceding week was that I'd be following Best Mate around on Wahiba Sands in the First National Bank Gold Cup. Best Mate, like Edredon Bleu, is owned by Jim Lewis and trained by Henrietta Knight. And for me he had been the best novice chaser of the previous season. He'd looked a class act again on his comeback in the Haldon Gold Cup at Exeter earlier in the month and although he'd been raised twelve pounds to a BHB mark of 169, I couldn't see him being beaten.

Norman Williamson came in for Edredon and I had to make the best of it with Wahiba Sands, whom I'd first won on as a novice hurdler with John Dunlop in 1997. David Johnson had bought him for 105,000 guineas at Doncaster Sales in August 1998 and the gelding had proved a good buy, but I was sure he had plenty on his plate at Ascot. He was getting twenty pounds from Best Mate, which I didn't think would be enough. I was more than happy to be wrong.

The ex-Australian chaser Logician led the field of four and I held Wahiba Sands in the rear while he jumped with little fluency in the early stages. Jim Culloty was happy to get a lead on Best Mate and took a narrow advantage two out. I was flat out on Wahiba Sands, but the horse found his rhythm as we turned for home and had enough momentum for me to force him into a narrow lead over Best Mate at the last. I got a three-quarter-length advantage and threw the lot at Wahiba Sands just as Jim asked Best Mate for a final burst. He couldn't concede the weight and we won all out by half a length. Time was to show that Best Mate stayed better than most people thought, and the near two and a half miles of that day was not far enough. That fact was rammed home to my cost on Boxing Day at Kempton.

November was my best-ever month for winners with forty. By contrast, towards the end it turned sour for Jim Culloty, who broke his arm when Abu Dancer fell at Taunton on 29 November. It meant that he would be out until the new year and would miss Best Mate in the King George at Kempton on Boxing Day. I knew I'd be offered the ride. The question was, would I be able to take it?

December was never going to see so many winners as November, but everything stayed on track and I clocked up my 1,500th winner when Celtic Native, trained by Philip Hobbs, won the novice chase at Exeter on 20 December. It was the right place to do it, too: just over seven years earlier I'd ridden my first English winner, Chickabiddy, there.

Two days later I almost reached the record books again at Ascot. Martin was gearing everything towards the valuable weekend meetings and he'd prepared five top-class chances on the six-race card. But the meeting hung in the balance until thirty minutes before the first due to frost in the ground. I knew I'd already had one winner when the stewards gave us the thumbs up.

Tarxien justified favouritism and won the opening three-runner novice hurdle, then Wahiba Sands outstayed Get Real in the Cantor Sport Handicap Chase. Shooting Light was still on the march and was a comfortable winner of the £32,500 Tote Silver Cup Handicap Chase. Three out of three and I had the next three favourites to ride. Could I do a Frankie Dettori and win all the races on an Ascot card, just as he'd done in October 1996? I soon knew the answer. Westender, for many the best of my rides that day, was a disappointing eighth to Marble Arch in the biggest race of the day, the Ladbroke Handicap Hurdle. I knew after three hurdles that he wasn't on a going day but it's at times like that that you have to try to understand why things went wrong. I weighed up the facts and reckoned I hadn't made enough use of him.

Sure enough, my next two rides won. Seebald looked a star in the making with an impressive win in the novice chase and Alvino, trained by Henrietta Knight, had five lengths to spare in the bumper. No super six to follow Dettori's magnificent seven, but that didn't stop the Italian making a friendly joke. I'd just reached the M4 when the mobile rang.

'Hey, Tony, you can't beat me. You're getting close, but not that close.'

Frankie had been watching the racing with Bill Gredley, who is a major Flat owner but has his jumpers with Martin. It was a nice gesture to call. He was saying well done, but also letting me know that he was still in front of me. It's what I'd expect from a fellow Arsenal supporter.

Frankie wasn't the only one to be quite pleased that Westender spoiled the party. The next morning I took a call from Nick

Cheyne, Ascot's clerk of the course. 'Tony, don't take this the wrong way, but thank God Westender got beaten. It would have broken my heart to have to fork out for another statue to go alongside Dettori!'

I have tremendous respect for Frankie and what he has achieved in raising the profile of racing among the public. And it was because of him that I knew I had no chance of being voted BBC Sports Personality of the Year. If Frankie didn't get it after winning all seven at the Festival of British Racing and the greatest of all, Lester Piggott, had never won, what chance did I have? Not that it stopped some well-respected people from other sports championing my cause. John Motson, the voice of football on BBC TV, nominated me as his sportsman of the year and sports journalist Sue Mott of the *Daily Telegraph* urged readers to phone in and vote for me. Claude Duval launched a 'Vote For Tony' campaign in the *Sun* and quoted Sir Peter O'Sullevan as saying it would be 'a betrayal of sport' not to vote for me. It was strong stuff.

The Friday night before the awards I was back early from racing and doing some work in the office with Gee when Jamie Osborne called and said they were talking about the Sports Review on John Inverdale's show and John Motson was on. I don't have a radio in the house so I ran out to the car, turned on the radio and listened to what John had to say. I felt a little embarrassed that someone as big in football was nominating me. He might have gone a bit over the top when he said I was the best pound-for-pound sportsman in Britain, but it was a kind gesture and one that made me proud to hear how highly some people rated me. John was also perceptive when he said that he was sure I wouldn't get into the top three. Make that top six. No disrespect to past winners and certainly not David Beckham, who justifiably won the award for some magical performances – not least against Greece, which saw England through to the World Cup Finals – but some have won that trophy when they haven't really won anything else.

Golf apart, football is my great love although playing it had nearly ruled me out of the previous season. I still like to get the boots on when I can, a bit like Sir Gordon: he often turned out for the Ogbourne stables of Martin Hartigan against the yards at Manton and Beckhampton. He was a life-long Wolves fan, too.

After the Ascot five there was no racing until Boxing Day and a Sunday morning game between the jockeys and Lambourn had been arranged for some time. The pitch was frozen and we definitely shouldn't have played, but I was up for it. My only concession to the freezing weather was a pair of black gloves. They were just like Thierry Henry's, and although I play up front that's where the similarity stopped – or so the spectators thought. About thirty minutes into the first half, John Francome stroked the ball to ex-pro Warren Aspinall – he qualified for our side by backing horses. He fed the ball through to Sean Curran who sent a high ball down the left-hand side, which I caught in mid-air and volleyed into the top left corner. Magic!

I couldn't believe it and I don't think anyone else could, either. I just stood there, arms in the air, bellowing with delight. At half-time someone said to me that I'd shown slightly more emotion than when I'd won the Cheltenham Gold Cup. I was able to look them squarely in the face and say, 'Listen, I might just win another Gold one day but I know for certain that I'll never score another goal like that.' It was a fluke, but I loved it.

But it's no good getting older if you don't get wiser and the frozen ground began to give me some pain at the back of my knees: I only lasted fifteen minutes of the second half before coming off. After all, there was still Boxing Day to come and plenty of action before that.

During late September I'd moved again, this time to Kingston Lisle, a village the other side of Lambourn and not far from Nicky Henderson's base at Seven Barrows. Seamus Durack decided it wasn't right for me to live in a big house on my own so he kindly rented out his house in Hungerford and came to lodge with me full-time as a non-paying guest. He cooks well and is house-trained. He and a few of the boys thought it would be a good idea if I held a house-warming on Christmas Eve before the builders and decorators got to work. They also convinced me that I needed a full-size karaoke machine. As usual I left all the organizing to Gee and by nine o'clock the house was heaving. It was nearly impossible to get trainer Richard Phillips and Jamie Blackshaw, one of the senior men at my sponsors, Cantor Index, off the karaoke. Durack decided to mime, which defeated the object, but most of the lads had a go, including Richard Dunwoody, Adrian Maguire, Mick FitzGerald and Johnny Kavanagh.

My old lodger Barney Clifford was the first to go. He's now clerk of the course at Kempton and had to be there early on Christmas Day to make certain that Florida Pearl and the other overseas runners had all they needed. I pulled up at around four, and Dunwoody and Durack made it no further than the sofa. But I had no chance of any sleep: my room was right over the karaoke amplifiers and all I could hear were two voices booming out. I went to discover that Barry Fenton and Timmy Murphy were having an in-depth discussion using two microphones that they hadn't realized were still switched on. Most of Kingston Lisle had been treated to their considered thoughts.

I usually like to get Christmas Day over as quickly as possible and get on with business on Boxing Day. Usually I'm doing light so a full-blown lunch is out, but this year ten stone twelve was my lightest and, with the cold weather holding, it was only evens that racing would go ahead.

Durack and I decided on lunch with my co-author and his family, who know that I like nothing more than to feed up, sleep, then watch the soaps. I didn't take any chances with my weight and drifted home at nine for a sweat to be ready for an early start at Kempton.

The meeting got the go-ahead early on Boxing Day morning. Best Mate was the pick of the day in the King George and I'd got over the first hurdle by being able to ride him. Owner Jim Lewis had asked me to take the mount when it became apparent that Jim Culloty wouldn't make it. Nothing had been written in the press and I knew that Martin had at least two possible runners, Upgrade and Toto Toscato. The week before Christmas I'd gone down to school at Pond House Stables and kept putting off asking him what was happening on Boxing Day. I shuffled around the kitchen, waiting for the right moment.

Carol Pipe can read me well and she said, 'What's the matter? You've got one to ride and you don't want to upset us?'

Martin chimed in, 'It's all right, you can upset me, what's up?'

'They've asked me to ride Best Mate in the King George.'

'No problem, go ahead.'

I think he'd had a good idea anyway, but it's in his mischievous nature to make me sweat a bit. It was a big weight off my mind.

I managed to get beaten by a short head on Island Sound in the first and, to make matters worse, it was by Thierry Doumen on Barito. The young Frenchman has had plenty of flak from the media in the past and some of the other jocks don't rate him very highly, but for me it's just a different style of riding. Anyway, it was good enough to beat me by a short head, and Norman Williamson, who was commentating for Channel Four, reckoned that he'd like to be in the changing room listening to me whinge. Well, he could have done what half my other friends did and sent a message.

No sooner had I sat down to get changed for the next than my phone was bleeping. Jamie Spencer and Richard Hughes in particular had plenty of time on their hands: 'That French fella's real strong.' And 'You should pay that French fella to stay at home over Christmas to save some embarrassment.'

With friends like that . . .

The messages stopped when I won the Feltham Chase on Maximize, beating Thierry and Innox, but the King George was the big one.

I'd schooled him before Christmas and was more than happy with him. In the paddock Henrietta Knight and her husband, the former champion jump jockey Terry Biddlecombe, gave me the final instructions. Although there was little doubt about his stamina, Best Mate still hadn't won beyond two and a half miles. They reasoned that if he had the pace to win over two miles one and a half furlongs in the Haldon Gold Cup he'd have much more pace than the others in the field. The instructions were not to get in front before the second last and to produce him to lead between the last two fences. That's what I tried to do, but unfortunately Adrian Maguire had gone to the front at the tenth on Florida Pearl and had dictated the pace to suit him. I was on Adrian's shoulder as we turned for home, but when I went for Best Mate at the second last he couldn't quicken up. Although we never stopped trying, Florida Pearl was always just holding him by three-quarters of a length.

If I had made more use of him Best Mate would have won. If I had been riding for Martin Pipe I would have won, because when I ride one of his I assume that if it doesn't stay it's not going to win so I ride accordingly. You can't make a horse stay: all you can do is help it a little bit.

I was absolutely gutted when I pulled up because I knew I should have won. Walking back, I said to Mick FitzGerald, 'If I rode this horse again I'd pop him out and make loads of use round here – all he does is gallop.'

Henrietta, Terry and Jim were excellent in defeat and I told them, 'Look, I'm not saying he's slow but he's not as quick as you think he is, and he stays a lot better than you think as well.'

I watched the tape over and over again that night and knew I was right. Jim Culloty was watching it too and would change the tactics when the Cheltenham Gold Cup came round in March.

On 29 December at Newbury, Classified, owned by David Johnson, continued his improvement to win the Grade Two Challow Hurdle. I was now seventy-five away from taking Sir Gordon, only to find the weather closing in. It was the one thing, apart from injury, that could put the skids under me but, of course, there was nothing I could do about it. There was no point in going on holiday because I didn't know when we'd start up again. I did something I've never done before: I went to the Harrods sale – and I won't be doing it again. Durack and I couldn't move. It turned out that we'd gone on the opening day, when Mrs David Beckham and the opera singer Lesley Garrett had also decided to attend. I bought six pairs of boxers and came home as soon as I could.

When there is no racing my system seems to shut down. I don't have any energy and I'll lie on the sofa or on the floor in the study while Gee tries to motivate me to do office work. It's a dangerous time, because there's always someone who wants to have lunch and, with no action to burn off the calories, I can be in trouble if I'm not careful.

It's amazing how just a short period of inactivity can take the edge off your fitness. Racing began again on 7 January at Fontwell, and I had to get after my first ride in the novice hurdle, Sterling Dot Com. I could feel the freezing cold wind burning as it hit the raw tissue of my lungs, but by the time I rode Claymore for Oliver Sherwood in the third, I was clear in the wind. We won that novice hurdle and later on I followed up with Possible Pardon for Philip Hobbs in the handicap chase.

Two winners the next day at Leicester put me on 199 and on the brink of breaking my fastest 200. Now I don't know why, but I've learned that whenever a record is looming something usually goes wrong. This time was no exception. Newbury would be as good a place as any for me to get the double century. It's a great course and it's easy for me to get to one of the pubs to celebrate on the way home. The record looked a formality with five rides, three of them well fancied.

Some hope. The first, Riyadh, was 11–8 for the opening novice hurdle and we were beaten by a neck by Norman Williamson on Sonevafushi. After that, things went downhill fast. In the second I was riding one Martin had bought from France, Jour J, who started 3–1 second favourite. At the first fence he gave me no warning and hardly rose. He turned a somersault and gave me a right slap as he fired me into the ground. I should probably have called enough, but with three rides to come I couldn't bear the idea of watching one win. Bow Strada was next in the novice hurdle and he'd won his last two. I thought, If you're able to walk you ride.

Bow Strada started 2–1 second favourite, but couldn't go on the tacky ground and was well beaten when he fell at the last. Although I was now very sore, temper as much as anything else made me go out on Strong Tel in the three-mile chase, even though he had no chance and I pulled him up before the fourteenth. I was stiffening up but there was no way I wasn't going to ride Baclama for Martin in the two-mile-one-furlong handicap chase. I knew that if that horse won I'd feel even worse if I wasn't on it.

Half-way down the back straight Baclama buried me at the seventh and this was a proper fall. I was lying on the ground and felt a strange numbing feeling going through my body. Instinctively I put my hand to the back of my head. When I looked at the black glove I was wearing it was wet.

One of the first-aid people came over. 'Am I bleeding?' I asked.

They looked at me with a mixture of disbelief and pity. When I glanced down I understood why. There was blood all over the colours and my white breeches.

As I walked into the ambulance I turned to one of the assistants. 'Is the cut bad?'

'Yes.'

'How bad?'

'It's a couple of inches long and about half an inch deep.'

'Is it going to need stitches?'

'Yeah.'

When I got to the first-aid room the doctor had a poke around at the damage. I wasn't the most patient of patients. 'Doc, if this needs stitches will you find out if I can ride with them, 'cos if I can't you're going to have to think of something else to do with it.'

He went away, made some inquiries and came back. 'You can ride with them.'

'All right, carry on.'

Five stitches were inserted towards the base of my head and neck, but that was the end of the day for me and I felt like shit. The local TV station, Meridian, was covering the meeting because they thought I'd get the 200 and the young fella who was fronting it asked for an interview. I was just on the way to get a tetanus jab but it wouldn't have been fair to blank him. I suppose I should be pleased that people are interested in me, though I must say I didn't feel that way at the time.

There was plenty of speculation that I wouldn't ride the next day and I didn't expect or get any sympathy from the boys at

Wincanton. I had a big plaster pad sticking out from the back of my helmet to protect the stitches, and at this time I was on the front page of the *Racing Post* most days. 'What's the picture going to be tomorrow – the back of McCoy's head?'

Sure enough, it was. But that had been as good a kicking as I've had in my time. It told on me on that day at Wincanton when I began to get tingling feelings up my arms and down my legs. As a result, I gave up my last two rides, which didn't have a chance in my book and I was right. I was stiffening up too but it was best not to think about it. My bloody-minded attitude eventually worked in my favour because, over the next few weeks, it gradually got better.

I should have taken it easy after coming home from Wincanton but I decided on a bit of interactive physiotherapy. For some reason best known to Durack and Bradley I ended up at the Brunel Rooms disco in Swindon. It wasn't, perhaps, the shrewdest move and I was extremely sore the next morning, but still determined to ride at Huntingdon. It seemed that everyone had an opinion on whether or not I should be riding, but it would have done my head in to stay at home and watch someone else win on a horse I should have been aboard. The pain would have been ten times worse.

The first half of the day at Huntingdon made me feel that I would have been better off at home. I was beaten on my first three rides, and all of a sudden that awkward drive home in the Friday-night traffic wasn't a pleasant prospect. Then Jonjo O'Neill came to the rescue. He produced Native Man to run for his life in the Insight Of Doncaster Handicap Chase over two and a half miles. Once we got to the front, two from home, it was all over. We beat Mill Orchid and young Paddy Aspell by eight lengths, and any twinges I might have had were numbed by pleasure. I'd beaten my previous best double hundred by thirty-eight days even though I knew I'd been pushing my luck during the last three. It was a nice touch that the winner was owned by Anne, Duchess of Westminster, which meant I carried the colours immortalized by the one and only Arkle.

There was no chance of celebrating that night. I had seven rides at Warwick the next day and two of them won, the Cheltenham hopes Seebald and Classified. Then it was off for a rare trip to Ireland on Sunday for Doonaree, trained by Pat Hughes, in the Pierse Handicap Hurdle. He'd been laid out for the race and I had to sweat to do the ten stone seven.

Although I love going home to Ireland I don't ride there very often: since I left in 1994 I have only managed twenty-eight winners there but I understand why: with my heavy commitments in England there's little chance of me being available on a regular basis for Irish horses and continuity with jockeys is important.

Unfortunately, I knew Doonaree wasn't going to win from an early stage, and after we finished eighth to Adamant Approach I told Pat that I reckoned the gelding now needed three miles, not two. I got back to Heathrow by seven o'clock and headed straight to Chris Maude's retirement party in Gloucestershire. Chris had done well as a jockey and had ridden plenty of winners for Martin. He took over John and Tom Buckingham's valeting business and now looks after me. I owed it to him to make his party.

Once a year I usually get a call to do *A Question of Sport* for the BBC, which is recorded in Manchester. They wanted me two days after Chris's party and as I was racing at Folkestone they sent a helicopter. I was meant to be with Ally McCoist and Robbie Fowler, but Robbie's dad had fallen ill so John Barnes took his place. It didn't stop me making a fool of myself on the picture round. I thought that the one I chose was Gary Carter, the Flat jockey, when it was the BBC racing correspondent Clare Balding, in her younger days as an amateur rider. In my defence, she was lady champion in 1990, the same year I had my first ride so I could hardly remember! Not that it stopped me getting plenty of flak.

Two days later Robbie, his dad and Steve McManaman had plenty to smile about after Samon landed a coup for them at Taunton on 17 January. Ever since we met in the late nineties we've been great mates, and Graham Bradley has done a brilliant job buying horses from Germany for the boys. They began with Auetaler, then Seebald and Major Lando, who was fatally injured in a fall. Then Brad bought them two more, Bernardon and Samon. Martin has trained them all and they've all won, but I don't think they have ever gone for a bigger punt than that day at Taunton. Samon had decent form in Germany but drifted out from 2–1 to 3–1 before the boys' cash got back and shortened him up to 6–4 favourite. Robbie had just finished training at Leeds but managed to watch the race on the Racing Channel and, with an hour's time difference in Spain, Steve had plenty of time to settle down and watch the race on satellite. The only worries they might have had were at the first and last flights, which Samon didn't take particularly well. I hardly saw another horse as Samon won by three and a half lengths. I got a kiss from their relieved racing manager as I dismounted.

Three days later Robbie invited me up to the Leeds–Arsenal game then did the dirty on me by scoring, but we came away with a 1–1 draw so the honours ended even.

Although the pressure was building on me at work, there was plenty of time to play and I agreed to attend the *Belfast Telegraph* Sports Awards on 21 January. I love going back to my roots because it's important to let those people who knew you in the early days know that you haven't forgotten them.

Ironically, it was another of my countrymen who presented me with the Sportsman of the Year award, the recently retired Flat jockey John Reid. I say ironically, because he lives barely two miles away in the next village. I shared a great table with two soccer legends from the North, George Best and the Celtic manager Martin O'Neill. All I was missing was Pat Jennings to make the night complete.

At this stage of the season the winners weren't exactly flowing, but twelve days after hitting 200 I reached 210 in the most bizarre circumstances I've ever raced under. Normally a jump jockey gets on the evening news for one of two reasons, winning either the Cheltenham Gold Cup or the Grand National. Piddling novice chases at Southwell in the East Midlands seldom generate much interest, but on 23 January I was responsible for the 'And finally . . .' bit that rounds off the late bulletin.

I was riding Family Business for Martin in the three-mile novice chase. It was a race on an ordinary enough horse and, what's more, we didn't get any further than the tenth. I was holding him just off the pace when he stopped as though he'd been shot, jinked out to the left and I fell off. It might have been only a small race but I was livid with myself and threw my skull cap on to the ground. I hopped into the Land Rover following the field and got a lift back. I suspected the runners had gone too fast on what was extremely holding ground but I had no idea of the carnage that was taking place while I was returning to the weighing room.

I got out at the winning post, walked across the all-weather track and saw that the stable girl had brought Family Business back and was making for the unsaddling boxes to wash him down. Then I looked across the course and saw that only three of the seven were still in the race.

Bob Hodge, who'd ridden plenty of winners as a conditional jockey before becoming Martin's travelling head lad, was moving towards the horse. I called over, 'Bob, get the girl to come back here with that horse, just in case.'

Sure enough, when I looked over again there were only three standing. 'Listen, I'm going back to pop this one round, you never know what might happen.'

I went back to the fence where I had been unseated and set off in pursuit. Two of the three had fallen and been remounted and going to the fourth last I needed something to happen. It did. What A Wonder was clear when he said enough was enough, put the brakes on and refused. Eaux Les Coeurs was left in front but downed tools at the same place and got rid of his rider, Rupert Wakley. Red Radish was now ambling along with the race for the taking, but he decided to join the party and whipped round at the fence, unseating Barry Keniry. I could only just make out what was happening because I was so far behind but I felt sure that some-one would have remounted again. The best I could hope for was second, so I found it hard to believe that the judge had got it right when he called Family Business first as we crossed the line alone. With the deviations it had taken ten and a half minutes to complete the course, an amazing four minutes above the standard time.

As I walked back to the unsaddling enclosure I was given dog's abuse by Carl Llewellyn and Warren Marston. 'It couldn't happen to anyone else, you jammy git.'

I'd hardly weighed in when the phone rang. It was Martin and he was still laughing. 'Well, I suppose I can forgive you for falling off in the first place.'

All I could think was, What happens if I only beat Sir Gordon by one?

Still, no one was injured and it made a good finish to the ITN news.

16. In the Shadow of a Legend

Although I missed over a week through bad weather I had a brilliant January and rode twenty-nine winners – and just as well. On 26 January the *Racing Post* began publishing a graph showing a line I had to stay above if I was going to better Sir Gordon's record. My face was superimposed on the graph with a picture of Sir Gordon underneath. I certainly didn't need reminding of what I had to do, but I felt honoured to be pictured alongside such a legend. I'd also managed one winner that wouldn't count towards the record bid, in Ireland on Direct Bearing for Dermot Weld at Leopardstown.

I was nicely on schedule with 224 winners stacked up, but once February arrives you have to start concentrating on the good horses that would be going to Cheltenham and picking up some of the big prizes on the way. They don't come much bigger outside the Festival than the Tote Gold Trophy Handicap Hurdle at Newbury. It is one of the great handicaps and I thought we had a certainty for it in Valiramix. The horse had never stopped improving since finishing third to Landing Light in the Championship Hurdle at Sandown the previous April, and had been doing fantastic work at home.

Valiramix looked a million dollars winning the Bula Hurdle, which had transferred from Cheltenham to Newbury in December because of bad weather, and had genuine star quality. Despite top weight of twelve stone I had no doubts about riding him. I was sure he'd produce a record weight-carrying performance and in doing so underline his chance in the Champion Hurdle. Unfortunately, the week before the Gold Trophy was very wet and Martin was worried that a hard race in testing ground might see us leave the Champion Hurdle at Newbury. He was absolutely right and also had a perfect substitute ride for me in Copeland, who had finished second and fifth in the last two renewals. He was in brilliant form, having been gelded during the summer, and had won easily at Cheltenham in late January. Also, he was eight pounds better in for the Gold Trophy than for future handicaps where he would be reassessed. What was more, he loved mud. When Martin gave me the news late on Thursday night, it wasn't too hard to take but I wasn't as buzzed up about the race as I would have been had I been on Valiramix. I just wanted more information on him and to show everyone what a superb horse he had become.

But business had to be attended to and, despite drifting out to 13–2, Copeland was never in much danger of losing the £64,000 first prize. He was cutting through the mud like a surfer when we moved ahead at the fourth last and he was clear by the next. With such a lumpy prize at stake, I punched him out to the line, beating Rooster Booster by six lengths.

Although the small races are important when you're chasing records it's the big ones that get you excited. I sometimes think I should take time to enjoy them more because I was delighted to win a race with the history of the Gold Trophy. Maybe I will when I've finished, but when I watch endless replays now it's not for self-gratification but to learn something. There'll be plenty of time to bask in past glories when I'm done for good.

As it was a Saturday night and there was no racing on Sunday I made my way to the Pheasant, a pub in Shefford Woodlands about a three-iron from the M4, for a celebratory Coke with Mick FitzGerald. Mick had also enjoyed a good day, thanks to Bacchanal's win in the AON Chase. When we got there we could hardly get in. It turned out that the part-owner's son was a finalist in the TV programme *Pop Stars* and every girl in the area was cramming the place. He won it, too.

As none of the girls seemed overly impressed by a jump jockey I took off for London to see my business agent, David Manasseh. He lives just off Hyde Park, which is a good base to begin a night's clubbing. I did most of my socializing in a great place called Mo Mo's and rose late before travelling home on Sunday afternoon. A nice little break to recharge the batteries. I'm not certain that such late-night activities warranted my inclusion in the list of the Fifty

Great Racing Elizabethans, one for each year of the Queen's reign. It was compiled by the most dedicated of racing statisticians, the *Racing Post*'s John Randall, and I was the choice for 1999. Martin Pipe was the year before. Sir Gordon was there for winning the 1953 Derby.

When it comes to deciding where I should ride you'd think I'd have learned enough to go where Martin wants me. However, I have that cussed streak and on 16 February I thought Warwick was the place to be. Martin said Ascot, so I went there, missed two winners at Warwick – and rode three at Ascot, including the big race of the day, the £38,000 Ritz Club Ascot Chase, on Tresor De Mai. I also won the Fernbank Novices' Chase on Iznogoud for Martin. Norman Williamson told me it was all down to him and Returning that I beat the 6–5 favourite Valley Henry in that race. 'I won that race for you, champ, by taking on Valley Henry at the downhill fences.'

Well, he certainly didn't do me any harm.

Perhaps the most relieving aspect of the afternoon was the third winner, Stormez, in the three-mile novice hurdle. He was one of the leading young hurdlers in France, beating the likes of Bilboa, and was priced accordingly when David Johnson bought him. He had disappointed in his two British outings, but the step up in distance worked ideally, and David was able to take a strong financial option at 2–1. It wasn't straightforward, though, and after looking sure to win easily I had to get quite vigorous on the run-in for a neck win.

Some sections of the press seemed to get a warped pleasure out of the apparent lack of success that David enjoyed with some of his more expensive purchases. It's worth pointing out that he's had plenty of success at Cheltenham and Aintree and most of the other big Festivals with horses that have come from the other end of the market. Fortunately he's philosophical, win or lose.

On 20 February I rode four winners at Ludlow, two for Martin and two for another great ally, Jonjo O'Neill. This put me on 248 and the bookmakers put the shutters up and stopped betting on whether I'd beat Sir Gordon's record. However, if they'd spoken to me a couple of days later I would have given them every encouragement to start up again. I went thirteen rides without a winner and, while there's nothing strange in that, I didn't feel I was riding well. There was nothing I could put a finger on but I wasn't happy with myself. I thought things were sure to pick up at the big Haydock meeting on the following Saturday, but it was rained off and that morning I switched to Kempton. I took over on two for Martin that didn't show anything, and Jonjo O'Neill let me back on Lorenzino in the handicap hurdle. This meant that I jocked off Dickie Johnson, who had been booked to ride in my absence – there was no problem with Dickie as I'd won on the horse previously. It was a close call but I just managed to get Lorenzino home by a head and I was happy to see the back of that week. However, if I thought that week was bad then the one that followed was uncomfortable for racing in general.

On Tuesday 26 February the Jockey Club swooped at dawn on Martin's yard to take blood samples that would be tested for possible use of banned drugs. Three other top jump trainers were also raided: Paul Nicholls, Venetia Williams and Len Lungo. The tiny yard of Alan Jones also got a visit.

The whole business had been stirred up by Upper Lambourn trainer Charlie Mann, who in December was quoted as saying that horses were running and winning 'every day of the week' having been given the illegal performance-enhancing drug erythropoetin, or EPO. Martin knew he had nothing to hide, and late the following afternoon it was announced that all the horses tested from each yard had come up clean.

With Cheltenham barely two weeks away it wasn't the sort of publicity racing needed but with Charlie Mann's whingeing to the press something had to be done. But, then, he is a trainer I had vowed I would never ride for again.

I used to ride a few for him and on 16 July 2000 he booked me for Bolton Forest in a three-mile novice chase at Stratford. The horse had won easily at Market Rasen two months earlier and started 5–2 favourite in a field of thirteen. Charlie gave me my orders, saying that the horse jumped well and suggesting that I should ride him how I wanted but preferably handy to the pace.

He was right: the horse jumped brilliantly and, after taking the lead at the thirteenth, we were soon in a clear lead. Unfortunately a horse ridden by David Dennis, Yer 'Umble, gradually wore us down, taking the lead on the run-in to win by a length and a half with the third beaten by fourteen lengths.

I came back to the unsaddling enclosure to see Charlie and the owners, and reported that Bolton Forest had jumped and run well. It was just a shame he got beaten. Everyone, including Charlie, seemed happy, and there wasn't a bother. That was on Sunday. The following day at Newton Abbot I was talking to Luke Harvey, who said that Charlie wasn't very pleased with the ride I'd given Bolton Forest. 'Well,' I said, 'he's said nothing to me and I'm down to ride Life Of Riley for him at Worcester on Wednesday.' I put in a call to Dave Roberts. 'Do I ride Life Of Riley for Charlie Mann at Worcester?'

'No, Dickie Johnson rides it.'

'Why?'

'Charlie says Bolton Forest's owners weren't happy at Stratford and none of his owners want you to ride their horses.'

Now, I didn't mind that the owners didn't want me to ride their horses. They were perfectly entitled to have who they wanted – after all, they paid the training fees. What really pissed me off was that Charlie had said nothing to me and I'd had to find out through third parties.

I was intent on having it out with him and waited for my moment in the old wooden weighing room at Worcester, which is a reminder of what jump racing used to be like. I kept my eye on Dickie to see when he went out to weigh for Life Of Riley and hand over the saddle. As he made for the door I shadowed him. Then, turning to Warren Marston, I said, 'I'm going to have this fella. I wouldn't mind if he told me afterwards that he thought I'd given his horse a bad ride but I don't want to learn it from other people.'

Charlie was standing by the scale. 'All right, AP?'

'I'll give you all right, now.' I'm afraid that I threw in a full range of expletives. 'You told Luke Harvey you weren't happy with the ride I gave your horse. You told Dave Roberts that none of your owners want me to ride for you again. Yet when I'm in the unsaddling enclosure after the race, everything's grand and everyone's happy as Larry. Not a word's said.'

Charlie said that he and the owners had gone home and, having looked at the video of the race, had felt I'd made too much use of the horse.

'Charlie, I'm not the brightest fella in the world, but you're telling me that you stood in the stand, watching me ride your horse, and then you have to watch a video to find out whether I'd given it a good or bad ride? I'm very pleased that I ride for someone like Martin Pipe, who trusts my judgement and knows right well that if I've given a horse a bad ride I'll have the balls to come back and tell him. But it's the last time I'll have to worry about it with you, I can assure you of that.'

I haven't worried him since that day and I never will. If Charlie Mann had the favourites for the Cheltenham Gold Cup, the Champion Hurdle and the Grand National I wouldn't ride them. Not if I was paid in gold bars.

As March approached Martin was doing everything he could to make sure I rode winners, even to the point that he was letting me off his less-fancied runners to go elsewhere. Instead of riding two beaten favourites for him at Taunton one day I rode two winners at Ludlow, one for Jonjo and the other for Mark Brisbourne. He did the same on 2 March, when I went to Huntingdon and rode a treble for Jonjo, which put me on 255 for the season, two ahead of my previous best in 1997–8.

The press were really playing up the comparison with Sir Gordon so I tried to put the thing in perspective: 'They were different times and other people are making a big thing of it. I definitely couldn't do it without the boss and I'm lucky that Jonjo lets me ride a lot of his. If you manage to stay in one piece in this game, you're going to be in a great position.'

The truth of that statement was brought home to me that night as I sat down for supper with friends at the Queen's Arms in East Garston. Not long after we'd finished the meal Seamus Durack hobbled in on crutches, having taken a heavy fall at Doncaster. He was hoping he hadn't broken the leg – it had kept him out for a long time the previous season. Sadly, an X-ray on Monday showed that he had, and therefore he was out for the rest of the season. It was impossible to raise his spirits and, as he was my lodger, I saw a lot of him. Poor old Seamus was a constant reminder to me of just how lucky I was.

The *Racing Post* was still doing a great job in reminding me of what I had to do. Each issue carried the graph with the number of winners to go and my rides for the day. However, all my thoughts were focused on Cheltenham and which of Martin's 101 entries I should ride. There was also the growing number of Cheltenham preview nights that I had been asked to attend and, while I can't do many, I always try to get back to Wexford for Jim Bolger's production. I might have thought it was a prison camp when I was a kid but I enjoy going back there as a visitor.

Sure enough, I arrived without a tie and Jim was on me in a flash: 'Didn't I teach you how to dress when you were here?'

I told the audience just how highly I rated Valiramix and a few days later I read a feature on his owner, seventy-three-year-old Jim Weeden, who also had Potentate and Doctor Green in training with Martin.

Jim had been forced to retire as a farmer in 1999 after suffering a stroke, which took the sight of one eye. In the story he revealed that his only hobby was following the progress and possibly the greatness of Valiramix: 'He is the only thing worth living for, and I wake up at night and think about him. I still get the effects of the stroke, but it is getting better and the horse helps me to stop thinking about it.'

The weekend before Cheltenham I began whittling down a short-list of horses I would ride for Martin, but there were constant reminders from elsewhere of how things can go wrong at the last minute. Martin had set up Sir Stanley Clarke's Polar Red for the same Imperial Cup–County Hurdle double that Blowing Wind had completed in 1998, but the handicapper had taken a stern view of his first win at Cheltenham in late January and hiked him twenty-three pounds. He was heavily backed at 6–4 in a field of sixteen and we just made it, beating Impek and Jim Culloty by a head.

However, events were once again put into perspective later in the afternoon when news came through that Adrian Maguire had badly damaged his neck in a fall at Warwick. It meant that he would miss Cheltenham for the fourth time in eight years.

On the Monday of Cheltenham week I had sorted out my rides and the bookmakers made me 5–4 favourite to be leading rider at the meeting. By the end of the second day you could have bet 3–1 that I wouldn't ride one winner.

17. You Only Sing When You're Winning

You need to understand that the Cheltenham Festival is the pinnacle of the jump season for everyone involved, from the newest stable lad to Martin Pipe. There was an added edge to 2002 as the previous year's meeting had been lost to foot-and-mouth.

When it came down to deciding which of Martin's fifty-seven five-day declarations I was eligible to ride I knew I wouldn't get it completely right. Martin gave me all the help he could. So, too, did his son, David, and Jonothan Lower. I kept bouncing options off Dave Roberts but in the end it was my decision. Horses can be flying at home only to run lifelessly in a race. Equally, a horse who has shown nothing like the required form will run better than it's ever done and for no apparent reason.

On the Flat it happens every week at the height of the season with operations like Coolmore and Godolphin. The top Flat jockeys can't choose right all the time.

But as I left Stratford on the Monday afternoon after riding a winner for Jonjo O'Neill and J. P. McManus, the owner of Istabraq who was going for an unprecedented fourth Champion Hurdle, I meant it when I told Jonjo, 'Valiramix is by far my best ride of the meeting.'

That win on Jonjo's Druid's Glen put me just eight short of breaking Sir Gordon Richards's record, but as I made my way to the house at Toddington that I'd rented with Graham Bradley for the three days my mind was a million miles away from breaking records. All I could centre on was the next day and the Champion Hurdle.

I had agreed to appear on the Morning Line for *Channel Four Racing*, which was coming live from the course, so I got there early. There had been persistent rumours about Istabraq's well-being and I said he'd have to be at his best to handle Valiramix.

After the show I slipped off to the first-aid room to get some sleep.

My first ride was Westender in the Gerrard Supreme Novices' Hurdle. I'd chosen him from five of Martin's entries including Bernardon, who was owned by Robbie Fowler and Steve McManaman. Steve was in Madrid while Robbie had hired a box for friends and family, but the boys understood that business was business and I had to ride the one I thought best.

Unfortunately, Robbie was the first casualty of the day. He came down to the paddock to give Bernardon a pat just as Richard Guest was mounting. In a split second his eyes puffed up like strawberries and began streaming. He watched the race on the big screen in the paddock with Brad, and after he'd seen his horse fall he was rushed to the ambulance room. He was given antihistamines but before they could give him a steroid jab they had to phone the Leeds United physio to make sure it was declared the next time he played. Robbie went back to his box, his eyes still watering, and one young lady remarked, 'Dear me, Robbie, do you always get so upset when your horses fall?'

I chose right, but Westender wasn't quite good enough to concede the five-pound mare's allowance to Like-A-Butterfly, ridden by Charlie Swan, and went down by a battling neck.

Next up was Robbie and Steve's pride and joy, Seebald, in the Irish Independent Arkle Trophy. Robbie didn't appear in the paddock this time but it was impossible not to be disappointed with Seebald, who might have been feeling the effects of a busy season. He was never going with any fire and I had to get after him from the sixth fence, which was much too soon for comfort. It was only the horse's courage that allowed me to force him alongside Armaturk at the third last and, although Seebald was flat to the boards, I knew we had that battle won. Then Barry Geraghty came swinging through to take the lead on Moscow Flyer two from home and I knew we were going to be second best.

Seebald kept trying but Moscow Flyer looked as though he had just jumped in and beat us by an easy four lengths. We were two races into the Festival and two of my best chances had finished second with no excuses. Perhaps I should have twigged that this wasn't going to be my meeting, but the ace in my hand was coming up in the third race of the day, Valiramix in the Champion Hurdle.

Make no mistake, this had been my horse of the season from the very start. My reports to Martin had got more enthusiastic each time I had ridden him, even when he'd been beaten.

In November 2000 after he'd won a two-mile handicap hurdle at Newbury with top weight of eleven stone thirteen I stated, 'He was very keen early on but stayed and was always going well.'

On his next run at Ascot he won the Knights Royal Hurdle by four lengths and I reported, 'Settled much better than last time and was going well to three out. Gurgled badly from then on.'

If a horse is messing with its tongue, it can make a noise in its throat. It can also be caused by a problem with the epiglottis or even by the stress of struggling through heavy ground as it was that day. It hadn't stopped Valiramix and I recommended, 'Might be better on faster ground.'

Valiramix was beaten in his two remaining races of 2000–01 but I never lost faith in him.

In the Sunderlands Imperial Cup at Sandown he had a massive twelve stone to carry and the ground was unsuitably heavy. He performed heroics to finish seven lengths second to Ibal, giving him thirty-three pounds, and I faxed to Martin, 'Travelled well all the way. Started to gurgle from three out but battled on well. Just too much weight. Will be better on faster ground. Should run in the Champion Hurdle – if there is one.'

There wasn't, but he ran in the substitute race on Whitbread Gold Cup day at Sandown, which finished the season. This was his first step into championship class and, despite jumping clumsily, he was a very fair third to Nicky Henderson's pair, Landing Light and Geos, with such top-quality performers as Barton, Bilboa and subsequent Champion Hurdle winner Hors La Loi III behind.

I was far from despondent and reported, 'Travelled very well but did not jump as well as normal and might have won if he'd jumped better.'

Martin had given Valiramix just the one prep race before the 2002

Champion Hurdle, heeding my warnings about the unsuitability of very soft ground and taking him out of the Tote Gold Trophy at Newbury. His sole run of the season was at the pre-Christmas meeting at Newbury, where he won the Bula Hurdle by nine lengths. My post-race report was brief: 'Always going well, won very easily and settled much better. Can run in any of the top two-mile races.'

Although he'd been off for three months I had been well pleased with Valiramix whenever I'd seen him on my visits to Pond House Stables. When anyone had asked me my best chance at the meeting I'd never hesitated to say Valiramix. I just had massive faith in him.

There is always an apprehensive air in the paddock before a big race like the Champion Hurdle, and I could sense the pride and anticipation in Valiramix's owner Jim Weeden. I was anxious to get going and do the business. I wanted people to know what I was certain I knew already: that Valiramix was a champion.

The fact that the reigning champion Istabraq pulled up lame after the second flight didn't alter my game plan at all. I was happy to hold Valiramix at the rear of the field; it wasn't until after the fourth that I began to creep closer. I moved him in behind the leaders as we freewheeled downhill after the third last flight and still had a tight hold of his head. There was no need to go just yet. Then, in a couple of strides, the dream died. Valiramix lurched on to his nose and came down. I knew the way he went down that he was gone. In those few seconds all the hopes of the year went.

I have replayed those final moments time and again, and I have never changed my immediate thoughts of that day. I'm sure something happened to him coming down the hill. When he went down on his nose he tried to save himself but couldn't. I didn't think he'd clipped heels. Horses do that every day in races then stumble on and regain their stride. The way he went down he was never going to be able to save himself.

Martin and his son, David, were soon with us and they were distraught. Although the horse ambulance had soon arrived we all knew there was no saving Valiramix.

I went back to the first-aid room behind the weighing room and thought of his owner. Jim had said that Valiramix was the only thing that made life worth living. Then there was Martin and his team, who had improved the horse by literally stones in the past year. For me he was my ride of the season and for the seasons to come. I'd never had a horse like Desert Orchid, One Man or Istabraq. They were the types who would dominate for years and I knew Valiramix was potentially just as good. I mumbled to myself, 'He'd got the Champion Hurdle won. He'd have pissed up.' And put my head in my hands and wept.

This was much worse than Gloria Victis. That had happened on the last day of the meeting and I could lose myself around the gaffs. Now I just didn't want to be at Cheltenham. There were three races to go and I had to perform. My riding wasn't affected because when I get on to a horse I instinctively block everything else out. If I could have come out of the weighing room and got down to the start without seeing anyone it would have been a little easier to bear. But you can't forget it in between.

The Champion Hurdle ended as a wonderful personal triumph for Dean Gallagher on Hors La Loi III, whom I'd ridden to win the 1999 Supreme Novices' before Martin and owner Paul Green had fallen out. Dean had rebuilt his life after testing positive for cocaine while riding in France and this was his highest point.

I couldn't have been any lower.

Carryonharry started second favourite but finished only ninth in the William Hill National Hunt Handicap Chase, which followed, and two of Martin's other runners finished ahead of him. I couldn't have cared less about that. It was the same in the last race of the day, the Pertemps Handicap Hurdle Final. I was on second favourite Ideal du Bois Beury and three of Martin's team finished nearer than I did. All I wanted to do was get away. I sent a message to Channel Four to say that I wouldn't be doing their morning programme for the remaining two days, and went to bed at nine fifteen. Sleep is my escape mechanism but I kept throwing the horrible events of the day around in my mind and the last time I looked at my watch it was one thirty.

When I got up on Wednesday morning I knew the next two

days were going to be tough but I didn't realize just how tough. Classified ran without much fire but still managed to finish fourth in the Royal & Sun Alliance Novices' Hurdle. The light in Edredon Bleu was dimming and, on unsuitably soft ground, he was only fourth in the Queen Mother Champion Chase.

Things got worse in the Coral Eurobet Cup Handicap Hurdle when I picked 11–2 favourite Golden Alpha from Martin's six runners. As I suspected, one horse ran out of his skin for no apparent reason and that was Martin's unconsidered outsider Ilnamar, who won by an easy eight lengths under Rodi Greene at 25–1. I finished last of the twenty-six that completed. Not that Martin had much to smile about afterwards. The stewards fined him £2,000 for not running Magnus on his merits after the horse finished one place ahead of me. The horse was banned from racing for forty days and his jockey, Barry Geraghty, was suspended for twelve days. Martin was fuming but, after he had submitted veterinary evidence at the subsequent appeal, the decisions were rightly overturned.

It shows the strength of Martin's team that I only failed by two lengths to win the Royal & Sun Alliance Chase on the 14–1 shot Iznogoud. Before racing, Norman Williamson, who was having a moderate time himself, tried to cheer me up: 'Champ, Lady Cricket's a certainty in the Mildmay Of Flete, isn't she?'

'Sure, the only one that can beat her is Blowing Wind.'

He did, and it was only in the final fifty yards that Ruby Walsh caught me. If that wasn't bad enough I got even more grief from the media the next day.

I had already received a text from Richard Dunwoody telling me not to worry. I sent him one back saying that was rich coming from him. I had another surprise when I met David Johnson and a group of friends in the paddock before the JCB Triumph Hurdle on Thursday. David did the introductions, but I wasn't paying any attention. In fact, I was in a world of my own as he said, 'And this is Alex.'

I didn't take a blind bit of notice and thought it was another of David's mates until, a few seconds later, I heard the Glasgow accent that has sent a shiver through some of the best players in the Premier

League. I looked at Sir Alex Ferguson and grinned. 'Jeez, they must think I'm going mad or bad if they've got you to come and sort me out.'

I'd met Sir Alex many times before and he beamed. 'I thought it might be a good idea to have a chat with you, but I took one look at you and thought it would be like trying to counsel Roy Keane after a defeat. I'd rather not waste my time. When he suffers, everyone suffers. You seem exactly the same. Better off leaving you alone.'

It's funny. You dream about meeting people like that when you're a kid, getting to shake their hand. The fact that he had come to see if I was all right was something I didn't appreciate at the time. When I got home that night I thought how kind he had been. I think he understood, probably better than most. That's why he's a great man manager.

Londoner showed no fight in the Triumph, and although It Takes Time ran above himself to finish third in the Bonusprint Stayers' Hurdle I never got into the Gold Cup on Shooting Light and pulled him up after the twelfth. At least I had been right about Best Mate: he stayed every bit as well as I'd thought he would and beat Commanche Court to give Henrietta Knight and Jim Culloty a day they will cherish for ever.

Exit Swinger tried his heart out for me in the Grand Annual Handicap Chase, but my former lodger David Casey always just had me on Fadoudal du Cochet. Time was running out, with only two races to go, and those who had taken the 3–1 about me not having a winner at the meeting must have been calculating their winnings.

Things suddenly changed in the Cathcart Chase. Royal Auclair had won his last two races and was still improving. The punters latched on to him and made him 2–1 favourite and I had him clear from the fifth fence. Everything seemed safe until Ruby Walsh appeared, looking a big danger, on Cregg House going to the last. Fortunately, when it came to a battle, Royal Auclair just had the greater stomach for it and stayed on to win all out by a length and a half. In a typically spontaneous gesture Ruby stretched out his hand in congratulation and I took it. Now people remembered that I hadn't been anywhere near as gracious in defeat over the previous three days. Also, I hadn't been interviewed on TV as I am usually. I was a sore loser.

I could never complain about the coverage I get in the press and on TV. I go out of my way to help when I can because I feel it is the right thing to do. I seldom refuse an interview because it is up to people like me to increase the profile of the sport. All year I'd had wonderful coverage and I knew that at some time something would be written that wasn't complimentary. People can't keep writing good things all the time – the media just don't work that way and if you're in any sport you've got to be able to take it.

On page three of the *Racing Post* on Friday morning Alastair Down wrote:

McCoy has ensured a rancid week and suffered the low point of his career with Valiramix's death on Tuesday.

But those who admire him both as man and jockey feel that he has overdone some of the despair.

When he won on Royal Auclair, runner-up Ruby Walsh was quickly over to shake his hand and the mutual congratulation between jockeys is a joyful aspect of this meeting. After all, these boys know what it means more than any to win here – and the brutality of the risks they all run in order to achieve it.

But this week AP has not congratulated anyone, not a pat on the back, not a shaken hand.

Frankly, it has been out of character as there is no finer gentleman in the weighing room and he is the best of company.

Hopefully, he will polish up his skills a bit. He's a fine winner and is a big enough man to master the art of being a more gracious loser.

Unfortunately, it's not in my nature to be congratulatory in the immediate aftermath of big races because I am not happy for someone else to beat me. I can't bring myself to throw my arms around someone or say well done when they've just beaten me, but I always say well done later. It's not my way to start embracing other jockeys. That doesn't mean I feel any different towards the lads or that I'm a horrible person. It's just not me. Nor was it a knock-on effect from what had happened to Valiramix, although I was deeply upset for everyone involved, especially his owner. I'm just not good at finishing second then celebrating with the person who's beaten me.

As for people writing about it and not being happy about it, well, they're perfectly entitled to. As I said in a letter to the *Racing Post* at the end of the season, 'Sorry if I upset you at Cheltenham, that was not the intention. Think yourself lucky – I have to live with me all the time!'

It was almost a relief to get back to the bread-and-butter stuff at Chepstow on the Friday. A win on Running Times for Martin in the claiming hurdle there put me just six behind the record on 264. There have been times when I've rattled six up in two days, but with Aintree coming up I knew there was going to be a dry spell and it would be tough. Most people had got used to me riding ten or twelve winners a week. By contrast, I felt that the record wasn't going to happen as soon as everyone thought. The horses just weren't there and I knew I'd have to grind out a winner here and there. In fact, I wasn't getting that many rides – I even flew up to Ayr for just one and that finished second.

On 19 March Martin and his family suffered a blow that put everything in perspective: his father, Dave, died at the age of seventy-eight after a long illness. Martin said, 'The whole yard is in mourning and everyone is very upset. Dad started everything here at Pond House and I owe him everything.'

He was 100 per cent right. Indeed, had it not been for Dave Pipe's encouragement and faith in his son I would not have been on the verge of breaking a record that had stood since 1947.

The death of his father really rocked Martin and he had hit a low by the following weekend. I opted for Bangor and drew a blank, while Ravenswood won at Newbury for Tom Scudamore. Martin could take no pleasure in the victory: 'I'm really sick of it all at the moment and feel like giving up. It's all getting to me a bit, with

Dad dying and Valiramix.' He was also still smarting from his treatment by the Cheltenham stewards over Magnus but that was soon to be overturned.

He had been stung, too, by the heavy-handed approach of the Jockey Club concerning the unfounded allegations about trainers using EPO. Fortunately, he was strong enough to put his anxieties to the back of his mind.

With a three-day break ahead, I decided to get some sun and flew to Marbella with Mick FitzGerald and Jamie Blackshaw, who works for Cantor Index, an arm of Cantor Fitzgerald, the firm who have sponsored me for the last two years. The nights were long, the golf was good, and when I got back late on Wednesday night, ready for action at Exeter the next day, I could have done with another week to recuperate. So much for holidays.

Some of the best news I read was the steady progress that Adrian Maguire was making, while Joe Tizzard was also coming to terms with a lengthy lay-off having injured his spine at Hereford a week earlier.

There was no joy for me at Exeter, and after I'd done a bungee jump at the Lambourn Open Day on Good Friday before a crowd of 10,000 I played a round of golf and got ready for seven rides at Newton Abbot. Five started favourite and only one, Polar Champ, won. He was my first winner for eight days, and things were tense. I just wanted to be done with the record.

I suppose I should have been wary of April Fool's Day. I went to Chepstow for five rides, all favourites, and only the first, Carandrew, won. Frankie Dettori and Jamie Spencer were travelling back to Newmarket from Kempton and had been listening to Radio Five Live, which mentioned that I'd now ridden 267 winners. I hadn't been on the M4 long when the mobile rang and Spencer's number flashed up. The pair said they'd called me up to ask what had happened to the seven hundred rides I'd had that hadn't won. Sometimes it's great to have friends.

April 2, 2002, started busy. Although I was riding at Warwick in the afternoon Martin wanted me to school the horses going to the Grand National meeting, which began two days later on Thursday.

My good friend Tom Butterfield, who made the Queen's Arms at East Garston legendary when he owned it, was my driver for the day. I'd long since decided to ride Blowing Wind in the National after his brave effort the previous year. His win at Cheltenham had underlined my determination. He was clearly in good order, as were the rest of the Aintree team, and I slept contentedly on the journey up the M5 to Warwick. With three winners needed to break Sir Gordon's record I didn't think today was likely to be the day. I had five rides, but the races were tough and competitive. Under those circumstances, and with the way my form had been, I told myself to be satisfied with one.

Later I took a call from Marcus Reader, owner of my second last ride of the day, Valfonic, in the Leek Wooton Novices' Handicap Hurdle. 'I'm just about to leave London and come up to Warwick. Do you think the horse has got any chance?'

'To be honest, Marcus, I think he's got plenty on his plate. I haven't ridden him since his first run when he was seventh at Plumpton in January but he unseated last time and didn't show much in the run in between. I think he's got plenty to do.'

I'd convinced him. 'OK, I'll stay at home and watch on the Racing Channel.'

My first ride, Shampooed, trained by Robin Dickin, hadn't won since the beginning of May when he was partnered by Chris Maude. It was the first time I'd ridden the horse that season and for Shampooed to start 13–8 favourite, I knew the Hampton Magna Novices' Chase must have been moderate. I was confident he'd jump, so we were either leading or pressing for the lead until we took a decisive advantage three fences out. He never felt like stopping and I pushed him out for a two-length win.

Martin provided my next ride, Sadler's Secret in the handicap hurdle, and when he weakened to finish fourth my forecast of one winner seemed fair. Next up was Shepherds Rest, trained by Charlie Morlock, in the Barford Handicap Chase. I knew that, despite starting second favourite at 5–1, this one had two ways of running and if he wasn't on a going day nothing I did would make the slightest difference.

I was in luck. The old horse was sweet as a nut and loved it as I held him up in the rear. He was full of running when I moved him in behind the leaders at the eleventh so I didn't ask him to do much until after the second last. He was never going to stop once he took the lead going to the last and we won by six lengths.

Whatever else happened, I had now drawn alongside Sir Gordon. Now it was a matter of time – not if but when. If my two remaining rides didn't do it, then I knew I had some good ones at Ascot the next day.

Although Valfonic started 4–1 favourite I found it hard to see him winning. He simply hadn't shown enough and when he made a mistake at the second I didn't hold out much hope. I gave him plenty of time to settle on the long four-furlong run to the fourth flight and, after we had jumped that, I realized he had plenty left. Creeping closer at the next, we were tucked in behind the leaders at the third last, but just as I moved him up to challenge Dunkerron and Ben Hitchcott at the second last he made another mistake. The last two flights at Warwick are quite close together. I had barely got Valfonic back on an even keel when he arrived at the last, where Barry Fenton had driven Tasbok up to dispute the lead. Luckily, Valfonic landed running and we got a narrow lead soon after touching down. Now it was head down and go for the line. Valfonic was with me all the way. He kept pulling out a little bit extra as the line came up and was still extending when we crossed it, a length and a quarter in front of Tasbok. The crowd wasn't massive, but as I pulled up I could see people rushing off the stands to get down to the unsaddling enclosure.

Barry finished upsides me and was first to shake my hand. Then the other lads milled round or called over their congratulations. Mick FitzGerald, Dean Gallagher and Mattie Bachelor were quick to grab me. Warwick might not have been the most romantic setting in which to reach such a milestone but in many ways it was fitting. So many of those 270 winners had been achieved around the small, unremarkable courses like Warwick.

Before I got back to unsaddle I felt the exhilaration bursting through me and I was soon punching the air with both hands. I was at once delighted and relieved to have the whole thing out of the way. I knew that I'd managed to do something that wasn't easy and it was a different kind of buzz from the one you get winning a big race like the Gold Cup or the Champion Hurdle. It was the long haul, not just the five minutes or so that it takes to win a race. This had been a war of attrition and I'd finally won it.

Perhaps one of the most satisfying aspects was that the boys in the weighing room seemed genuinely pleased for me. As much as anything, I think it is important to have the respect and friendship of your peers.

I came out wearing my back protector and was given a bottle of champagne to celebrate, although I said a Coke would have been better. The media people had been following me around for days but it was clear that some of them still didn't know me very well. 'Tony, take a swig of champagne.'

'Not on your life! Can't stand the stuff.'

Still, I had to do something with it, so I did a Michael Schumacher and sprayed whoever was in range. I didn't mind who got hit so long as none ended up spilling on to my lips.

I hadn't prepared a speech, but I knew right enough who were the people to thank for getting me to this memorable stage. First and foremost I felt real pleasure for my mother, father, sisters and brother. Then there was my extended family headed by Billy Rock, the man who had had almost blind faith in me. He had kept telling my dad that I'd make it when it might have looked as though I wouldn't. I ended one interview with the throwaway line: 'Perhaps my mum and dad think it was worth my while going into racing now!' In fact, they couldn't have been more supportive.

People also had to understand that I had been moulded by a good man in Jim Bolger, and after him Toby Balding had always had my best interests at heart. I needed to give credit to Martin, because I knew that without him it would have been an impossibility to ride such a number of winners. What was more, if I had needed to go down to the wire of the last days of the season I knew that Martin would have kept finding horses for me. In many ways it was as much his success as mine.

Martin paid me a wonderful compliment when he said later, 'Only this morning he schooled his National mount Blowing Wind, but he also schooled as many of our other National runners as he could, which just proves he is a team player. That is why we all love him so much at Pond House – he is part of the team, part of the family.'

And then there was my back-up team. I wanted everyone to be aware of just how big a part they had played and said, 'Dave Roberts knows the form book inside out and has booked every single ride I've ever had since I came to England. Gee Armytage does a wonderful job organizing me away from racing and takes the pressure off.'

Because I wasn't riding in the next race I could make time for everyone who needed an interview and the public who wanted their racecards autographed. At least they'd have proof that they were there with me when I did it.

The question I was asked continually was: 'What does it feel like to have beaten Sir Gordon Richards's record?'

It was as easy to answer then as it is now. In many ways I felt embarrassed to be mentioned alongside him and I wouldn't dream of comparing myself with someone like him. He'd won the Flat championship twenty-six times. If I wanted to do that jumping I'd have to ride until I was fifty – and even I know my limits. When someone showed me the Flat form book for 1947 it looked a puny little volume compared to its jumping brother of 2001–02. Just how had the man got 269 winners out of it?

No one will ever surpass what Sir Gordon achieved over fifty years ago, no matter how many winners they ride in a season. But there are certain things that I would like to share with him. From what I have read and been told by those who knew him, he was dead straight, spoke the truth and, above everything else, had the respect of his fellow men. On a wonderful afternoon in early April, I would gladly settle for that.

I finished third on my final ride of the day, Sure Touch for Jonjo in the bumper, and set off for home – although I knew I wouldn't be there for very long. The fact that I had to do light at Ascot the next day wasn't excuse enough to put off a party at the Pheasant — it's not every day you make it to 270 winners.

I spoke to Radio Five Live and finally made it to the pub at around eight forty-five, only to find that Dave Roberts had been there for an hour having come straight from his Reigate home. It's not often you get Dave out in the middle of the week. Marcus Reader, who clearly held no grudges that I'd put him off Valfonic, had come down from London and also beaten me to it. By the time I arrived nearly everyone I wanted to be there, except my family, was present. It was wonderful to see Adrian Maguire, albeit with his head pinned into a horrendous-looking cage, among the crowd. He had been driven over from Faringdon by his wife Sabrina, who had seen me, years ago, come into Jim Bolger's weighing barely six stone. And I had another reminder of just how much luck I had on my side when Seamus Durack limped through the door on crutches, having travelled back from Ireland with Norman Williamson.

The late evening news put together a package from Warwick that afternoon intercut with black-and-white newsreel footage of Sir Gordon. I suppose that in years to come they'll wheel out some old shots of me when I'm knocked off my perch by some youngster.

It wasn't a particularly late night, by our standards, and I was home by around one and soon out for the count.

I was back on the wheel next morning, but I hadn't checked the fax when I came back the previous night and now it had run on to the floor. As I looked through the list of messages there were many, many names from the past, sending me congratulations. Among them was Jim Bolger, and a long one from Coolmore with the signatures of Aidan O'Brien and all his team, including my friend from way back, T. J. Comerford.

With ten stone seven to do on Spy Knoll at Ascot I took the *Racing Post* into the bath for company. I found it hard to accept that all the tributes were about me, but back came that old chestnut about me burning myself out and the possibility of snapping mentally and physically. I know it was well meant, but I also know that

I've got the best job in the world and the easiest lifestyle – because it's the one I choose.

Winners are a bit like buses: nothing for a while and then there are three. Sure enough, my first ride at Ascot won, so the BBC were unlucky in that they missed covering me breaking the record by just one day. But that had been yesterday, and the following day the Grand National meeting opened at Liverpool and there was no point in dwelling on the past. As my counsellor Sir Alex Ferguson has said: 'The past is never enough. A victory only lasts a moment. It's where the next one is that matters.'

18. Absent Friends

Although the Grand National is watched all over the world, the Aintree meeting is only the second biggest of the year, next to Cheltenham. It's still a great one, though, and I was keen to make the right choices and not miss out as I had done at the Festival in March. After the Ascot meeting on Wednesday I drove straight to Liverpool to avoid any travel hassle and booked into my usual base, the Moat House. Most of the lads stay there so you're never short of company.

Cyfor Malta ran well, though not well enough to match Florida Pearl in the Martell Cup Chase. It wasn't until the last race of the day, the Martell Mersey Novices' Hurdle, that I managed a winner. Classified was tough enough to shrug off his hard race at Cheltenham and held off Eternal Spring to put me on the scoreboard.

However, the next day things took a big dive and, in the end, I was lucky to be riding in the National on Saturday. I gave Take Control one more chance in the three-mile-one-furlong handicap chase, which opened the card, and Cadougold finished just ahead of him. We were fourth and fifth, so there was no damage done, but later in the month Take Control had the last laugh.

Westender was favourite for the following race, the Martell Top Novices' Hurdle, but unlike Classified he was probably still feeling the effects of his hard second at Cheltenham and couldn't confirm that form with In Contrast. Dickie Johnson on In Contrast came up my inside after the third last and I held my line and tried to keep him out. It was something and nothing, but I felt it was my right to be there, not his. It wouldn't have mattered who it was, I'd have still done the same. I didn't feel that I'd come off a true line any more than he had and the stewards decided that any interference had been accidental and took no action.

I went for the wrong one in the Mumm Melling Chase in choosing Upgrade over Wahiba Sands, who responded to a strong ride from Norman Williamson and was beaten by a length by Native Upmanship. Northern Starlight, trying to repeat his Topham Chase win of 2000, had just been headed when he blundered four out and got rid of me. There were no excuses for Tarxien, who finished second to Stromness in the Martell Sefton Novices' Hurdle, but I felt sure that whatever else happened I'd be justified in getting down to ten stone five to finish the day on a winner with Ravenswood in the two-and-a-half-mile handicap hurdle. He was the one horse we sent to Aintree that I knew would take a lot of beating. He'd just started to get things right with his Newbury win and, having missed Cheltenham, was running as a fresh horse.

The trouble was that I still had to ride Iznogoud in the Martell Mildmay Novices' Chase. We were tracking Phar From A Fiddle when Iznogoud turned over at the fourth and gave me a proper bang. I didn't know where I was and felt badly shaken. I tried to convince the course doctor that I was fit to ride. Wisely, he stood me down. I was still gutted to see Ravenswood win under Tom Scudamore, but I made my way back to the Moat House and stayed in my room, dozing and trying to watch TV. Tomorrow was a massive day but I felt progressively worse as I drifted into a deep sleep at about ten o'clock.

More worryingly, when National morning dawned I felt like shit. I had to pass the doctor, along with Dickie Johnson and Mick FitzGerald, who were in second and third place behind me in the championship and had also taken heavy falls on Friday.

I'd got a graze along my nose, which was superficial, but with the sort of fall Iznogoud had given me you feel tired and lethargic, and carry a desperate headache. It's like someone has drugged you and sleep becomes very deep. It just knocks everything out of you for two or three days. Any other day, apart from this one or Cheltenham, and I'd probably have taken it off. That wasn't an option. I went through the usual routine with the doctor, who checked my sight and watched me touch my toes without any difficulty.

With it being the day it was, the more it went on the less I remembered how bad I felt. I picked the wrong one of Martin's pair for the opener, finishing sixth on Golden Alpha, but it wouldn't have mattered who was on the second, Idaho D'Ox, because Intersky Falcon won, easing up by fifteen lengths. I was really pumped up for the ride on Seebald in the Martell Maghull Novices' Chase. Even though Robbie Fowler and Steve McManaman couldn't be there it would mean a lot to the boys and their families to have a winner on National day at their local course. Unfortunately, the hard season and tight track were too much for Seebald and he was beaten into second by Armaturk, who had been thirteen lengths behind him at Cheltenham. Still, he owed no one anything.

The next race, the Martell Aintree Hurdle, which was the one before the National, got to me. I'd had to choose between Martin's pair It Takes Time and Ilnamar, the horse who had sprung the 25–1 surprise at Cheltenham. It was a tough call, but It Takes Time was officially rated two pounds better than Ilnamar and had run a good third in the Stayers' Hurdle. Although the two-and-a-half-mile trip was on the short side I thought he'd get away with it. He didn't. Ilnamar was still improving and, under a strong ride from Ruby Walsh, just got the better of Grimes in the final hundred yards. It Takes Time was finishing better than anything and would have won in another furlong. As it was we were third.

Although Martin had eight runners in the National I was always going to ride Blowing Wind, and in finishing third to Bindaree and What's Up Boys I had no excuses. At least I was now in the habit of getting round. Unfortunately 2001 was probably his year to win, and I remain convinced that he would have done but for being badly hampered and getting rid of me. That year's race wasn't so good as the 2002 renewal and the ground was much softer, which, in my opinion, helped him.

At the same time I felt sorry for Dickie Johnson and pleased for Jim Culloty. Dickie had taken the lead on What's Up Boys at the last and looked sure to win at the elbow only to be overtaken by Bindaree and Jim near the finish. It must have shattered Dickie to have the world's most famous chase snatched away when he'd almost had his hands round the trophy. That said, I was pleased things had come right for Jim. He'd had a poor year until Cheltenham but had always been a good rider. I don't think he needed the

Gold Cup and the Grand National to prove it – but a double like that doesn't half help.

A few of us, including Norman, Fitzy and Seamus Durack, decided to have Saturday night in Liverpool. There wasn't much point getting stuck in heavy traffic so we did the clubs and travelled home on Sunday morning. Seamus and I were keener than the others to get back: we'd arranged four days away in Marbella – I'd got a two-day ban for careless riding on Copeland at Chepstow, and with me being knocked about and Seamus laid up with his broken leg, we couldn't wait to hit the runway. Then a nightmare.

I got home around midday to pack and was just hunting for my passport when the car arrived. A few minutes later, still no passport. Because I'd had the builders in I had moved bedrooms, but I was positive the passport was on my bedside table. It wasn't. Gee Armytage looked in every cupboard and suitcase I possessed, but after half an hour I let the car and Seamus go and said I'd catch a later flight. I never dreamed how late it would be.

The passport didn't surface, so next morning I was up at six and drove to the passport office in London to try for a new one. No chance. Because it was lost it would take five days to replace.

I was home by nine thirty and, with the effects of the fall still on me, I fell into a deep sleep until mid-afternoon. A four-day break might not mean much to the average person but to me, feeling like shit and looking forward to some sun, the situation was an absolute bummer. At times such as this you need your mother, and mine came through for me yet again. She called to see how I was, which wasn't brilliant, and when she heard what had happened said she knew someone at British Airways in Terminal One, Heathrow. I didn't hold out much hope but, sure enough, I got a call from a lady, Breda Walls. She said it was a pleasure to be able to help Claire McCoy and that if I got to Heathrow the next morning someone would take me through Customs. She also alerted the Spanish authorities that I was coming so I made it. I am always amazed by the people my mother knows.

Seamus, Tom Butterfield and Marcus Reader were already installed at the Marbella Club, just about the most expensive place

Absent Friends   271

in the town. The only problem was that we were hardly ever in it to sleep. All the plans for golf had to be abandoned due to late nights. By the time I got back to Heathrow on Thursday night my headache was gone but I was still in desperate need of sleep.

I managed a couple of winners at Uttoxeter on Friday and had an important date at Ascot the next day. My sponsors, Cantor Index, were opening the charity Race To A Million, which aimed to raise funds for the many children of the employees of Cantor Fitzgerald who lost their lives in the World Trade Center atrocity of 11 September 2001. The Olympic super-heavyweight champion Audley Harrison, who is also sponsored by Cantor, was alongside for the launch.

Although I managed a couple of winners that afternoon I knew that my chance of reaching 300 was now impossible. As the Scottish Grand National meeting at Ayr came up I was on 281 with only eight days of the season remaining. Still, there was good money on offer. There was also only one race where I'd have to make a serious decision about Martin's runners and that was the big one, the Scottish National.

On the first day I got on Ravenswood and we won the last race. Martin had left me the choice of two in the National, Cyfor Malta and Take Control. Both had run at Liverpool: Cyfor Malta had run another sound race to be second to Florida Pearl, while Take Control had been on and off the bit before finishing a moderate fifth in the Martell VS Handicap Chase. In fact, he hadn't run two races alike all season. It had to be Cyfor Malta, even if there was a doubt about him getting the four miles one furlong. As it turned out it wouldn't have mattered what the trip was: Cyfor Malta was empty after a tough season while Take Control decided it was a going day. Responding to a tremendous ride from Ruby Walsh, who had got the better of me on Blowing Wind at Cheltenham the previous month, he beat Shotgun Willy by half a length.

There was nothing I could do except say well done and mean it because it had turned out a fabulous day for Ruby, one of the great talents in jump racing on either side of the water. He'd won the race prior to the National on Kadarann for Paul Nicholls, then taken the two races after the National for Paul on Saint Par and Maybe The Business. A good day for a grand fellow, but I wasn't the only member of the McCoy family who was delighted. As I was travelling back from Ayr and contemplating what I might have changed, my mother phoned. She'd met Ruby and his father Ted, the trainer and RTE racing pundit, several times before and is very fond of them. 'Anthony, I've just phoned Ted to tell him how delighted I am, over the moon. Sure, isn't it great for Ruby?'

'Well, maybe, but not as great as all that. It might have been even better if I'd ridden the bloody thing in the National.'

But she didn't seem to think so. Maybe she thought I'd won enough that season and it was time for someone else to have a go. That just about sums up my mother, genuinely pleased for everyone.

Fortunately for me, there was still the last big race of the season to come at Sandown the following weekend – and, once again, Martin was going to make me think hard before making my decision.

The Whitbread Gold Cup, along with the Hennessy and the Tote Gold Trophy, are the outstanding handicaps of the season. I'd missed out on the first, won the second and now had to choose from the six Martin had entered for the race, which had been renamed the Attheraces Gold Cup.

Martin didn't push me one way or another. Dark Stranger was running into form but he only had ten stone, while Iris Bleu was on ten stone five, light enough. Royal Predica, You're Agoodun and Majed had all had hard races in the Grand National, which left me with Bounce Back. He was the first horse that John and Belinda Harvey had placed with Martin and had cost plenty from François Doumen after showing decent form in staying hurdles in France. He'd won a moderate novice chase for Tom Scudamore at Chepstow back in December but had been largely disappointing since. He had switched back to hurdles and produced a fair run at Aintree to finish sixth to Ilnamar. I reasoned that he was still relatively unexposed and had plenty of ability if he wanted to use it. Also, he was running over three miles five furlongs, his longest distance yet.

John and Belinda had made the trip from their home in Barbados and had what they later described as one of the most exciting days of their lives.

From the start, Bounce Back was interested and enjoying himself, showing no signs of the reluctance to jump that had hindered him earlier in the season. Turning to go down the back straight for the last time, I began to pick up and could see that Dark Stranger and young David Howard had the field stretched. I was sure he wouldn't stop in this mood so we began to close going to the first of the railway fences, six from home. However, as I made my move I felt certain that I'd be giving speed horses like Frenchman's Creek and Carbury Cross a tow through. It wasn't until jumping three out that I knew we were in business. I pushed Bounce Back ahead after the second last. He still had plenty left to give, putting eight lengths between himself and Dark Stranger at the finish to give Martin a memorable one-two.

It was the final race of what had been the most wonderful season for me. Sure there had been setbacks, but I had arrived at the end in one piece, unlike Adrian Maguire and Joe Tizzard. Mick FitzGerald was missing, too, with a fractured arm and Norman Williamson had broken his leg just above the ankle. I knew I was a lucky man and said so as I faced the media with Martin after the race.

I apologized if I had antagonized them at Cheltenham but said again that the loss of Valiramix was something that would not go away. Martin was also facing life for the first time without the support of his late father.

This seemed as good a time as any to remember absent friends.

I stayed around the racecourse for a while after then headed back to the Queen's at East Garston for some serious celebrating. I was joined by, among many others, the Irish champion Barry Geraghty, my friend of long ago Paul Carberry, and my former lodger Jamie Spencer, now the shooting star of the Flat. The party lasted until around three and I had to be up by eight the next morning for a pro-am golf day at Woburn Abbey.

I won't pretend I was at my best, but when we arrived I couldn't have bumped into a more welcome sight than my boyhood hero, Pat Jennings. I'd met the former Arsenal and Spurs keeper several times before, but he is an icon as far as I am concerned and I still remember lining up to get that ball signed all those years ago. We talked for quite a while about home, his job as goal-keeping coach at Spurs, as well as my job and the season I'd had. I still find it strange that he knows who I am.

When the final statistics of the 2001–02 season were printed, they showed that Bounce Back was my 289th winner of the season, and 187 had been supplied by Martin Pipe, who was once again champion trainer. It Takes Time, in the opening race on the final day of the season at Sandown, was the last winner of the season for David Johnson who regained the title of leading owner over jumps.

I could look back on a season when fortune had favoured me, and the hard work by all those around me had been justified in my breaking of a record that had stood for over half a century. It is foolish to compare them as they were achieved in different eras, but I hope history will allow the two to stand together.

The future? I think the elusive 300 winners is a distinct possibility. If you can ride 289 what's to stop you riding a few more?

As for the big races, well, I won some but I won't be happy until I've ridden more, especially the Grand National.

Above all, I'm pleased to have justified the faith that people have shown in me.

As for those who worry about me, the short message is, don't: I appreciate the thought and there are times when I get low, but when I'm on a horse the world looks a wonderful place and I'm doing a job I dreamed of doing when I was a small boy.

On the Monday after the season ended I was given a wonderful celebration dinner at the Ritz in London by Cantor Index where Martin and David Johnson were also honoured. As we walked out at twelve forty-five into the cool air of London and headed for a nightclub, someone asked me what I'd be doing tomorrow.

'I'm going to Hexham for three.'

'Hexham? That's nearly five bloody hours in the car. Are you mad?'

'It's a new season, I'm back to zero and I'm a jump jockey. That's what I do.'

Epilogue: 27.8.02.

A sportman's story is ever changing until the day he gives his particular game away to the younger, hungrier man. Then the columns of figures are added for the final time and there he stands as a target for someone, possibly yet unborn, who will take him down in years to come.

The time of my life that this book records was meant to finish at the end of the 2001–2 jump season when I managed to surpass the wonderful record of 269 winners in a season set by Sir Gordon Richards back in 1947.

The next milestone was the 1,699 record for winners ridden by a jump jockey in Britain set by my childhood hero, Richard Dunwoody. Barring accidents I knew it would come, but nowhere near as quickly as it did.

When the 2002–3 season began on 29 April I was 97 winners away from 1,700, but it was a dream summer and the victories flowed. When Mighty Montefalco, my 6,366th ride in Britain, won the 2.50 at Uttoxeter on 27 August I was truly on top of the world.

I savoured that day but know there is more to do. 300 winners in a season? 3,000 before I retire? Who knows, but be sure of one thing: I will try.

Index

Names in italics are those of horses unless otherwise stated.